INSIDE MACINTOSH

PowerPC System Software

Addison-Wesley Publishing Company

Reading, Massachusetts   Menlo Park, California   New York
Don Mills, Ontario   Wokingham, England   Amsterdam   Bonn
Sydney   Singapore   Tokyo   Madrid   San Juan
Paris   Seoul   Milan   Mexico City   Taipei

ISBN 0-201-40727-2
1 2 3 4 5 6 7 8 9-CRW-9897969594
First Printing, February 1994

The paper used in this book meets the EPA standards for recycled fiber.

Library of Congress Cataloging-in-Publication Data

Inside Macintosh. PowerPC system software / Apple Computer, Inc.
    p. cm.
    Includes index.
    ISBN 0-201-40727-2
    1. Macintosh (Computer) 2. PowerPC (Microprocessor) 3. Systems
software. I. Title: PowerPC system software.
QA76.8.M3I528 1994
005.4'469—dc20   93-50182
                                                                          CIP

Contents

Figures, Tables, and Listings   vii

Preface   **About This Book**   ix

Related Documentation   xi
Format of a Typical Chapter   xi
Conventions Used in This Book   xii
  Special Fonts   xii
  Types of Notes   xii
  Bit Numbering and Word Size   xii
  Assembly-Language Information   xiv
Development Environment   xiv
For More Information   xv

Chapter 1   **Introduction to PowerPC System Software**   1-1

Overview of the PowerPC System Software   1-4
The 68LC040 Emulator   1-6
  Emulator Operation   1-7
  Emulator Limitations   1-8
    Coprocessors   1-9
    Instruction Timings   1-9
    Deleted Instructions   1-9
    Unsupported Instruction Features   1-10
    Instruction Caches   1-10
    Address Error Exceptions   1-10
    Bus Error Exceptions   1-11
    Memory-Mapped I/O Locations   1-11
Mixed Mode   1-13
  Cross-Mode Calls   1-14
  Routine Descriptors   1-15
  Memory Considerations   1-19
The PowerPC Native Environment   1-19
  Fragments   1-20
    The Structure of Fragments   1-22
    Imports and Exports   1-23
    The Table of Contents   1-26
    Special Routines   1-29
    Fragment Storage   1-30
    Executable Resources   1-34

Calling Conventions   1-41
 The 680x0 Calling Conventions   1-42
 The PowerPC Calling Conventions   1-43
 Parameter Passing   1-47
Import Libraries   1-50
The Organization of Memory   1-52
 File Mapping   1-53
 The System Partition   1-56
 Application Partitions   1-57
 Data Alignment   1-63
Compatibility and Performance   1-65
 Patches   1-66
 The Memory Manager   1-68
 Performance Tuning   1-70
  Mode Switches   1-71
  Routine Parameters   1-72

Chapter 2	Mixed Mode Manager 2-1

About the Mixed Mode Manager   2-4
 External Code   2-4
 Procedure Pointers   2-5
 Mode Switches   2-7
  Calling PowerPC Code From 680x0 Code   2-8
  Calling 680x0 Code From PowerPC Code   2-12
Using the Mixed Mode Manager   2-14
 Specifying Procedure Information   2-14
 Using Universal Procedure Pointers   2-21
 Using Static Routine Descriptors   2-22
 Executing Resource-Based Code   2-24
Mixed Mode Manager Reference   2-26
 Constants   2-27
  Routine Descriptor Flags   2-27
  Procedure Information   2-27
  Routine Flags   2-34
  Instruction Set Architectures   2-35
 Data Structures   2-36
  Routine Records   2-36
  Routine Descriptors   2-37
 Mixed Mode Manager Routines   2-38
  Creating and Disposing of Routine Descriptors   2-39
  Calling Routines via Universal Procedure Pointers   2-42
  Determining Instruction Set Architectures   2-44

Summary of the Mixed Mode Manager   2-45
    C Summary   2-45
        Constants   2-45
        Data Types   2-48
        Mixed Mode Manager Routines   2-49

Chapter 3   Code Fragment Manager   3-1

About the Code Fragment Manager   3-3
    Fragments   3-4
    Import Library Searching   3-5
    Version Checking   3-7
Using the Code Fragment Manager   3-10
    Loading Code Fragments   3-10
    Creating a Code Fragment Resource   3-12
    Getting Information About Exported Symbols   3-14
Code Fragment Manager Reference   3-15
    Data Structures   3-15
        Fragment Initialization Block   3-15
        Fragment Location Record   3-16
        Memory Location Record   3-17
        Disk Location Record   3-17
        Segment Location Record   3-18
    Code Fragment Manager Routines   3-18
        Loading Fragments   3-19
        Unloading Fragments   3-23
        Finding Symbols   3-24
    Fragment-Defined Routines   3-26
    Resources   3-28
        The Code Fragment Resource   3-28
Summary of the Code Fragment Manager   3-32
    C Summary   3-32
        Constants   3-32
        Data Types   3-33
        Code Fragment Manager Routines   3-34
        Fragment-Defined Routines   3-35
    Result Codes   3-35

Chapter 4   Exception Manager   4-1

About the Exception Manager   4-3
    Exception Contexts   4-4
    Types of Exceptions   4-5

Using the Exception Manager   4-6
    Installing an Exception Handler   4-6
    Writing an Exception Handler   4-7
Exception Manager Reference   4-9
    Constants   4-9
        Exception Kinds   4-9
        Memory Reference Kinds   4-11
    Data Structures   4-12
        Machine Information Records   4-12
        Register Information Records   4-12
        Floating-Point Information Records   4-14
        Memory Exception Records   4-15
        Exception Information Records   4-16
    Exception Manager Routines   4-17
    Application-Defined Routines   4-17
Summary of the Exception Manager   4-19
    C Summary   4-19
        Constants   4-19
        Data Types   4-19
        Exception Manager Routines   4-22
        Application-Defined Routines   4-22

Glossary   GL-1

Index   IN-1

Figures, Tables, and Listings

Preface   About This Book   ix

| Figure P-1 | 680x0 bit numbering   xiii |
| Figure P-2 | PowerPC bit numbering   xiii |

Table P-1   Sizes of memory operands   xiii

Chapter 1   Introduction to PowerPC System Software   1-1

Figure 1-1   The system software for PowerPC processor-based Macintosh computers   1-5
Figure 1-2   Creating imports in a fragment   1-24
Figure 1-3   A transition vector   1-27
Figure 1-4   The structure of a PowerPC application   1-31
Figure 1-5   The structure of a 680x0 application   1-32
Figure 1-6   The structure of a fat application   1-33
Figure 1-7   The structure of an accelerated resource   1-35
Figure 1-8   The structure of a private resource   1-36
Figure 1-9   A 680x0 stack frame   1-42
Figure 1-10   The PowerPC stack   1-44
Figure 1-11   The structure of a stack frame's linkage area   1-45
Figure 1-12   The Red Zone   1-46
Figure 1-13   The organization of the parameter area on the stack   1-49
Figure 1-14   Organization of memory when virtual memory is enabled   1-54
Figure 1-15   Organization of memory when virtual memory is not enabled   1-56
Figure 1-16   The structure of a PowerPC application partition   1-60
Figure 1-17   The Memory control panel for PowerPC processor-based Macintosh computers   1-69

Listing 1-1   Creating a routine descriptor   1-17
Listing 1-2   The definition of the NewControlActionProc routine   1-18
Listing 1-3   Creating a routine descriptor for a control action procedure   1-19
Listing 1-4   Testing for unresolved soft imports   1-25
Listing 1-5   The Rez input for a sample 'cfrg' resource   1-32
Listing 1-6   Rez input for a list definition procedure stub   1-35
Listing 1-7   Using an accelerated resource   1-37
Listing 1-8   Some acceptable global declarations in an accelerated resource   1-39
Listing 1-9   Some unacceptable global declarations and code in an accelerated resource   1-39
Listing 1-10   Using a private resource   1-40
Listing 1-11   Declaring an application's QuickDraw global variables   1-59
Listing 1-12   A sample 680x0 VBL task definition   1-61
Listing 1-13   A conditionalized VBL task definition   1-62
Listing 1-14   Patching an Operating System trap   1-67
Listing 1-15   Waiting to call the WaitNextEvent function   1-72

Chapter 2   Mixed Mode Manager   2-1

Figure 2-1   680x0 and PowerPC procedure pointers   2-5
Figure 2-2   Calling PowerPC code from a 680x0 application   2-9
Figure 2-3   The stack before a mode switch   2-10
Figure 2-4   A 680x0-to-PowerPC switch frame   2-11
Figure 2-5   A PowerPC-to-680x0 switch frame   2-13
Figure 2-6   Procedure information for a stack-based routine   2-17
Figure 2-7   Procedure information for a register-based routine   2-19
Figure 2-8   General structure of an executable code resource   2-25
Figure 2-9   General structure of a fat resource   2-26

Table 2-1   Limits on the number of specifiable parameters in a procedure information   2-20

Listing 2-1   Sample glue code for a 680x0 routine   2-12
Listing 2-2   Creating global routine descriptors   2-21
Listing 2-3   Creating local routine descriptors   2-22
Listing 2-4   Creating static routine descriptors   2-23
Listing 2-5   Building a static routine descriptor   2-23

Chapter 3   Code Fragment Manager   3-1

Figure 3-1   Structure of a compiled code fragment ('cfrg') resource   3-29
Figure 3-2   The format of a code fragment information record   3-30

Listing 3-1   Pseudocode for the version-checking algorithm   3-9
Listing 3-2   Loading a resource-based fragment   3-11
Listing 3-3   Loading a disk-based fragment   3-11
Listing 3-4   The Rez input for a typical application's 'cfrg' resource   3-12
Listing 3-5   The Rez input for a typical import library's 'cfrg' resource   3-13
Listing 3-6   Finding symbol names   3-14

Chapter 4   Exception Manager   4-1

Listing 4-1   Installing an exception handler   4-6
Listing 4-2   A native exception handler   4-8

About This Book

This book, *Inside Macintosh: PowerPC System Software*, describes the new process execution environment and system software services provided with the first version of the system software for Macintosh on PowerPC computers. It contains information you need to know to write applications and other software that can run on PowerPC processor-based Macintosh computers.

The first release of the system software for Macintosh on PowerPC computers provides a mixed or hybrid environment: the system software provides the ability to execute both applications that use the native instruction set of the PowerPC microprocessor and applications that use the 680x0 instruction set. It accomplishes this by providing a very efficient 68LC040 Emulator that emulates 680x0 instructions with PowerPC instructions. As a result, virtually all existing 680x0-based Macintosh applications and other software modules that conform to the programming interfaces and techniques documented in the *Inside Macintosh* suite of books will execute without modification on PowerPC processor-based Macintosh computers.

To take maximum advantage of the much greater processing speed of the PowerPC microprocessor, however, you'll need to recompile your application's source code into a PowerPC application. Apple Computer, Inc., provides MPW-based C and C++ compilers and other tools that you can use to create native PowerPC applications. In general, if your source code is already compliant with ANSI C standards or the de facto ANSI C++ standards, you should be able, with moderately little effort, to rework your source code so that it can be compiled and built using the Apple-supplied tools into a PowerPC application. This book is intended to provide much of the information you need to port your existing 680x0 application (or other software) to the PowerPC platform.

Note

There will also be third-party compilers and development environments capable of generating PowerPC code. ◆

Although the native run-time execution environment of the first version of the system software for PowerPC processor-based Macintosh computers is significantly different from the execution environment of current 680x0-based Macintosh computers, you won't need to worry about those differences unless your existing code relies on specific information about the 680x0 execution environment. For example, if for some reason you directly access information in your application's A5 world, you'll need to rewrite those parts of code when porting your application to the PowerPC environment. Similarly, you'll need to rewrite any parts of your code that depend on data being passed in certain 680x0 registers. VBL tasks, for instance, very often depend on the fact that a pointer to the VBL task record is passed in register A0.

The first chapter in this book, "Introduction to PowerPC System Software," provides a general overview of the system software that runs on PowerPC processor-based Macintosh computers. It also describes in detail the mixed environment provided by the 68LC040 Emulator and the Mixed Mode Manager, as well as the new run-time environment used for native PowerPC applications. You should read this chapter for general information about porting your existing software to the PowerPC environment. Even if you do not intend to port your existing 680x0 software, you might still want to read this chapter for information about running under the 68LC040 Emulator.

The remaining chapters in this book provide reference material for the three new system software managers introduced in the first version of the system software for PowerPC processor-based Macintosh computers. You should read these chapters for specific information on using the services provided by those managers. The new system software managers are

- the Mixed Mode Manager, which manages the mixed environment of PowerPC processor-based Macintosh computers running 680x0-based code

- the Code Fragment Manager, which loads fragments (blocks of executable PowerPC code and their associated data) into memory and prepares them for execution

- the Exception Manager, which handles exceptions that occur during the execution of PowerPC applications or other software

IMPORTANT

Some of the system software services introduced in the first version of the system software for PowerPC processor-based Macintosh computers might in the future be available on Macintosh computers that are not based on the PowerPC microprocessor. For example, it's possible that the Code Fragment Manager (and the entire run-time environment based on fragments) will be included in future versions of the system software for 680x0-based Macintosh computers. As a result, some of the information in this book might eventually be more generally applicable than the title of this book might suggest. ▲

If you are new to programming for Macintosh computers, you should read the book *Inside Macintosh: Overview* for an introduction to general concepts of Macintosh programming. You should also read other books in the *Inside Macintosh* series for specific information about other aspects of the Macintosh Toolbox and the Macintosh Operating System. In particular, to benefit most from this book, you should already be familiar with the run-time environment of 680x0 applications, as described in the two books *Inside Macintosh: Processes* and *Inside Macintosh: Memory*.

Related Documentation

This book is part of a larger suite of books that contain information essential for developing PowerPC applications and other software.

■ For information about the PPCC compiler that you can use to compile your source code into a PowerPC application, see the book *C/C++ Compiler for Macintosh With PowerPC.*

■ For information about the PPCAsm assembler, see the book *Assembler for Macintosh With PowerPC.*

■ For information about debugging and measuring the performance of PowerPC applications, see the book *Macintosh Debugger Reference.*

■ For information about performing floating-point calculations in PowerPC applications, see the book *Inside Macintosh: PowerPC Numerics.*

■ For information about building PowerPC applications and other kinds of PowerPC software for Macintosh computers, see *Building Programs for Macintosh With PowerPC.*

Format of a Typical Chapter

Almost all chapters in this book follow a standard structure. For example, the chapter "Mixed Mode Manager" contains these sections:

■ "About the Mixed Mode Manager." This section describes the Mixed Mode Manager. You should read this section for a general understanding of what the Mixed Mode Manager does and when you might need to call it explicitly.

■ "Using the Mixed Mode Manager." This section provides detailed instructions on using the Mixed Mode Manager. You should read this section if you need to use the services provided by the Mixed Mode Manager.

■ "Mixed Mode Manager Reference." This section provides a complete reference to the constants, data structures, and routines provided by the Mixed Mode Manager. Each routine description also follows a standard format, which presents the routine declaration followed by a description of every parameter of the routine. Some routine descriptions also give additional descriptive information, such as circumstances under which you cannot call the routine or result codes.

■ "Summary of the Mixed Mode Manager." This section provides the C interfaces for the constants, data structures, routines, and result codes associated with the Mixed Mode Manager.

Conventions Used in This Book

Inside Macintosh uses various conventions to present information. Words that require special treatment appear in specific fonts or font styles. Certain information, such as parameter blocks, appears in special formats so that you can scan it quickly.

Special Fonts

All code listings, reserved words, and the names of actual data structures, constants, fields, parameters, and routines are shown in Courier (`this is Courier`).

Words that appear in **boldface** are key terms or concepts and are defined in the glossary at the end of this book. Note that numerical entries (for example, **32-bit clean**) are sorted before all alphabetical entries in the glossary and in the index.

Types of Notes

There are several types of notes used in *Inside Macintosh*.

Note

A note like this contains information that is interesting but possibly not essential to an understanding of the main text. (An example appears on page 1-6.) ◆

IMPORTANT

A note like this contains information that is essential for an understanding of the main text. (An example appears on page 1-19.) ▲

▲ **WARNING**

Warnings like this indicate potential problems that you should be aware of as you design your application. Failure to heed these warnings could result in system crashes or loss of data. (An example appears on page 1-8.) ▲

Bit Numbering and Word Size

This book departs from the conventions followed in previous *Inside Macintosh* books in regard to the numbering of bits within a range of data. Previously, for example, the bits in a 32-bit data type were numbered 0 to 31, from right to left, as shown in Figure P-1 on the following page. The least significant bit of a 32-bit data type was addressed as bit 0, and the most significant bit was addressed as bit 31. This convention was in accordance with that used by

Motorola in the books documenting their 680x0 family of microprocessors (for example, the *MC68040 32-Bit Microprocessor User's Manual*).

Figure P-1   680x0 bit numbering

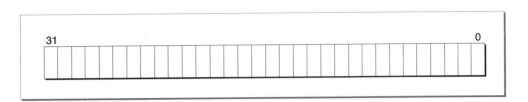

In this book, the bits in a 32-bit data type are numbered 0 to 31, from left to right. The most significant bit of a 32-bit data type is addressed as bit 0, and the least significant bit is addressed as bit 31. This convention, illustrated in Figure P-2, is in accordance with the bit-numbering conventions used by Motorola in the books documenting the PowerPC family of microprocessors (for example, the *PowerPC 601 RISC Microprocessor User's Manual*).

Figure P-2   PowerPC bit numbering

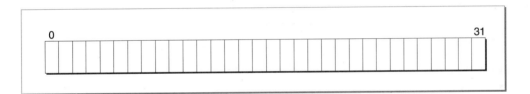

In addition, there are differences between 680x0 and the PowerPC terminology to describe the sizes of certain memory operands, as shown in Table P-1.

Table P-1   Sizes of memory operands

Size	680x0 terminology	PowerPC terminology
8 bits	Byte	Byte
2 bytes	Word	Half word
4 bytes	Long word	Word
8 bytes	N/A	Double word
16 bytes	N/A	Quad word

To avoid confusion, however, this book generally uses bytes to give the sizes of objects in memory.

Assembly-Language Information

Inside Macintosh presents information about the fields of a parameter block in this format:

Parameter block

↔	`inAndOut`	`Handle`	Input/output parameter.
←	`output1`	`Ptr`	Output parameter.
→	`input1`	`Ptr`	Input parameter.

The arrow in the far-left column indicates whether the field is an input parameter, output parameter, or both. You must supply values for all input parameters and input/output parameters. The routine returns values in output parameters and input/output parameters.

The second column shows the field name as defined in the MPW C interface files; the third column indicates the C data type of that field. The fourth column provides a brief description of the use of the field. For a complete description of each field, see the discussion that follows the parameter block or the description of the parameter block in the reference section of the chapter.

Development Environment

The system software routines described in this book are available using C or assembly-language interfaces. How you access these routines depends on the development environment you are using. This book shows system software routines in their C interface using the Macintosh Programmer's Workshop (MPW).

All code listings in this book are shown in C (except for listings that describe resources, which are shown in Rez-input format). They show methods of using various routines and illustrate techniques for accomplishing particular tasks. All code listings have been compiled and, in most cases, tested. However, Apple Computer does not intend that you use these code samples in your application. You can find the location of this book's code listings in the list of figures, tables, and listings.

To make the code listings in this book more readable, only limited error handling is shown. You need to develop your own techniques for detecting and handling errors.

This book occasionally illustrates concepts by reference to a sample application called *SurfWriter* and a sample import library called *SurfTools*; these are not actual products of Apple Computer, Inc.

For More Information

APDA is Apple's worldwide source for over three hundred development tools, technical resources, training products, and information for anyone interested in developing applications on Apple platforms. Customers receive the quarterly *APDA Tools Catalog* featuring all current versions of Apple development tools and the most popular third-party development tools. Ordering is easy; there are no membership fees, and application forms are not required for most of our products. APDA offers convenient payment and shipping options, including site licensing.

To order products or to request a complimentary copy of the *APDA Tools Catalog*, contact

APDA
Apple Computer, Inc.
P.O. Box 319
Buffalo, NY 14207-0319

Telephone	800-282-2732 (United States)
	800-637-0029 (Canada)
	716-871-6555 (International)
Fax	716-871-6511
AppleLink	APDA
America Online	APDA
CompuServe	76666,2405
Internet	APDA@applelink.apple.com

If you provide commercial products and services, call 408-974-4897 for information on the developer support programs available from Apple.

For information on registering signatures, file types, Apple events, and other technical information, contact

Macintosh Developer Technical Support
Apple Computer, Inc.
20525 Mariani Avenue, M/S 303-2T
Cupertino, CA 95014-6299

Introduction to PowerPC System Software

Contents

Overview of the PowerPC System Software   1-4
The 68LC040 Emulator   1-6
  Emulator Operation   1-7
  Emulator Limitations   1-8
    Coprocessors   1-9
    Instruction Timings   1-9
    Deleted Instructions   1-9
    Unsupported Instruction Features   1-10
    Instruction Caches   1-10
    Address Error Exceptions   1-10
    Bus Error Exceptions   1-11
    Memory-Mapped I/O Locations   1-11
Mixed Mode   1-13
  Cross-Mode Calls   1-14
  Routine Descriptors   1-15
  Memory Considerations   1-19
The PowerPC Native Environment   1-19
  Fragments   1-20
    The Structure of Fragments   1-22
    Imports and Exports   1-23
    The Table of Contents   1-26
    Special Routines   1-29
    Fragment Storage   1-30
    Executable Resources   1-34
  Calling Conventions   1-41
    The 680x0 Calling Conventions   1-42
    The PowerPC Calling Conventions   1-43
    Parameter Passing   1-47

Import Libraries   1-50
The Organization of Memory   1-52
    File Mapping   1-53
    The System Partition   1-56
    Application Partitions   1-57
    Data Alignment   1-63
Compatibility and Performance   1-65
    Patches   1-66
    The Memory Manager   1-68
    Performance Tuning   1-70
        Mode Switches   1-71
        Routine Parameters   1-72

This chapter is a general introduction to the system software provided on PowerPC processor-based Macintosh computers. It describes the mixed environment provided by the 68LC040 Emulator and the Mixed Mode Manager. These two new system software services work together to allow existing 680x0 applications, extensions, drivers, and other software to execute without modification on PowerPC processor-based Macintosh computers. The 68LC040 Emulator and the Mixed Mode Manager also make it possible for parts of the system software to remain as 680x0 code, while other parts of the system software are reimplemented (primarily for reasons of speed) as native PowerPC code.

This chapter also describes the native PowerPC execution environment. Although the process-scheduling mechanism used for both native and emulated applications has not changed, the run-time environment for PowerPC applications is significantly different from the run-time environment used for 680x0-based Macintosh applications. In cases where your application (or other software) relies on features of the 680x0 run-time environment, you'll need to modify your application before recompiling it as a PowerPC application. For example, if your application directly accesses information stored in low memory (such as system global variables) or in its A5 world, you might need to rewrite parts of your application to remove the dependence on that information. See "The PowerPC Native Environment" beginning on page 1-19 for complete instructions on doing this.

You should read this chapter if you want your application to run on PowerPC processor-based Macintosh computers, either under the 68LC040 Emulator or in the PowerPC native environment. If you choose not to rebuild your application for the PowerPC environment, you should at least make certain that it doesn't violate any of the known restrictions on the emulator. See "Emulator Limitations" on page 1-8 for specific information about the known operational differences between the 68LC040 Emulator and a 680x0 microprocessor.

You should also read this chapter for information about the PowerPC execution environment. Although the existing software development tools build your source code into executable PowerPC code that conforms to the requirements of this new environment, you might need to know about the native run-time environment for debugging purposes or if your application uses external code modules. Otherwise, the new execution environment should be completely transparent to your application.

You should be able to accomplish much of the work involved in porting your application from the 680x0 platform to the PowerPC platform using the information in this chapter. If your application installs callback routines with nonstandard calling conventions, however, you might need to read the chapter "Mixed Mode Manager" in this book. In addition, if your application explicitly loads external code modules (such as file translators or custom definition procedures), you might need to read the chapter "Code Fragment Manager" in this book. Read the chapter "Exception Manager" if you want your native application to handle any exceptions that arise while it is executing.

To use this chapter, you should already be generally familiar with the Macintosh Operating System. See the books *Inside Macintosh: Processes* and *Inside Macintosh: Memory* for information about the run-time environment of 680x0-based Macintosh computers.

This chapter begins with a description of the mixed environment provided by the PowerPC system software. Then it gives information about the native PowerPC run-time environment. This chapter ends by explaining how to perform a number of specific tasks in the PowerPC environment, such as patching system software traps.

Note

For ease of exposition, this book occasionally focuses on porting applications from the 680x0 environment to the PowerPC environment. In general, however, any changes required for applications are required also for all other kinds of software. ◆

Overview of the PowerPC System Software

The system software for PowerPC processor-based Macintosh computers is System 7.1, with suitable changes made to support the **mixed environment** that allows both 680x0 software and PowerPC software to execute on a computer. The mixed environment provides virtually complete compatibility for existing 680x0 software, as well as vastly increased performance for applications and other software that are built to use the native instruction set of the PowerPC microprocessor.

Because the system software for PowerPC processor-based Macintosh computers is derived from System 7.1 for 680x0-based Macintosh computers, your application—whether 680x0 or PowerPC—must conform to the basic requirements imposed by system software versions 7.0 and later. In particular, your application (or other software) must be

- 32-bit clean

- compatible with the operations of the Virtual Memory Manager

- able to operate smoothly in the cooperative multitasking environment maintained by the Process Manager

If your 680x0 software conforms to these specific requirements and to the general requirements for Macintosh software documented throughout *Inside Macintosh*, it is highly probable that it will execute without problems on PowerPC processor-based Macintosh computers. This is because the system software for PowerPC processor-based Macintosh computers includes a very efficient 68LC040 Emulator that emulates 680x0 instructions with PowerPC instructions. In addition, the system software includes the Mixed Mode Manager, which is responsible for handling any necessary mode switches between the native PowerPC environment and the 680x0 environment.

Figure 1-1 shows a general overview of the system software for PowerPC processor-based Macintosh computers. A small kernel, called the **nanokernel,** communicates directly with the PowerPC processor and provides very low-level services (such as interrupt handling and memory management).

Figure 1-1   The system software for PowerPC processor-based Macintosh computers

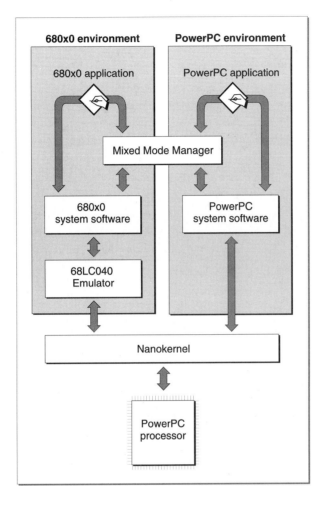

Even applications written entirely in 680x0 code might cause mode switches while they are executing, because some portions of the Macintosh Operating System have been rewritten in PowerPC code for increased performance. For example, the Memory Manager has been rewritten in C and recompiled into PowerPC code. In general, however, mode switches occur completely transparently to 680x0 software. Only native PowerPC software needs to worry about mode switches. See "Mixed Mode" beginning on page 1-13 for details.

As you would expect, the emulation environment provided by the 68LC040 Emulator uses the standard 680x0 run-time model. The organization of an application partition and the run-time behavior of emulated software are identical to what is provided on 680x0-based Macintosh computers. However, the execution environment for native PowerPC software is significantly different from the standard 680x0 run-time environment. The PowerPC environment provides a much simpler and easier-to-use run-time model based on fragments. A **fragment** is any block of executable PowerPC code and its associated data. Fragments are created by your development system's linker.

Note

The term *fragment* is not intended to suggest that the block of code and data is in any way either small, detached, or incomplete. Fragments can be of virtually any size, and they are complete, executable entities. The term *fragment* was chosen to avoid confusion with the terms already used in *Inside Macintosh* to describe executable code (such as *component* and *module*). ◆

Fragments use a method of addressing the data they contain that is different and more general than the A5-relative method that 680x0 applications use to address their global data. One important consequence is that any PowerPC software packaged as a fragment has easy access to global data. In the 680x0-based system software, it was sometimes difficult to use global data within types of software other than applications.

In addition, it was often complicated for a routine installed by some code to gain access to the code's global variables. For example, you cannot—in the current 680x0 environment—write a VBL task that uses your application's global variables without somehow passing your application's A5 value to the VBL task. (A **VBL task** is a task that executes during a vertical blanking interrupt.) In the PowerPC environment, any routine contained in an application has automatic access to the application's global variables. You do not need to devise special ways to pass the address of your application's A5 world to the installed routine. More generally, any routine executing in the PowerPC environment has access to the global data of the fragment it's contained in.

The new run-time model used for native PowerPC software incorporates other important simplifications as well. In native applications, there is no segmentation of the executable code. The existing compilers that produce PowerPC code ignore any segmentation directives you include in your source code. In addition, any calls you make to the Segment Manager's `UnloadSeg` procedure are simply ignored by the PowerPC system software. The task of keeping required code in memory is handled completely by the Virtual Memory Manager or the Process Manager, not by your application.

The remaining sections in this chapter describe in greater detail the mixed environment of PowerPC processor-based Macintosh computers and the new native run-time environment. If you're interested mainly in rebuilding your application as native PowerPC code, you can skip to the section "Mixed Mode" beginning on page 1-13, which describes the ways in which you might need to use the Mixed Mode Manager to make your native application compatible with the mixed environment.

The 68LC040 Emulator

The **68LC040 Emulator** is the part of the PowerPC system software that allows 680x0 applications and other software to execute on PowerPC processor-based Macintosh computers. This emulator provides an execution environment that is virtually identical to the execution environment found on 680x0-based Macintosh computers. The emulator converts 680x0 instructions into PowerPC instructions, issues those instructions to the PowerPC microprocessor, and updates the emulated environment (such as the emulated 680x0 registers) in response to the operations of the PowerPC microprocessor.

In general, the 680x0 emulation environment supports all existing 680x0 applications that already work correctly on all Macintosh computers containing a Motorola 68020, 68030, or 68040 microprocessor. There are, however, some differences between the operation of the 68LC040 Emulator and an actual 68040 microprocessor. The following two sections provide some information on the general operation and limitations of the 68LC040 Emulator.

Note

Unless you are programming in assembly language or doing very low-level debugging, you're not likely to need the information in the following two sections. ◆

Emulator Operation

The 68LC040 Emulator implements the basic Motorola 68040 user mode instruction set. It does not, however, support any of the instructions from the optional 68881 or 68882 floating-point coprocessors. Moreover, although the emulator supports the operations of the Virtual Memory Manager, it does not support instructions from the 68851 Paged Memory Management Unit (PMMU). The 680x0-based Macintosh computer whose hardware configuration most closely resembles the software configuration of the 68LC040 Emulator is the Macintosh Centris 610, which contains the Motorola 68LC040 microprocessor. (The 68LC040 microprocessor is identical to the 68040 microprocessor except that it has no floating-point unit.) As a result, if your application or other software runs without problems on the Macintosh Centris 610, it is very likely to run without problems under the 68LC040 Emulator.

Note

For the complete specification of how you can expect both a real 68040 and the 68LC040 Emulator to behave, see the *MC68040 32-Bit Microprocessor User's Manual*. ◆

The `Gestalt` function returns the value `gestalt68020` when you pass it the selector `gestaltProcessorType` and the calling software is executing under the emulator. This return value is intended to highlight the two ways in which the 68LC040 Emulator more closely resembles a 68020 processor than a 68040 processor:

■ The emulated environment does not support either the FPU or the MMU contained in an actual 68040 processor.

■ The emulated environment creates exception stack frames in accordance with the 68020 exception frame model.

The 68LC040 Emulator consists of two main parts, a main dispatch table and a block of additional code called by entries in the main dispatch table. The main dispatch table contains two native PowerPC instructions for each recognized 680x0 operation code (or opcode). In cases where a 680x0 opcode can be handled by a single PowerPC instruction, the first native instruction in the dispatch table is enough to complete the requested operation. In most cases, however, the handling of a 680x0 opcode requires more than one PowerPC instruction. In that case, the first native instruction in the main dispatch table simply begins the emulation process.

The second native instruction in the emulator's main dispatch table is usually a PC-relative branch into the block of additional code. The additional code continues the emulation of the 680x0 opcode begun by the first instruction.

The emulator's main dispatch table also includes entries that support private opcodes reserved for use by the system software, including both A-line and F-line instructions. For example, the Mixed Mode Manager communicates with the 68LC040 Emulator using A-line instructions embedded in routine descriptors. (See "Routine Descriptors" beginning on page 1-15 for details.) Other system software services, including the Virtual Memory Manager, also issue reserved opcodes to the emulator.

When the emulator is active, it maps all 680x0 registers to the registers on the PowerPC microprocessor, including the 680x0 program counter (PC) and Status Register (SR). The general-purpose register GPR1 serves as both the 680x0 and native stack pointer. The emulator also dedicates a native register to point to the **680x0 context block,** a block of data containing information that needs to be preserved across mode switches. The context block contains all the 680x0 registers, the addresses of the main dispatch table and the block of additional code, and other information used internally by the emulator. The emulator saves information into the context block when it is about to exit (for example, when a 680x0 application calls a piece of native code) and restores the information from the block when it is subsequently activated.

▲ **WARNING**
You should not rely on any specific information about the 68LC040 Emulator's private data structures or opcodes. ▲

Emulator Limitations

Largely because it is a purely software implementation of a hardware microprocessor, the 68LC040 Emulator sometimes exhibits behavior that differs from that of an actual 680x0 microprocessor. These operational differences can lead to problems, ranging from the obvious (for example, using the floating-point coprocessor instruction set, which is not supported by the 68LC040 Emulator) to the subtle (for example, depending upon a value in an undefined condition code bit). If your application or other software depends on 680x0 behavior that is not reproduced exactly by the 68LC040 Emulator, your product might have problems when executing under the emulator. The known exceptions to the documented 680x0 specifications concern

- coprocessors and instruction sets
- instruction timings
- deleted instructions
- unsupported instruction features
- instruction caches
- address error exceptions
- bus error exceptions
- memory-mapped I/O locations

The following sections describe these limitations in greater detail.

Coprocessors

As previously indicated, the 68LC040 Emulator does not support the instruction sets of either the 68881 or the 68882 floating-point coprocessor or of the 68851 PMMU. Any software that uses floating-point instructions is therefore not compatible with the 68LC040 Emulator. Because there are several 680x0-based Macintosh computers that do not contain floating-point coprocessors, this restriction is not likely to cause new compatibility problems for your software. It's possible that you have used SANE to perform hardware-independent floating-point arithmetic. If so, you'll probably notice that floating-point calculations are performed even faster under the 68LC040 Emulator than on a real 680x0-based Macintosh computer. This is because PowerPC processor-based Macintosh computers include an accelerated version of SANE written in native PowerPC code.

The 68LC040 Emulator does not support the 68851 PMMU instruction set (which also includes the 68030 and 68040 internal PMMUs). The Virtual Memory Manager is still supported, but using a different mechanism. Very few applications address the PMMU directly, so this restriction is not likely to affect many developers. Those applications that do address the PMMU directly are very likely already incompatible with A/UX and with the Virtual Memory Manager.

More generally, the 68LC040 Emulator does not support the coprocessor bus interface. As a result, the emulator does not support any externally connected hardware coprocessors.

Instruction Timings

The 68LC040 Emulator executes 680x0 instructions as fast as possible, making no attempt to maintain the same number of clock counts as on a real 68040 microprocessor. There are classes of instructions that execute in the same number of cycles whether on a real 68040 or under the 68LC040 Emulator, but you should not depend on this. In general, of course, your 680x0 application is most likely already independent of instruction timing, because it should run without problem on a wide range of 680x0 microprocessors having quite different clock rates.

Deleted Instructions

Several instructions included in the instruction set of the 68020 microprocessor were removed from the instruction sets of the 68030 and 68040 microprocessors. The deleted instructions are the CALLM and RTM instructions, which were intended for use in module calls. These instructions are not supported by the 68LC040 Emulator, and any attempt to execute them will result in an illegal instruction exception. However, because these instructions are not present in any 680x0 microprocessor either before or after the 68020, this restriction is not likely to present compatibility problems for your software.

Unsupported Instruction Features

Several instruction or addressing mode fields and encodings are documented by Motorola as reserved. In addition, many instructions are documented as producing undefined condition code result bits or undefined register results. Accordingly, the behavior of these reserved fields and undefined results differs across the various members of the 680x0 family of microprocessors and under the 68LC040 Emulator. It is unlikely that any existing software intentionally depends on either reserved fields or undefined results. It is, however, remotely possible that through a programming error some software might be depending on these results and hence might behave differently under the emulator than on an actual 680x0.

Instruction Caches

The operation of the instruction cache in the 68040 microprocessor is not supported by the 68LC040 Emulator, although all of the bits in the Cache Control Register (CACR) and Cache Address Register (CAAR) related to the instruction cache are supported. In general, of course, your code should not address the cache registers directly.

Because both emulated code and data reside in the PowerPC data cache, the performance benefits associated with caching are still present. Indeed, the caching scheme used transparently by the 68LC040 Emulator results in a higher level of software compatibility than is found on actual 680x0 microprocessors. Some older versions of software that are incompatible with the 68040 cache mechanism can run without problem under the emulator.

Requests to invalidate the 68040 instruction cache are ignored by the 68LC040 Emulator. However, you should continue to issue those calls in order to remain compatible with 680x0-based Macintosh computers. Moreover, all cache flushing required for PowerPC code fragments is performed automatically by the Code Fragment Manager.

Note
For details on invalidating the 680x0 instruction cache, see the chapter "Memory Management Utilities" in *Inside Macintosh: Memory*. ◆

It is possible, although unlikely, that an application depends on the ability of the 68040 instruction cache to retain a stale copy of instructions after the RAM copy of them has been changed. Such applications do not work correctly with 68000-based Macintosh computers (for example, the Macintosh Plus, SE, Classic®, or PowerBook 100) and any 68040-based computers (for example, the Macintosh Quadra 950) when the Cache CDEV is used to disable caching. As a result, this nonemulated behavior should not present any new compatibility problems.

Address Error Exceptions

To improve the performance of branch instructions, the 68LC040 Emulator is not completely compatible with an actual 68040 microprocessor when detecting and reporting address error exceptions. A 680x0 microprocessor checks for address errors before completing the execution of a branch instruction; if it finds an address error, the microprocessor reports (in an address error exception frame that it creates on the stack) the PC at the beginning of the branch instruction. By contrast, the 68LC040 Emulator checks for address errors *after* executing a branch instruction; as a result, it reports the odd branch address as the PC in the exception frame. Because the PC of the instruction that caused the branch is not reported, you might find it more difficult to debug an application that commits address errors. You might also have compatibility problems if you install an address error exception handler.

Bus Error Exceptions

The 68LC040 Emulator handles bus error exceptions slightly differently than does a real 680x0 microprocessor. If you install a bus error handler, you might need to be aware of these differences. You also need to be aware of these differences when debugging your software, because most debuggers need to handle bus error exceptions.

The 68LC040 Emulator creates format $B exception frames when generating and handling bus errors. However, several fields within the exception frame are documented by Motorola as internal fields, and the contents of those fields are very likely to differ between the 68LC040 Emulator exception stack frame and the exception stack frame created by a 680x0 microprocessor. You should not rely on these reserved fields. To avoid any possible confusion that the internal state information in the emulated exception frame is compatible with the internal state information created by the 680x0 micro-processors, the exception frame created by the emulator intentionally uses a value in the Version Number field of the exception frame that is different from the value put there by any 680x0 microprocessor.

In addition, there are several documented fields of the bus error exception frame that have slightly different values in the emulator than on a 680x0-based Macintosh computer. As long as bus error exception handlers do not modify these fields, it is still possible to use the RTE instruction to continue execution of the instruction that caused the exception. In particular, the PC field of the exception frame might not point to the exact beginning of the instruction that generated the exception. Instead, it might point to some location near the beginning of that instruction. Also, the Stage B address field and the Stage B and Stage C instruction pipe fields might not contain valid information.

Finally, the Special Status Word (SSW) differs under the 68LC040 Emulator. The 68LC040 Emulator does not distinguish between instruction space and data space accesses; instead, it converts instruction fetches to data space reads. As a result, the FC2–FC0 field always indicates either a supervisor or a user data space reference. In addition, the emulator never sets the FC, FB, or RM bits, and it ignores the RC and RB bits. The DF bit is fully supported, however, allowing both program completion of bus cycles and rerunning of bus cycles with the RTE instruction. The 68LC040 Emulator also puts valid values in the RM and SIZ bits.

Memory-Mapped I/O Locations

In general, most applications do not directly access memory-mapped I/O locations. Instead, they call device drivers or other system software routines to perform the requested I/O operations. For code (such as a device driver) that does directly access memory-mapped I/O locations, there are a number of compatibility issues. In some cases, the 680x0 emulation environment might not perform some write operations that a real 680x0 performs:

■ The BSET and BCLR instructions might not write back an operand if none of the bits were changed as a result of the operation.

■ Some memory-to-memory MOVE instructions might not write to memory if the source and destination addresses are the same.

You might need to modify your application to use different sequences of instructions to perform the operations if an I/O device was expecting these write bus cycles.

The TAS, CAS, and CAS2 instructions in the 68040 instruction set perform indivisible read, modify, and write memory operations. The 68040 bus architecture provides a special locked bus cycle for a read-and-write operation without allowing any other devices to request the bus between them. These indivisible bus cycles cannot be emulated. As a result, an alternate bus master type of I/O device might be allowed to modify a memory location between the read and the write operations.

The 68020 and 68030 bus interface supports a feature called **dynamic bus sizing** that allows 8- or 16-bit-wide I/O devices to work with the 32-bit-wide data bus. If the processor has a memory request for a data width that was larger than the data width of the device connected to the bus, the memory interface breaks the request into multiple requests that are the width of the device. For example, if a 32-bit read request is made to an 8-bit device, the memory interface actually performs four separate 8-bit reads to assemble the 32-bit data. This feature cannot be emulated. Any application or other software that depends upon this feature must to be modified to use separate instructions to access and assemble each piece of data.

The 68020 and 68030 bus interface also supports a feature called **byte smearing** that allows 8- or 16-bit data to be duplicated on a write operation across all 32 bits of the data bus. The 68040 processor does not support this feature. This feature cannot be emulated, but solutions that were used for the 68040 should be compatible with the 68LC040 Emulator.

The 68020, 68030, and 68040 microprocessors define the NOP instruction as having the effect of synchronizing the pipeline and waiting for all prior bus operations to complete. The 68020 and 68030 have a very small pipeline, and bus operations normally finish soon after they are issued. However, the 68040 and the PowerPC architecture let memory operations be queued and issued out of order. Because of this, the NOP instruction might be needed to ensure that accesses to memory-mapped I/O devices occur in the proper order. The 68LC040 Emulator supports the features of the NOP instruction. Any application that includes NOP instructions should be compatible with all Macintosh computers.

If an I/O device causes a bus timeout that results in a bus error exception, it might not be possible for the PowerPC microprocessor—and therefore the 68LC040 Emulator—to determine the memory address that was accessed. If all locations within a 4 KB I/O page consistently time out, this problem might not occur, but if accesses to some locations within a page sometimes succeed, it is possible for this situation to occur. A bus error exception is generated in that case, but the Data Fault Address field in the exception frame will not be accurate and the DF bit in the SSW will not be set.

Mixed Mode

An **instruction set architecture** is the set of instructions recognized by a particular processor or family of processors. The **Mixed Mode Manager** is the part of the Macintosh system software that manages **mode switches** between code in different instruction set architectures, switching the execution context between the CPU's native PowerPC context and the 68LC040 Emulator. The 68LC040 Emulator is responsible for handling all code in the 680x0 instruction set. This includes existing 680x0 applications, device drivers, system extensions, and even parts of the system software itself that have not yet been rewritten to use the PowerPC instruction set.

Mode switches are required not only when the user switches from an emulated to a native application (or vice versa), but also when any application calls a system software routine or any other code that exists in a different instruction set. For example, the Memory Manager has been reimplemented in the first version of system software for PowerPC processor-based Macintosh computers as native PowerPC code. When an existing 680x0 application running under the 68LC040 Emulator calls a Memory Manager routine such as `NewHandle`, a mode switch is required to move out of the emulator and into the native PowerPC environment. Then, once the Memory Manager routine completes, another mode switch is required to return to the 68LC040 Emulator and to allow the 680x0 application to continue executing.

Similarly, PowerPC applications cause mode switches whenever they invoke routines that exist only as 680x0 code. For example, if a PowerPC application calls a part of the Macintosh Toolbox or Operating System that has not been ported native, a mode switch is required to move from the native environment to the environment of the 68LC040 Emulator.

The Mixed Mode Manager exists solely to manage these kinds of mode switches. It makes it possible for the execution environment of PowerPC processor-based Macintosh computers to accommodate a mixture of 680x0 applications, PowerPC applications, 680x0 system software, PowerPC system software, 680x0 executable resources, PowerPC executable resources, 680x0 device drivers, PowerPC device drivers, and so forth. The 68LC040 Emulator and the Mixed Mode Manager together allow both 680x0 code and PowerPC code to execute on the PowerPC microprocessor.

The Mixed Mode Manager is designed to hide, as much as possible, the hybrid nature of the mixed environment supported on PowerPC processor-based Macintosh computers. Occasionally, however, some executable code needs to interact directly with the Mixed Mode Manager to ensure that a mode switch occurs at the correct time. Because the 68LC040 Emulator is designed to allow existing 680x0 applications and system software to execute without modification, it's always the responsibility of native applications and system software to implement any changes necessary to interact with the Mixed Mode Manager.

This section describes the basic operation of the Mixed Mode Manager. It shows you how, if you're writing a native application, you might need to modify your application to make it compatible with the mixed environment of the system software for PowerPC processor-based Macintosh computers. If you use fairly simple techniques for calling code external to your application and use only the standard types of callback routines, the information in this section might be sufficient for your needs. If not, see the chapter "Mixed Mode Manager" in this book for complete information about the Mixed Mode Manager.

Cross-Mode Calls

The Mixed Mode Manager is intended to operate transparently to most applications and other kinds of software. This means, in particular, that most **cross-mode calls** (calls to code in a different instruction set from the caller's instruction set) are detected automatically by the Mixed Mode Manager and handled without explicit intervention by the calling software. For instance, when a 680x0 application calls a Memory Manager routine—which, as you have already learned, exists as PowerPC code in the system software for PowerPC processor-based Macintosh computers—the Trap Manager dispatches to the code pointed to by the appropriate entry in the trap dispatch table. For routines that are implemented as native code, the entry in the trap dispatch table is a pointer to a routine descriptor, a data structure used by the Mixed Mode Manager to encapsulate information about a routine. The first field in a routine descriptor is an executable 680x0 instruction that invokes the Mixed Mode Manager. The Mixed Mode Manager handles all the details of switching to the native mode, calling the native code, and then returning to the 68LC040 Emulator. The calling application is completely unaware that any mode switches have occurred.

The operation of the Mixed Mode Manager is also completely transparent when a PowerPC application calls a system software routine that exists as 680x0 code, although the exact details are slightly different. When a native application calls a system software routine, the Operating System executes some glue code in an import library of executable code. The glue code inspects the trap dispatch table for the address of the called routine. If the called routine exists only as 680x0 code, the Mixed Mode Manager switches modes and calls the 680x0 routine. When the 680x0 code returns, the Mixed Mode Manager switches back to the native PowerPC environment and the execution of the PowerPC application continues.

Note

See "The PowerPC Native Environment" beginning on page 1-19 for information about the native execution environment, including import libraries. ◆

When writing PowerPC code, you need to explicitly intervene in the mode-switching process only when you execute code (or have code executed on your behalf) whose instruction set architecture might be different from that of the calling code. For example, whenever you pass the address of a callback routine to the Operating System or Toolbox, it's possible that the instruction set architecture of the code whose address you are passing is different from the instruction set architecture of the routine you're passing it to. In such cases, you need to explicitly signal the type of code you're passing and its calling conventions. Otherwise, the Mixed Mode Manager might not be called to make a required mode switch.

To see this a bit more clearly, suppose that you are writing a native PowerPC application that calls the Control Manager procedure `TrackControl`. `TrackControl` accepts as one of its parameters the address of an action procedure that is called repeatedly while the user holds down the mouse button in a control. `TrackControl` has no way of determining in advance the instruction set architecture of the code whose address you will pass it. Moreover, you have no way of determining in advance the instruction set architecture of the `TrackControl` procedure, so you cannot know whether your action procedure and the `TrackControl` procedure are of the same instruction set architecture. As a result, you must explicitly indicate the instruction set architecture of any callback routines whose addresses you pass to the system software.

Routine Descriptors

You indicate the instruction set architecture of a particular routine by creating a **routine descriptor** for that routine. Here is the structure of a routine descriptor.

```
struct RoutineDescriptor {
    unsigned short      goMixedModeTrap;    /*mixed-mode A-trap*/
    char                version;            /*routine descriptor version*/
    RDFlagsType         routineDescriptorFlags;
                                            /*routine descriptor flags*/
    unsigned long       reserved1;          /*reserved*/
    unsigned char       reserved2;          /*reserved*/
    unsigned char       selectorInfo;       /*selector information*/
    short               routineCount;       /*index of last RR in this RD*/
    RoutineRecord       routineRecords[1];/*the individual routines*/
};
typedef struct RoutineDescriptor RoutineDescriptor;
```

As you can see, the first field of a routine descriptor is an executable 680x0 instruction that invokes the Mixed Mode Manager. When the Mixed Mode Manager is called, it inspects the remaining fields of the routine descriptor—in particular the `routineRecords` field—to determine whether a mode switch is required. The `routineRecords` field is an array of **routine records,** each element of which describes a single routine. In the simplest case, the array of routine records contains a single element. Here is the structure of a routine record.

```
struct RoutineRecord {
    ProcInfoType        procInfo;           /*calling conventions*/
    unsigned char       reserved1;          /*reserved*/
    ISAType             ISA;                /*instruction set architecture*/
    RoutineFlagsType    routineFlags;       /*flags for each routine*/
    ProcPtr             procDescriptor;     /*the thing we're calling*/
    unsigned long       reserved2;          /*reserved*/
    unsigned long       selector;           /*selector for dispatched calls*/
};
typedef struct RoutineRecord RoutineRecord;
typedef RoutineRecord *RoutineRecordPtr, **RoutineRecordHandle;
```

The most important fields in a routine record are the `procInfo` field and the `ISA` field. The `ISA` field encodes the instruction set architecture of the routine being described. It must always contain one of these two constants:

```
enum {
    kM68kISA            = (ISAType)0,      /*MC680x0 architecture*/
    kPowerPCISA         = (ISAType)1       /*PowerPC architecture*/
};
```

The `procInfo` field contains the routine's **procedure information,** which encodes the routine's calling conventions and information about the number and location of the routine's parameters. For the standard kinds of callback procedures and other types of "detached" code, the universal interface files include definitions of procedure information. For example, the C language interface file `Controls.h` includes this definition:

```
enum {
    uppControlActionProcInfo = kPascalStackBased
        | STACK_ROUTINE_PARAMETER(1, SIZE_CODE(sizeof(ControlHandle)))
        | STACK_ROUTINE_PARAMETER(2, SIZE_CODE(sizeof(short)))
};
```

This procedure information specification indicates that a control action procedure follows standard Pascal calling conventions and takes two stack-based parameters, a control handle and a part code; the action procedure returns no result. Similarly, the file `Controls.h` defines the procedure information for a control definition function as follows:

```
enum {
    uppControlDefProcInfo = kPascalStackBased
        | RESULT_SIZE(SIZE_CODE(sizeof(long)))
        | STACK_ROUTINE_PARAMETER(1, SIZE_CODE(sizeof(short)))
        | STACK_ROUTINE_PARAMETER(2, SIZE_CODE(sizeof(ControlHandle)))
        | STACK_ROUTINE_PARAMETER(3, SIZE_CODE(sizeof(short)))
        | STACK_ROUTINE_PARAMETER(4, SIZE_CODE(sizeof(long)))
};
```

You can create a routine descriptor by calling the Mixed Mode Manager function NewRoutineDescriptor, as shown in Listing 1-1.

Listing 1-1   Creating a routine descriptor

```
UniversalProcPtr myActionProc;
myActionProc = NewRoutineDescriptor((ProcPtr)MyAction,
                                    uppControlActionProcInfo,
                                    GetCurrentISA());
```

Here, MyAction is the address of your control action procedure and GetCurrentISA is a C language macro that returns the current instruction set architecture. When executed in the PowerPC environment, the NewRoutineDescriptor function creates a routine descriptor in your application heap and returns the address of that routine descriptor. When executed in the 680x0 environment, the NewRoutineDescriptor function simply returns its first parameter. Notice that the result returned by the NewRoutineDescriptor function is of type UniversalProcPtr. A **universal procedure pointer** is defined to be either a 680x0 procedure pointer or a pointer to a routine descriptor, essentially as follows:

```
#if !USESROUTINEDESCRIPTORS
typedef ProcPtr UniversalProcPtr, *UniversalProcHandle;
#else
typedef RoutineDescriptor *UniversalProcPtr, **UniversalProcHandle;
#endif
```

Once you've executed the code in Listing 1-1 (probably at application launch time), you can later call TrackControl like this:

```
TrackControl(myControl, myPoint, myActionProc);
```

If your application is a PowerPC application, the value passed in the gActionProc parameter is not the address of your action procedure itself, but the address of the routine descriptor created in Listing 1-1. When a 680x0 version of TrackControl executes your action procedure, it begins by executing the instruction contained in the first field of the routine descriptor. That instruction invokes the Mixed Mode Manager, which inspects the instruction set architecture of the action routine (contained in the ISA field of the routine record contained in the routine descriptor). If that instruction set architecture differs from the instruction set architecture of the `TrackControl` routine, the Mixed Mode Manager causes a mode switch. Otherwise, if the two instruction set architectures are identical, the Mixed Mode Manager simply executes the action procedure without switching modes.

In short, you solve the general problem of indicating a routine's instruction set architecture by creating routine descriptors and by using the addresses of those routine descriptors where you would have used procedure pointers in the 680x0 programming environment. You have to do this, however, only when you need to pass the address of a routine to some external piece of code (such as the Toolbox or Operating System or some other application) that might be in a different instruction set architecture from that of the routine. There are quite a number of cases in which you pass procedure pointers to the system software and which therefore require you to use the techniques illustrated above for Control Manager action procedures. Some of the typical routines you need to create routine descriptors for include

- grow-zone functions
- control action procedures
- event filter functions
- VBL tasks
- Time Manager tasks
- trap patches
- completion routines

The interface files for the PowerPC system software have been revised to change all references to parameters or fields of type `ProcPtr` to references of type `UniversalProcPtr`. In addition, these new **universal interface files** contain procedure information definitions for all the standard kinds of callback routines. Moreover, the universal interface files define new routines that you can use in place of the more general code shown in Listing 1-1 on page 1-17. For example, the interface file `Controls.h` contains the definition shown in Listing 1-2 for the `NewControlActionProc` function.

Listing 1-2   The definition of the `NewControlActionProc` routine

```
typedef UniversalProcPtr ControlActionUPP;
#define NewControlActionProc(userRoutine) \
    (ControlActionUPP) NewRoutineDescriptor((ProcPtr)userRoutine, \
    uppControlActionProcInfo, GetCurrentISA())
```

Because this routine is defined in the universal header files, you can replace the code in Listing 1-1 with the simpler code shown in Listing 1-3.

Listing 1-3 Creating a routine descriptor for a control action procedure

```
ControlActionUPP myActionProc;
myActionProc = NewControlActionProc((ProcPtr)MyAction);
```

In general, you should use the specific routines defined throughout the universal header files instead of the general technique illustrated in Listing 1-1.

IMPORTANT

You do not need to create routine descriptors for routines that are called only by your application. More generally, if you know for certain that a routine is always called by code of the same instruction set architecture, you can and should continue to use procedure pointers instead of universal procedure pointers. If, however, the address of one of your application's routines might be passed to a Toolbox or Operating System routine, you should make sure to use a routine descriptor. ▲

Memory Considerations

The technique described in the previous section for using routine descriptors is by far the simplest and easiest to implement: any routine descriptors needed by an application are allocated in the application heap at application launch time. The descriptors remain allocated until the application terminates, at which time the entire application heap is reclaimed by the Process Manager. As a result, you don't have to dispose of any routine descriptors created in this way.

If, in some case, you know that you won't be needing a routine descriptor any more during the execution of your application, you can explicitly dispose of it by calling the `DisposeRoutineDescriptor` function. This is most useful when you allocate a routine descriptor for temporary use only. For example, you might call some code that uses a callback procedure only very infrequently. In that case you can allocate the routine descriptor when the code is called and then release it when the code is done.

Finally, you can create a routine descriptor on the stack if you intend to use it only within a single procedure. The Mixed Mode Manager interface file `MixedMode.h` defines the C language macro `BUILD_ROUTINE_DESCRIPTOR` that you can use for this purpose, as well as for initializing static routine descriptors. For details, see "Using Static Routine Descriptors" on page 2-22 in the chapter "Mixed Mode Manager" in this book.

The PowerPC Native Environment

A **run-time environment** is a set of conventions that determine how code is loaded into memory, where data is stored and how it is addressed, and how functions call other functions and system software routines. The run-time environment available on a specific Macintosh computer is determined jointly by the Macintosh system software (which manages the loading and scheduling of executable code) and your software development system (which generates code to conform to the documented run-time conventions).

The run-time environment for native PowerPC code is significantly different from the run-time environment for 680x0 code with which you are probably already familiar. In general, however, the PowerPC run-time environment is both simpler and more powerful than the 680x0 run-time environment. This increased simplicity and power are due primarily to the use of *fragments* as the standard way of organizing executable code and data in memory. In the native PowerPC run-time environment, all discrete collections of executable code—including applications, code resources, extensions, and even the system software itself—are organized as fragments when loaded into memory. Accordingly, all executable code shares the benefits that derive from the organization of fragments, including

■ a uniform set of calling conventions

■ the ability to store code called by many applications or other software in import libraries

■ a simplified means of addressing global data

■ the ability to execute special initialization and termination routines when the fragment is loaded into and unloaded from memory

This section describes the run-time environment for applications and other software executing on PowerPC processor-based Macintosh computers. It describes in detail

■ the structure of fragments

■ how to address global code and data

■ subroutine invocation

■ PowerPC stack frames

■ import libraries

■ the organization of memory

IMPORTANT

Keep in mind that the run-time environment defined by the use of fragments might in the future be available on 680x0-based Macintosh computers (and not solely on PowerPC processor-based Macintosh computers). The new run-time environment based on fragments is intended to be as processor independent as possible. ▲

Fragments

In the run-time environment introduced in the first version of the system software for PowerPC processor-based Macintosh computers, the basic unit of executable code and its associated data is a **fragment.** All fragments share a number of fundamental properties, such as their basic structure and their method of accessing code or data contained in themselves or in other fragments. There are, however, different *uses* for fragments, just as there are different uses for executable code in the 680x0 environment.

Fragments can be loosely differentiated into three categories, based on how they are used.

- An **application** is a fragment that can be launched by the user from the Finder (which calls the Process Manager to do the actual launching), typically to process documents or other collections of information. An application almost always has a user interface and uses standard event-driven programming techniques to control its execution.

- An **import library** is a fragment that contains code and data accessed by some other fragment or fragments. The Macintosh system software, for instance, is an import library that contains the code (and data) implementing the Macintosh Toolbox and Operating System routines. When you link an import library with your application, the import library's code is not copied into your application. Instead, your application contains symbols known as **imports** that refer to some code or data in the import library. When your application is launched, the system software automatically resolves any imports your application contains and creates a connection to the appropriate import libraries.

- An **extension** is a fragment that extends the capabilities of some other fragment. For example, your application might use external code modules like menu definition functions, control definition functions, or data-conversion filters. Unlike import libraries, extensions must be explicitly connected to your application during its execution. There are two types of extensions: application extensions and system extensions. An **application extension** is an extension that is used by a single application. A **system extension** is an extension that is used by the Operating System or by multiple applications; it is usually installed at system startup time from a resource of type `'INIT'`, `'DRVR'`, or `'CDEV'`.

Import libraries and system extensions are sometimes called **shared libraries,** because the code and data they contain can be shared by multiple clients. Import libraries and system extensions are also called **dynamically linked libraries,** because the link between your application and the external code or data it references occurs dynamically at application launch time.

The physical storage for a fragment is a **container,** which can be any kind of object accessible by the Operating System. The system software import library, for example, is stored in the ROM of a Macintosh computer. Other import libraries are typically stored in files of type `'shlb'`. The fragment containing an application's executable code is stored in the application's data fork, which is a file of type `'APPL'`. An extension can be stored in a data file or in a resource in some file's resource fork.

IMPORTANT

In general, it's best to put an application extension into the data fork of some file (possibly even the application's data fork itself), not into a resource. There is, however, one notable exception to this rule, namely when the extension is PowerPC code that is intended to operate in the same way as a 680x0 stand-alone code module. See "Executable Resources" on page 1-34 for more information. ▲

Before the code or data in a fragment can be used, it must be loaded into memory from its container and prepared for execution. This process is usually handled automatically by the **Code Fragment Manager,** the part of the Macintosh Operating System responsible for loading and preparing fragments. Fragment **preparation** consists mainly in resolving any imports in the fragment; the Code Fragment Manager searches for another fragment (an import library) that exports the symbols imported by the fragment being loaded. Of course, the import library containing the code or data imported by the first fragment might itself contain imported symbols from yet a third fragment. If so, the Code Fragment Manager needs to load and prepare the third fragment, then the second fragment, and finally the first fragment.

IMPORTANT

In general, the Code Fragment Manager is called by the Operating System in response to a request to load some specific fragment (for example, when the user launches an application). The import libraries used by that fragment are loaded automatically, if the Code Fragment Manager can find them. The Code Fragment Manager usually operates completely transparently, just like the 680x0-based Segment Manager. You need to use the Code Fragment Manager only if your application uses custom application extensions. See the beginning of the chapter "Code Fragment Manager" in this book for details. ▲

To load fragments into memory from the containers they are stored in, the Code Fragment Manager uses the **Code Fragment Loader,** a set of low-level services called mainly by the Code Fragment Manager. The Code Fragment Loader is responsible for knowing about container formats, such as PEF and XCOFF. Unless you need to design a new container format, you do not need to use the Code Fragment Loader. Currently, however, the application programming interface to the Code Fragment Loader is private.

The following sections describe the organization and operation of fragments in greater detail.

The Structure of Fragments

Once a fragment has been loaded into memory and prepared for execution, the code and data it contains are available to itself and to any fragments that import parts of that code and data. The code and data of a particular fragment are loaded into separate **sections** or regions of memory. In general, the code and data sections of a loaded fragment are not contiguous with one another in memory. Instead, the data section of a fragment is loaded either into your application's heap or into the system heap. The code section of a fragment is usually loaded elsewhere in memory. (See "File Mapping" beginning on page 1-53 for details on the location of the code sections of a fragment.) Regardless of where it is loaded, there is no segmentation within a code section of a fragment.

Because every fragment contains both code and data sections, it follows that any code executing in a fragment-based run-time environment—not just application code—can have global variables. (In the 680x0 run-time environment, it's difficult for some kinds of code to have global variables.) In addition, there is no practical limit on the size of a fragment's data section. By contrast, the total size of an application's global variables in the 680x0 environment is 32 KB, unless your development system provides special capabilities to exceed that limit.

Fragments created by the currently available linkers contain one section of code and one section of static data (although it's theoretically possible to have more than one of each type of section). A fragment's **code section** must contain pure executable code, that is, code that is independent of the location in memory where it is loaded. Pure code can be loaded anywhere in memory. As a result, it cannot contain any absolute branches. In addition, any references to the fragment's data must be position-independent: there can be no absolute data addresses in the code. Because the code contained in a fragment's code section must be pure and position-independent, and because a code section is always read-only, a fragment can be put into ROM or paged directly from an application file. In addition, it's much easier to share pure code than it is to share impure code. This makes it very easy to implement import libraries as fragments.

A fragment's **data section** contains the static data defined by the fragment. An application's data section is typically loaded into the application's heap. An import library's data section can be loaded into the system heap or into the heap of any application that uses the import library. Indeed, it's possible for an import library's data section to be loaded into memory at multiple locations, thereby creating more than one copy of the data. This is especially useful for providing different applications with their own copy of a library's data. See "Import Libraries" beginning on page 1-50 for more details on this.

Even though a fragment's code and data sections can be loaded anywhere in memory, those sections cannot be moved within memory once they've been loaded. Part of the process of loading a fragment into memory is to resolve any dependencies it might have upon other fragments. This preparation involves inserting into part of the fragment's data section a number of pointers to data and code imported by the fragment from other fragments, as described in the following section. To avoid having to perform this fragment preparation more than once, the Operating System requires that a loaded fragment remain stationary in memory for as long as it is loaded.

Note
In the 680x0 environment, an application's code can be unloaded (by the Memory Manager) and later reloaded into a different place in memory. This difference in run-time behavior leads to some important restrictions on stand-alone PowerPC code resources (called *accelerated* resources) that mimic the behavior of existing kinds of 680x0 code resources. See "Executable Resources" beginning on page 1-34 for details. ◆

Imports and Exports

As you've seen, a fragment (for example, an application) can access the code and data contained in some other fragment (typically an import library) by importing that code and data. Conversely, an import library can **export** code and data for use by other fragments (applications, extensions, or even other import libraries). It's the responsibility of the linker to resolve any imports in your application (or other code fragment) to exports in some import library. The linker generates symbols that contain the name of the exporting library and the name of the exported symbol and inserts those symbols into your linked application.

Figure 1-2 illustrates how the linker resolves imports in an application. The SurfWriter object module contains a number of unresolved symbols. Some of the symbols reference code that is part of the system software contained in the InterfaceLib import library. Other unresolved symbols reference code in the SurfTool import library. The linker resolves those symbols and creates the SurfWriter application, which contains the names of the appropriate import library and function.

Figure 1-2   Creating imports in a fragment

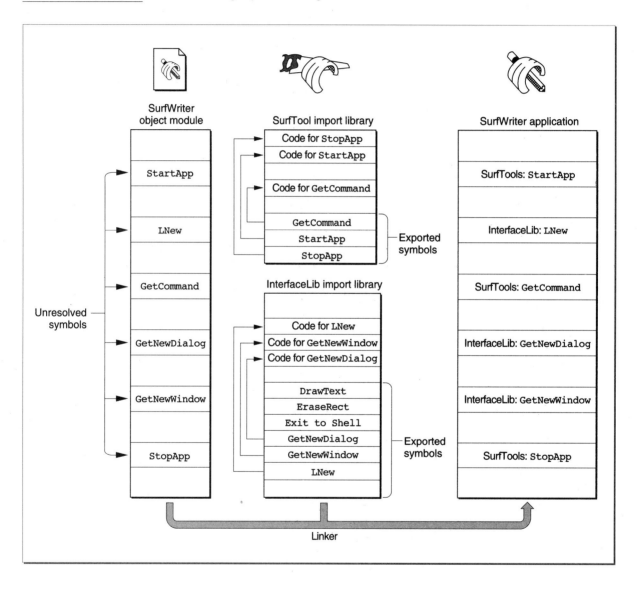

When your application is launched, the Code Fragment Manager searches for the linker-generated import symbols and replaces them with the addresses of the imported code or data. To do this successfully, the Code Fragment Manager needs to find the appropriate import library and load it into memory if it isn't already in memory. Then, it needs to **bind** the imported symbols in your application to the actual addresses, in the import library, of the imported code or data. Once the loading and binding of import libraries are complete, your application can execute.

Note

When binding imported symbols to external code and data, the Code Fragment Manager ensures that the version of the import library used at link time to resolve external symbols is compatible with the version used at fragment loading time. See the chapter "Code Fragment Manager" in this book for a description of this version-checking capability. In general, this all happens transparently to your application or other code. ◆

It's possible to designate some of the imports in your application (or other software) as soft. A **soft import** is an imported symbol whose corresponding code or data might not be available in any import library on the host machine and which is therefore undefined at run time. For example, a particular system software component such as QuickTime might not be available on all Macintosh computers. As a result, if you call QuickTime routines, you should mark all those imports as soft. When the Code Fragment Manager loads and prepares your application, it resolves the soft imports if the QuickTime code and data are available. If the QuickTime code and data aren't available, the Code Fragment Manager inserts an invalid address (namely, `kUnresolvedSymbolAddress`) into your fragment's table of contents entry for any QuickTime routines or data items.

▲ **WARNING**

You should always check to see that any imports declared as soft by your software were successfully resolved at load time. Trying to access code or data referenced by an unresolved soft import will cause your software to crash. ▲

For most system software services, you can use the `Gestalt` function to determine if the necessary code or data is available in the current operating environment. Note that this is not a new requirement and should not cause you to change your existing source code; existing 680x0 software should also call `Gestalt` to ensure that needed system software services are available. When no `Gestalt` selector exists to test for the existence of a particular routine or data item, you can check for unresolved soft imports by comparing the address of the import to `kUnresolvedSymbolAddress`. Listing 1-4 illustrates this technique.

Listing 1-4   Testing for unresolved soft imports

```
extern int printf (char *, ...);
...
if (printf == kUnresolvedSymbolAddress)
   DebugStr("\printf is not available.");
else
   printf("Hello, world!\n");
```

See the description of the MakePEF tool in the book *Building Programs for Macintosh With PowerPC* for exact details on how to specify imports as soft.

The Table of Contents

The imported symbols in a fragment are contained in a special area in the fragment's data section known as the **table of contents (TOC).** Prior to preparation by the Code Fragment Manager, a table of contents contains unresolved references to code and data in some other fragment. After preparation, the table of contents contains a pointer to each routine or data item that is imported from some other fragment. This provides a means of global addressing whereby a fragment can locate the code or data it has imported from other fragments.

Note

As you can see, the phrase "table of contents" is a slight misnomer, because a fragment's table of contents does not supply a list of the addresses of routines or data in the fragment itself. Rather, a fragment's table of contents consists (in part) of the addresses of code and data that the fragment imports, which reside in some other fragment. The table of contents is more akin to a personal address book. A fragment's table of contents is private to the fragment itself and exists solely to provide external linkage for the code in the fragment. ◆

A fragment's table of contents also contains pointers to the fragment's own static data. Because the code and data sections of a fragment are usually loaded into different locations in memory, and because they must both be position-independent, the code section needs a method of finding its own data, such as data addressed by global variables. Global variables are addressed through the fragment's table of contents. Within the compiled code of your application, references to global variables appear as indirect references via offsets into the table of contents.

Of course, for this scheme to work, the code section of a fragment needs to know where in memory its TOC begins. The address of the TOC cannot be compiled into the fragment; instead, the address of the TOC of the currently executing fragment is maintained in a register on the microprocessor. Currently, the general-purpose register GPR2 is dedicated to serve as the **Table of Contents Register (RTOC).** It contains the address in memory of the beginning of the TOC of the currently executing fragment.

It's easy to see how a code fragment can find its own global data. It simply adds the compiled-in offset of a global variable within the TOC to the address of the TOC contained in the RTOC. The result is the address of a pointer to the desired data.

It's slightly more complicated to see how a code fragment can execute an external piece of code. As it does with global data, the linker accesses external code via an offset into the TOC. The corresponding address in the TOC, however, is not the address of the piece of external code itself. Instead, the TOC of the calling fragment contains the address—in the static data section of the called fragment—of a **transition vector,** a data structure that contains two pointers: the address of the routine being called and the address of the called fragment's TOC. The basic structure of a transition vector is shown in Figure 1-3.

Figure 1-3   A transition vector

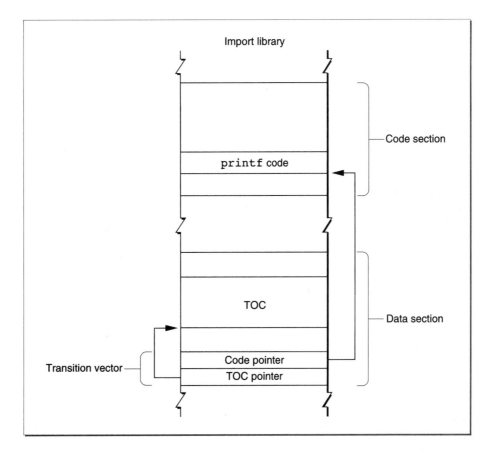

Note

Strictly speaking, a transition vector can contain any number of pointers, as long as there are at least two. The first pointer is always the address of the routine being called, and the second pointer is always a value to be loaded into GPR2 prior to the execution of that routine. The second pointer in a transition vector can serve any purpose appropriate to the called routine. In the PowerPC environment for Macintosh computers, the second pointer is almost always the TOC address of the fragment containing the called routine. However, the callee is free to use the second pointer in other ways, if this is deemed useful. Your development system's compiler ultimately determines the size and contents of a transition vector. ◆

A TOC entry for an external routine points to a transition vector largely so that the calling routine can set up an RTOC with the called fragment's TOC value. Then, when the called routine exits, the caller restores the RTOC to its original value, pointing to the TOC of the calling fragment. This kind of function call is known as a **cross-TOC call.** During a cross-TOC call, GPR12 is assumed to point to the transition vector itself; this convention allows the called routine to access any additional fields in the transition vector beyond the first two.

To access data stored in another fragment, there is no need for the caller to install the TOC address of the other fragment in the RTOC. Instead, the TOC entry of the calling fragment contains a pointer to the external data, in exactly the same way that a TOC entry for global data in the same fragment contains a pointer to that data.

In short, a fragment's table of contents contains

- one pointer for each imported routine called by the fragment; this pointer is the address of a transition vector in the data section of the import library.

- one pointer for each external data item used by the fragment; this pointer is the address of the data in the data section of the import library.

- one pointer for each global variable.

- one pointer for each pool of C static data internal to the fragment.

Note

Compilers and assembly-language programmers may place additional items in a fragment's table of contents. ◆

The size of a fragment's TOC is determined at the time your source code is compiled and linked, but the actual values in the TOC cannot be determined until the fragment is loaded and prepared for execution. When the Code Fragment Manager loads a fragment, it also loads any fragments that contain exports used by that fragment; at that time, the addresses of those exports can be determined and placed into the original fragment's TOC.

The TOC provides the means whereby a routine in a given fragment can find its own static data and any external routines it calls. In providing access to a fragment's own data, the TOC is analogous to the A5 world in applications created for the 680x0 run-time environment. The TOC is more general than the A5 world, however, at least insofar as it allows stand-alone code to have global data; in the 680x0 environment, only applications have an A5 world and its resulting easy access to global data.

The Code Fragment Manager is responsible for dynamically resolving symbols in an unprepared TOC by binding them with their referents. This process involves finding unresolved imported symbols in the TOC, searching for the code or data they refer to, and replacing the symbols with the relevant addresses. This indirection through the TOC gives rise to a number of useful features.

- Routines external to a fragment can be specified by name, not by address. This allows routines to be grouped into import libraries.

- Data can be specified by name, not by address.

- Callback routines can be specified by name, not by address.

- Initialization and termination routines can be included in a fragment and are executed automatically by the Code Fragment Manager when the fragment is connected and disconnected, respectively.

- A fragment's data can be either shared among multiple applications or instantiated separately for each application that uses the fragment. This feature is especially useful for fragments that are import libraries.

■ The Code Fragment Manager can treat two import libraries as a single import library for the purposes of symbol resolution. This feature is especially useful for creating an update library—an import library that contains enhancements or bug fixes for an existing import library.

■ A fragment's code and data can be loaded anywhere in memory, because the address of a routine or a piece of data is always relative to the address contained in the RTOC.

Notice that TOC entries that point into another fragment always point into the data section of that fragment. This is a consequence of the fact that code is exported only through a transition vector in the fragment's data section. Code symbols are never exported directly, but only via data symbols.

Because entries in a TOC are addressed using a register value plus an offset, and because offsets are signed 16-bit quantities, a table of contents can be at most 64 KB in size, with at most 16,384 entries. As already noted, current compilers and linkers create only one TOC per fragment. If you need to work with more than 16,384 pointers, you can create one or more import libraries, each of which can itself contain up to 16,384 pointers. As a practical matter, this is not a serious limitation.

Note
Future development tools might not create a TOC at all. The method of collecting a fragment's imported symbols and global data references into a table of contents is independent of the method of packaging code and data into a fragment. A fragment doesn't need to have a table of contents, but all current development systems that create fragments do in fact create a single table of contents in each fragment. ◆

Although transition vectors are used primarily for cross-TOC calls (as described above), they are also used for pointer-based function calls. Whenever your application takes the address of a function (even one inside the same fragment), a transition vector is allocated to point to that function. Indeed, all function pointers in PowerPC code are actually pointers to transition vectors. If you are writing in assembly language, you need to be sure to export pointers to transition vectors instead of to actual code.

Special Routines

A fragment can define three special symbols that are separate from the list of symbols exported by the fragment. These symbols define an initialization routine, a termination routine, and a main routine (or block of data). These routines, if present, are called at specific times during the loading, unloading, or normal execution of a fragment. A fragment that is an application must define a main symbol that is the application's entry point. Import libraries and extensions may or may not define any of these symbols.

A fragment's **initialization routine** is called as part of the process of loading and preparing the fragment. You can use the initialization routine to perform any actions that should be performed before any of the fragment's other code or static data is accessed. When a fragment's initialization routine is executed, it is passed a pointer to a fragment initialization block, a data structure that contains information about the fragment. In particular, the initialization block contains information about the location of the fragment's container. (For example, if an import library's code fragment is contained in some file's data fork, you can use that information to find the file's resource fork.)

It's important to know when the initialization routine for a fragment is executed. If the loading and preparation of a fragment cause a (currently unloaded) import library to be loaded in order to resolve imports in the first fragment, the initialization routine of the import library is executed before that of the first fragment. This is obviously what you would expect to happen, because the initialization routine of the first fragment might need to use code or data in the import library. In case there are two import libraries that depend upon each other, their developer may specify which should be initialized first.

A fragment's **termination routine** is executed as part of the process of unloading a fragment. You can use the termination routine to undo the actions of the initialization routine or, more generally, to release any resources or memory allocated by the fragment.

Note

See "Fragment-Defined Routines" beginning on page 3-26 in the chapter "Code Fragment Manager" in this book for more information about a fragment's initialization and termination routines. ◆

The use of a fragment's **main symbol** depends upon the type of fragment containing it. For applications, the main symbol refers to the **main routine,** which is simply the usual entry point. The main routine typically performs any necessary application initialization not already performed by the initialization routine and then jumps into the application's main event loop. For import libraries, the main symbol (if it exists) is ignored. For extensions having a single entry point, a main routine can be used instead of an exported symbol to avoid having to standardize on a particular name.

IMPORTANT

In fact, the main symbol exported by a fragment does not have to refer to a routine at all; it can refer instead to a block of data. You can use this fact to good effect with application extensions, where the block of data referenced by the main symbol can contain essential information about the extension. For instance, a loadable tool contained in a fragment might store its name, icon, and other information in that block. The Code Fragment Manager returns the address of the main symbol when you programmatically load and prepare a fragment. ▲

Fragment Storage

As you've learned, the physical storage for a fragment is a container. A container can be any logically contiguous piece of storage, such as the data fork of a file (or some portion thereof), the Macintosh ROM, or a resource. In the first version of the system software for PowerPC processor-based Macintosh computers, the Code Fragment Loader can recognize two kinds of container formats, the **Extended Common Object File Format (XCOFF)** and the **Preferred Executable Format (PEF).**

XCOFF is a refinement of the Common Object File Format (COFF), the standard executable file format on many UNIX®-based computers. XCOFF is supported on

Macintosh computers primarily because the early development tools produce executable code in the XCOFF format.

IMPORTANT

Not all object code in the XCOFF format will execute on Macintosh computers. Any XCOFF code that uses UNIX-style memory services or that otherwise depends on UNIX features will not execute correctly on Macintosh computers. ▲

PEF is an object file format defined by Apple Computer. A container in the PEF format is dramatically smaller than the corresponding container in the XCOFF format. This smaller size reduces both the disk space occupied by the container and the time needed to load the container's code and data into memory. More importantly, PEF provides support for a fragment's optional initialization and termination routines and for the version checking performed by the Code Fragment Manager when an import library is connected to a fragment.

As you know, the mixed environment provided by the first version of the system software for PowerPC processor-based Macintosh computers allows the user to run both 680x0 and PowerPC applications. The Process Manager needs some method of determining, at the time the user launches an application, what kind of application it is. Because the mixed environment is intended to support existing 680x0 applications unmodified, the Process Manager assumes that an application is a 680x0 application, unless you specifically indicate otherwise. You do this by including, in the resource fork of your PowerPC application, a **code fragment resource.** This resource (of type `'cfrg'` and ID 0) indicates the instruction set architecture of your application's executable code, as well as the location of the code's container. Typically, the code and data for a PowerPC application are contained in your application's data fork, as shown in Figure 1-4.

Figure 1-4   The structure of a PowerPC application

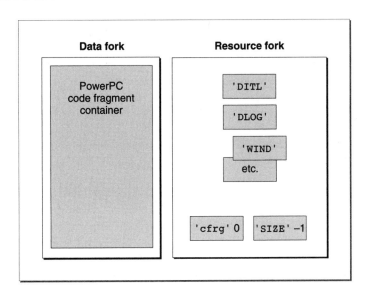

If your application contains a code fragment resource, the Process Manager calls the
Code Fragment Manager to load and prepare your application's code and data. If, on the
other hand, your application does not contain a code fragment resource, the Process
Manager assumes that your application is a 680x0 application; in this case, the Process
Manager calls the Segment Manager to load your application's executable code from
resources of type 'CODE' in your application's resource fork, as illustrated in Figure 1-5.

Figure 1-5   The structure of a 680x0 application

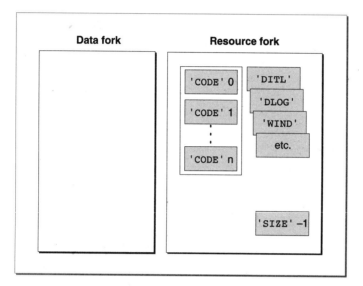

Listing 1-5 shows the Rez input for a sample code fragment resource.

Listing 1-5   The Rez input for a sample 'cfrg' resource

```
#include "CodeFragmentTypes.r"
resource 'cfrg' (0) {
    {
        kPowerPC,                /*instruction set architecture*/
        kFullLib,                /*no update level for apps*/
        kNoVersionNum,           /*no implementation version number*/
        kNoVersionNum,           /*no definition version number*/
        kDefaultStackSize,       /*use default stack size*/
        kNoAppSubFolder,         /*no library directory*/
        kIsApp,                  /*fragment is an application*/
        kOnDiskFlat,             /*fragment is on disk*/
        kZeroOffset,             /*fragment starts at fork start*/
        kWholeFork,              /*fragment occupies entire fork*/
```

```
    "SurfWriter"                    /*name of the application*/
  }
};
```

The `'cfrg'` resource specification in Listing 1-5 indicates, among other things, that the application consists of PowerPC code, that the code is contained in the application's data fork, and that the code container occupies the entire data fork. It's possible to have the container occupy only part of the data fork, if you need to put other information in the data fork as well. (Some applications, for instance, put copyright or serial number information in their data fork.) You do this by specifying a nonzero offset for the beginning of the code fragment. Alternatively, you can move the information previously contained in the data fork into one or more resources in your application's resource fork, thereby reserving the entire data fork for the PowerPC code fragment.

Note
For information about the other fields in a code fragment resource, see the chapter "Code Fragment Manager" in this book. ◆

This recommended placement of an application's PowerPC code in the data fork makes it easy to create **fat applications** that contain both PowerPC and 680x0 executable code. A fat application contains 680x0 code in `'CODE'` resources in the resource fork and PowerPC code in the data fork, as shown in Figure 1-6.

Figure 1-6   The structure of a fat application

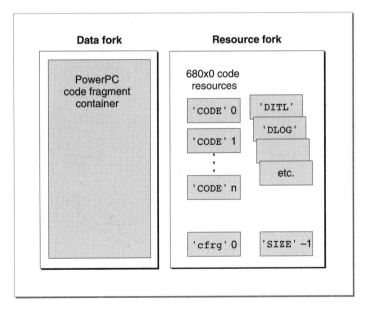

The advantage of a fat application is that it can be executed on either 680x0-based or PowerPC processor-based Macintosh computers. The Process Manager on 680x0-based Macintosh computers knows nothing about `'cfrg'` resources. As a result, it ignores the code contained in the data fork and uses the code contained in the application's 'CODE' resources. The Process Manager on PowerPC processor-based Macintosh computers, however, reads the 'cfrg' resource and uses the code in the specified location (usually, the data fork); the 680x0 'CODE' resources in the resource fork are ignored.

Ideally, you should package your application as a fat application, to give your users maximum flexibility in how they manage their working environment. For example, a user might move a storage device (such as a hard disk) containing your application from a 680x0-based Macintosh computer to a PowerPC processor-based Macintosh computer. If your application is fat, it can be launched successfully in either environment.

For various reasons, however, you might decide not to package your application as a fat application. If so, you should at the very least include an executable 680x0 'CODE' resource that displays an alert box informing the user that your application runs only on PowerPC processor-based Macintosh computers.

Note

Import libraries also need a code fragment resource, to indicate the location of the container and the appropriate version information. See the chapter "Code Fragment Manager" in this book for information about creating a 'cfrg' resource for an import library. ◆

Executable Resources

The Code Fragment Manager is extremely flexible in where it allows fragments to be stored. As you've seen, an application's executable code and global data are typically stored in a container in the application's data fork. Import libraries supplied as part of the Macintosh system software are often stored in ROM, while import libraries created by third-party developers are usually stored in the data forks of files on disk. It's also possible to use resources as containers for executable PowerPC code. This section describes how to work with executable resources in the PowerPC environment.

There are two kinds of executable resources you can create that contain PowerPC code: resources whose behavior is defined by the system software (or by some other software) and those whose behavior is defined by your application alone. For present purposes, these two kinds of resources are called *accelerated* and *private* resources, respectively.

Note

The terms *accelerated* and *private* are used here simply to help distinguish these two kinds of executable resources containing PowerPC code. They are not used elsewhere in this book or in *Inside Macintosh*. ◆

First, you can put an executable PowerPC code fragment into a resource to obtain a PowerPC version of a 680x0 stand-alone code module. For example, you might recompile an existing menu definition procedure (which is stored in a resource of type 'MDEF') into PowerPC code. Because the Menu Manager code that calls your menu definition procedure might be 680x0 code, a mode switch to the PowerPC environment might be required before your definition procedure can be executed. As a result, you need to prepend a routine descriptor onto the beginning of the resource, as shown in Figure 1-7. These kinds of resources are called **accelerated resources** because they are faster implementations of existing kinds of resources. You can transparently replace 680x0 code resources by accelerated PowerPC code resources without having to change the software (for example, the application) that uses them.

Figure 1-7   The structure of an accelerated resource

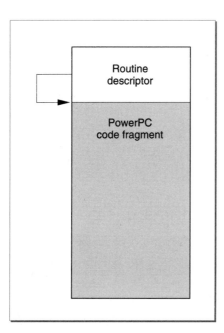

Sometimes it's useful to keep the executable code of a definition function in some location other than a resource. To do this, you need to create a **stub definition resource** that is of the type expected by the system software and that simply jumps to your code. For example, Listing 1-6 shows the Rez input for a stub list definition resource.

Listing 1-6   Rez input for a list definition procedure stub

```
data 'LDEF' (128, "MyCustomLDEF", preload, locked) {
   /*need to fill in destination address before using this stub*/
   $"41FA 0006"   /*LEA PC+8, A0      ;A0 <- ptr to destination address*/
   $"2050"        /*MOVEA.L (A0), A0  ;AO <- destination address*/
   $"4ED0"        /*JMP (A0)          ;jump to destination address*/
   $"00000000"    /*destination address*/
};
```

Your application (or other software) is responsible for filling in the destination address before the list definition procedure is called by the List Manager. For 680x0 code, the destination address should be the address of the list definition procedure itself. For

PowerPC code, the destination address should be a universal procedure pointer (that is, the address of a routine descriptor for the list definition procedure).

By contrast, you can create a resource containing executable PowerPC code solely for the purposes of your application (perhaps on analogy with the standard kinds of code-bearing resources used by the system software). Because these kinds of executable resources do not conform to a calling interface defined by the system software (or by some other widely available software, such as HyperCard), they are called **private resources.** The code in private resources is called only by your application, not by any other external code. As a result, there is no need to put a routine descriptor onto the beginning of the executable code. Figure 1-8 shows the general structure of a private resource.

Figure 1-8   The structure of a private resource

It's important to understand the distinction between accelerated and private resources, so that you know when to create them and how to load and execute the code they contain. An accelerated resource is any resource containing PowerPC code that has a single entry point at the top (the routine descriptor) and that models the traditional behavior of a 680x0 stand-alone code resource. There are many examples, including menu definition procedures (stored in resources of type 'MDEF'), control definition functions (stored in resources of type 'CDEF'), window definition functions (stored in resources of type 'WDEF'), list definition procedures (stored in resources of type 'LDEF'), HyperCard extensions (stored in resources of type 'XCMD'), and so forth. A private resource is any other kind of executable resource whose code is called directly by your application.

IMPORTANT

For several reasons, it's generally best to avoid using private resources unless you absolutely must put some code into a resource. As you'll see later (in "File Mapping" on page 1-53), the executable code of a private resource is loaded into your application's heap and is not eligible for file mapping. Whenever possible, you should put executable PowerPC code into your application's data fork or create your own application-specific files. ▲

In most cases, you don't need to do anything special to get the system software to recognize your accelerated resource and to call it at the appropriate time. For example, the Menu Manager automatically loads a custom menu definition procedure into memory when you call `GetMenu` for a menu whose `'MENU'` resource specifies that menu definition procedure. Similarly, HyperCard calls code like that shown in Listing 1-7 to load a resource of type `'XCMD'` into memory and execute the code it contains.

Listing 1-7   Using an accelerated resource

```
Handle      myHandle;
XCmdBlock   myParamBlock;

myHandle = Get1NamedResource('XCMD', '\pMyXCMD');
HLock(myHandle);

/*Fill in the fields of myParamBlock here.*/

CallXCMD(&myParamBlock, myHandle);
HUnlock(myHandle);
```

The caller of an accelerated resource executes the code either by jumping to the code (if the caller is 680x0 code) or by calling the Mixed Mode Manager `CallUniversalProc` function (if the caller is PowerPC code). In either case, the Mixed Mode Manager calls the Code Fragment Manager to prepare the fragment, which is already loaded into memory. With accelerated resources, you don't need to call the Code Fragment Manager yourself. In fact, you don't need to do anything special at all for the system software to recognize and use your accelerated resource, if you've built it correctly. This is because the system software is designed to look for, load, and execute those resources in the appropriate circumstances. In many cases, your application passes to the system software just a resource type and resource ID. The resource must begin with a routine descriptor, so that the dereferenced handle to the resource is a universal procedure pointer.

IMPORTANT

The MPW interface file `MixedMode.r` contains Rez templates that you can use to create the routine descriptor that appears at the beginning of an accelerated resource. If you want to build the routine descriptor yourself or if you want to build a fat accelerated resource (which contains both PowerPC and 680x0 code), see the section "Executing Resource-Based Code" beginning on page 2-24 in the chapter "Mixed Mode Manager" in this book. ▲

The code shown in Listing 1-7—or similar code for any other accelerated resource—can be executed multiple times with no appreciable performance loss. If the code resource remains in memory, the only overhead incurred by Listing 1-7 is to lock the code, fill in the parameter block, jump to the code, and then unlock it. However, because of the way in which the system software manages your accelerated resources, there are several key restrictions on their operation:

■ An accelerated resource cannot contain a termination routine, largely because the Operating System doesn't know when the resource is no longer needed and hence when the resource can be unloaded. The Code Fragment Manager effectively forgets about the connection to your resource as soon as it has prepared the resource for execution.

■ An accelerated resource must contain a main symbol, which must be a procedure. For example, in an accelerated `'MDEF'` resource, the main procedure should be the menu definition procedure itself (which typically dispatches to other routines contained in the resource).

■ You cannot call the Code Fragment Manager routine `FindSymbol` to get information about the exported symbols in an accelerated resource. More generally, you cannot call any Code Fragment Manager routine that requires a connection ID as a parameter. The connection ID is maintained internally by the Operating System and is not available to your application.

■ The fragment's data section is instantiated in place (that is, within the block of memory into which the resource itself is loaded). For in-place instantiation, you need to build an accelerated resource using an option that specifies that the data section of the fragment not be compressed. See the documentation for your software development system for instructions on doing this.

Note

If you use the MakePEF tool to help build an accelerated resource, you should specify the –b option to suppress data section compression. ◆

You might have noticed that the code shown in Listing 1-7 unlocks the `'XCMD'` resource after executing it. By unlocking the resource, the caller is allowing it to be moved around in memory or purged from memory altogether. This behavior—which is perfectly acceptable in the 680x0 environment—contradicts the general rule that fragments are not allowed to move in memory after they've been loaded and prepared (see page 1-23). To allow accelerated PowerPC resources to be manipulated just like 680x0 code resources, the Mixed Mode Manager and the Code Fragment Manager cooperate to make sure that the code is ready to be executed when it is called. If the resource code hasn't been moved since it was prepared for execution, then no further action is necessary. If, however, the code resource has moved or been reloaded elsewhere in memory, some of the global data in the resource might have become invalid. For example, a global pointer might become dangling if the code or data it points to has moved. To help avoid dangling pointers, the Code Fragment Manager updates any pointers in the fragment's data section that are initialized at compile time and not modified at run time. However, the Code Fragment Manager cannot update all global data references in an accelerated resource that has moved in memory. There is, therefore, an important restriction on using global data in accelerated resources:

■ An accelerated resource must not use global pointers (in C code, pointers declared as `extern` or `static`) that are either initialized at run time or contained in dynamically allocated data structures to point to code or data contained in the resource itself. An accelerated resource can use uninitialized global data to point to objects in the heap. In addition, an accelerated resource can use global pointers that are initialized at compile time to point to functions, other global data, and literal strings, but these pointers cannot be modified at run time.

Listing 1-8 shows some declarations that can be used in an accelerated resource, provided that the resource code does not change the values of the initialized variables.

Listing 1-8   Some acceptable global declarations in an accelerated resource

```
int a;          /*uninitialized; not modified if resource moves*/
Ptr myPtr;      /*uninitialized; not modified if resource moves; */
                /* can be assigned at run time to point to heap object*/
Handle *h;      /*uninitialized; not modified if resource moves; */
                /* can be assigned at run time to point to heap object*/
int *b = &a;                    /*updated each time resource moves*/
char *myStr = "Hello, world!";   /*updated each time resource moves*/
extern int myProcA(), myProcB();
struct {
   int   (*one)();
   int   (*two)();
   char  *str;
} myRec = {myProcA, myProcB, "Hello again!"};
            /*all three pointers are updated each time resource moves*/
```

Listing 1-9 shows some data declarations and code that will not work in an accelerated resource that is moved or purged.

Listing 1-9   Some unacceptable global declarations and code in an accelerated resource

```
int a;
int *b;
int *c = &a;
Ptr (*myPtr) (long) = NewPtr;
```

```
static Ptr MyNewPtr();
struct myHeapStruct {
    int       *b;
    Ptr       (myPtr) (long);
} *hs;

b = &a;          /*b does not contain &a after resource is moved*/
c = NULL;        /*c does not contain NULL after resource is moved*/
c = (int *) NewPtr(4);      /*dangling pointer after resource is moved*/
myPtr = MyNewPtr;           /*dangling pointer after resource is moved*/
hs = NewPtr(sizeof(myHeapStruct));
                 /*hs still points to nonrelocatable heap block after move*/
hs->b = &a;      /*hs->b will not point to global a after move*/
hs->myPtr = MyNewPtr;
                 /*hs->myPtr will not point to MyNewPtr after move*/
```

Note that a code fragment stored as an accelerated resource can import both code and data from an import library. The code and data in the import library do not move in memory. As a result, you can sidestep the restrictions on global data in an accelerated resource by putting the global data used by the accelerated resource into an import library. The import library is unloaded only when your application terminates, not when the accelerated resource is purged.

To load and prepare a *private* resource, you need to call the Resource Manager, Memory Manager, and Code Fragment Manager explicitly, as shown in Listing 1-10.

Listing 1-10   Using a private resource

```
Handle         myHandle;
OSErr          myErr;
ConnectionID   myConnID;
Ptr            myMainAddr;
Str255         myErrName;

myHandle = Get1NamedResource('RULE', '\pDeM');
HLock(myHandle);
myErr = GetMemFragment(*myHandle, GetHandleSize(myHandle),
            '\pDeM', kLoadNewCopy, &myConnID, (Ptr*)&myMainAddr,
            myErrName);

/*Call the code in here.*/

myErr = CloseConnection(myConnID);
HUnlock(myHandle);
```

None of the restrictions on accelerated resources listed above applies to your own private code-bearing resources. For instance, you do have access to the connection ID to the resource-based fragment (as you can see in Listing 1-10), so you can call Code Fragment Manager routines like `CloseConnection` and `FindSymbol`. However, the overhead involved in loading the code fragment and later unloading it is nontrivial, so you should avoid closing the connection to a private resource (that is, calling `CloseConnection`) until you're done using it.

Because a private resource is just a fragment stored in a resource, it's preferable to avoid using private resources, whenever possible, by putting that code and data into some file. By doing this, you gain the benefits afforded by the system software to file-based fragments (such as file mapping directly from the file's data fork). You should use private executable resources only in cases where your code absolutely must be packaged in a resource.

Calling Conventions

The software development tools and the system software for PowerPC processor-based Macintosh computers dictate a set of calling conventions that are significantly different from those you might be used to in the 680x0 execution environment. The new calling conventions are designed to reduce the amount of time required to call another piece of code and to simplify the entire code-calling process. In the 680x0 environment, there are many ways for one routine to call another, depending on whether the called routine conforms to Pascal, C, Operating System, or other calling conventions. In the PowerPC environment, there is only one standard calling convention, having these features:

- Most parameters are passed in registers dedicated for that purpose. The large number of general-purpose and floating-point registers makes this goal quite easy to achieve. Parameters are passed on the stack only when they cannot be put into registers.

- The size of a stack frame is determined at compile time, not dynamically at run time.

- Stack frames are subject to a strict set of rules governing their structure. The new run-time architecture reserves specific areas of a stack frame for saved registers, local variables, parameters, and stack frame linkage information (such as the return address and the beginning of the previous stack frame).

The following sections describe these differences in greater detail. They begin by reviewing the procedure calling conventions that exist on 680x0-based Macintosh computers. Then they describe the calling conventions adopted for PowerPC processor-based Macintosh computers and show how those conventions affect the organization of the stack.

IMPORTANT

The information in the following sections is provided primarily for debugging purposes or for compiler writers and assembly-language programmers, who need to conform to the new calling conventions. Because generating code conforming to these conventions is handled automatically by your compiler, you might not need this information for writing applications in a high-level language. ▲

The 680x0 Calling Conventions

To appreciate how different the PowerPC calling conventions are from the 680x0 calling conventions, it's useful to review the model used on 680x0-based Macintosh computers. On 680x0-based computers, there is a conventional grow-down stack whose parts are delimited by two pointers: a stack pointer and a frame pointer. Figure 1-9 illustrates a typical 680x0 stack frame.

Figure 1-9   A 680x0 stack frame

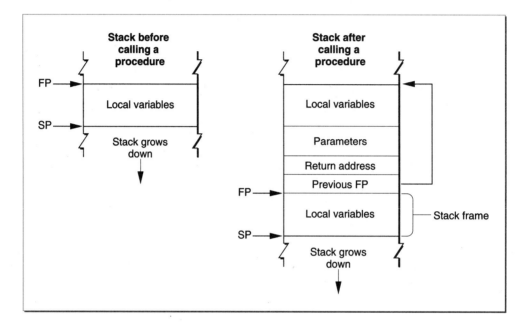

Note

By convention, the stack grows from high memory addresses toward low memory addresses. The end of the stack that grows or shrinks is usually referred to as the "top" of the stack, even though it's actually at the lower end of memory occupied by the stack. ◆

The **stack pointer (SP)** points to the top of the stack and defines its current downward limit. All operations that push data onto the stack or pop data off it do so by reading and then modifying the stack pointer. The Operating System uses the 680x0 register A7 as the stack pointer.

The **frame pointer (FP)** points to the base in memory of the current **stack frame,** the area of the stack used by a routine for its parameters, return address, local variables, and temporary storage. Because the Operating System maintains the frame pointer, it can easily find the beginning of the stack frame when it's time to pop it off the stack. The Operating System uses the 680x0 register A6 as the frame pointer.

A routine's parameters are always placed on the stack above the frame pointer, and its local variables are always placed below the frame pointer. The 680x0 hardware enforces

16-bit alignment for parameters on the stack. So, for example, if you push a single byte onto the stack, the stack pointer is decremented by 2 bytes rather than 1.

The order of the parameters on the stack differs according to the language type of the called routine. When you call a C routine on a 680x0-based Macintosh computer, the parameters are pushed onto the stack in order from right to left. This order is dictated by the fact that the C language allows routines with a variable number of parameters. The first parameter (which often indicates how many parameters are being passed) must always be pushed onto the stack last, so that it resides at a fixed offset from the frame pointer. Moreover, because only the caller knows how many parameters it pushed onto the stack, it is always the caller's responsibility to pop the parameters off the stack. Finally, with C routines, a function result is returned in register D0 (or, for floating-point results, in register FPR0). However, structures and other large values are handled differently: the caller allocates space for the result and passes a pointer to that storage as the first (that is, leftmost) parameter.

The calling conventions for Pascal routines are different from those for C routines. For Pascal routines, the caller pushes space for the return result onto the stack before pushing the parameters. The caller pushes parameters onto the stack from left to right. Because Pascal does not allow routines with a variable number of parameters, the size of a stack frame can be determined at compile time. It is therefore the responsibility of the called routine to remove the parameters from the stack before returning.

Note

These differences between C and Pascal are due entirely to historical factors, not to any requirements of the 680x0 environment. It would have been possible for Pascal routines to follow the C calling conventions. ◆

There are still other calling conventions followed on 680x0-based Macintosh computers. Macintosh Toolbox managers generally follow Pascal conventions, although some of the most recent additions to the Toolbox follow C conventions. More importantly, the Macintosh Operating System typically ignores the stack altogether. Instead, Operating System calls generally pass parameters and return results in registers.

The PowerPC Calling Conventions

The native run-time environment on PowerPC processor-based Macintosh computers uses a set of uniform calling conventions:

- Parameters are processed from left to right and are placed into general-purpose registers GPR3 through GPR10 and (when necessary) floating-point registers FPR1 through FPR13.

- Function results are returned in GPR3, FPR1, or by passing a pointer to a structure as the implicit leftmost parameter (as in the 680x0 C implementation).

- Any parameters that do not fit into the designated registers are passed on the stack. In addition, enough space is allocated on the stack to hold all parameters, whether they are passed in registers or not.

Like the 680x0 run-time environment, the PowerPC run-time environment uses a grow-down stack that contains areas for a routine's parameters, for linkage information, and for local variables. However, the organization of the stack in the PowerPC environment is significantly different from that in the 680x0 environment. The PowerPC run-time environment uses a single stack pointer and no frame pointer. To achieve this simplification, the PowerPC stack has a much more rigidly defined structure than does the stack in the 680x0 environment. Figure 1-10 illustrates the general structure of the stack in the PowerPC environment.

Figure 1-10 The PowerPC stack

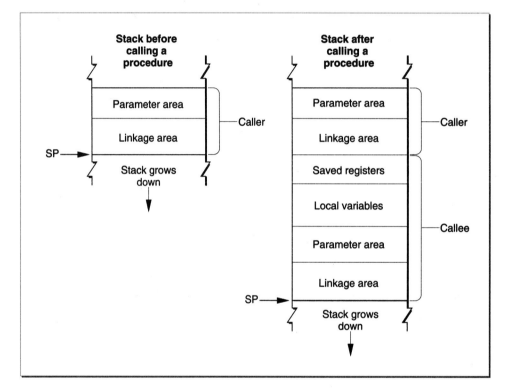

The caller's stack frame includes a parameter area and some linkage information. The **parameter area** in each stack frame is used by the caller to hold the parameters of any routines the caller calls (*not* the parameters of the caller itself). Of course, a given routine might in turn call several other routines; if so, the parameter area in the caller's stack frame is made large enough to accommodate the largest parameter list of all routines the caller calls. It is the caller's responsibility to set up the parameter area before each call to some other routine, and the callee's responsibility to access its parameters from that parameter area. See the following section, "Parameter Passing" on page 1-47, for details on the structure of a routine's parameter area.

Once the caller has set up the parameters for a call to some other routine, it then stores its own RTOC value in its **linkage area,** an area of the caller's stack frame that holds the saved stack pointer, Condition Register (CR), Link Register (LR), and RTOC values. It is necessary to save the caller's RTOC value because the callee might reside in another fragment, a situation that would require that the callee's RTOC value be installed in the RTOC. The caller always restores its RTOC value immediately upon return from the callee. The callee's prolog writes the saved Condition Register and Link Register into the caller's linkage area. The structure of a linkage area is illustrated in Figure 1-11.

IMPORTANT

The RTOC value is saved and restored only for two kinds of subroutine calls: cross-TOC calls and pointer-based calls. In all other cases, the RTOC field of the caller's linkage area is ignored. ▲

Figure 1-11   The structure of a stack frame's linkage area

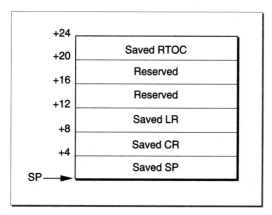

Notice that the linkage area always appears at the "top" of the stack, adjacent to the stack pointer. This positioning is necessary to allow the caller to find and restore the values saved there, and to allow the callee to find the caller's parameter area. One consequence of this requirement, however, is that a routine cannot push and pop arbitrary values on the stack after a stack frame is set up.

A PowerPC stack frame also includes space for the callee's local variables. In general, the general-purpose registers GPR13 through GPR31 and the floating-point registers FPR14 through FPR31 are reserved for a routine's local variables. If a particular routine has more local variables than fit entirely into the registers reserved for them, it uses additional space on the stack. The size of the area used for local variables is determined at compile time; once a stack frame is allocated, the area for local variables cannot grow or shrink.

The callee is responsible for allocating its own stack frame, making sure to preserve 8-byte alignment on the stack. The callee allocates its stack frame by decrementing the stack pointer, then writes the previous stack pointer into its own linkage area and saves all nonvolatile general-purpose and floating-point registers into the **saved registers area** of its stack frame. All of these actions are performed by a standard piece of compiler-generated code called the **prolog.**

Note

The order in which the callee's prolog performs these actions is determined by convention, not by any requirements of the PowerPC run-time architecture. Also, the callee saves only those nonvolatile registers it uses; if the callee doesn't change a particular nonvolatile register, it doesn't bother to save and restore it. ◆

When the callee exits, its **epilog** code restores the nonvolatile registers that its prolog previously saved. The Link Register and Condition Register are restored from the linkage area in the caller's stack frame. The nonvolatile general-purpose registers (namely, GPR13 through GPR31) and floating-point registers (namely, FPR14 through FPR31) are restored from the saved register area in the callee's stack frame. The RTOC value of the caller is, however, restored by the caller immediately upon return from the called routine.

There is one special case in which a callee's stack usage does not conform to the structure shown in Figure 1-10—namely, when the callee is a leaf procedure. A **leaf procedure** is a procedure that calls no other procedures. Because it doesn't call any procedures, it doesn't need to allocate a parameter area on the stack. If, in addition, a leaf procedure doesn't need to use the stack for any local variables, it needs to save and restore only those nonvolatile registers that it uses for local parameters.

Leaf procedures, due to their limited stack requirements, can use a special area on the stack called the Red Zone. The **Red Zone** is the area just below the stack pointer, in the area where a new stack frame normally would be allocated (see Figure 1-12). Because by definition only one leaf procedure can be active at any time, there is no possibility of multiple leaf procedures competing for the same Red Zone space.

Figure 1-12   The Red Zone

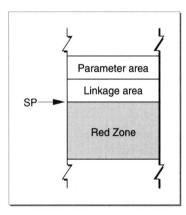

It's important to realize that a leaf procedure doesn't actually allocate a stack frame for itself and that it doesn't decrement the stack pointer. Instead, it stores its LR and CR values in the linkage area of the routine that calls it (if necessary) and stores the values of any nonvolatile registers it uses in the Red Zone. As a result, the epilog of a leaf procedure doesn't need to tear down a stack frame. Instead, the epilog needs at most to restore the calling routine's LR and CR values. This allows leaf procedures to execute faster than they would if they had to set up and later tear down a complete stack frame.

Note

A leaf procedure uses the Red Zone in place of a stack frame only when your code is compiled with speed optimization enabled. ◆

Using the Red Zone in this way can, however, cause problems for native exception handlers, because an exception handler cannot know in advance if a leaf procedure is executing at the time the exception occurs (and hence cannot know if the Red Zone contains information that should be preserved). A native exception handler must therefore decrement the stack pointer by 224 bytes (the largest possible register save area) before using the stack, to skip over any Red Zone that might currently be in use.

Note

The value 224 is the space occupied by nineteen 32-bit general-purpose registers plus eighteen 64-bit floating-point registers, rounded up to the nearest 8-byte boundary. If a leaf procedure's Red Zone usage would exceed 224 bytes, then the leaf procedure is forced to use a stack frame, like any other procedure. ◆

In general, you should use the new Exception Manager to install any native exception handlers your application or other software defines. The Exception Manager automatically adjusts the stack pointer before calling your exception handler and then restores it after your handler exits. See the chapter "Exception Manager" in this book for complete details on writing and installing a native exception handler.

IMPORTANT

The calling conventions and stack usage described in this section are those of the PPCC compiler and the Macintosh Operating System. Other compilers may employ different calling conventions. ▲

Parameter Passing

In the PowerPC run-time environment, as you've already learned, parameters are usually passed from a caller to a callee in registers. The fact that there are many general-purpose and floating-point registers dedicated for parameter passing makes it extremely likely that all of a subroutine's parameters can be passed in registers. Passing parameters in registers reduces the number of memory accesses required (namely, to read the stack frame) and thereby increases the performance of your software.

Any parameters that cannot be passed in registers are instead passed in the parameter area of the caller's stack frame. This section describes the way in which a caller prepares the registers and the parameter area for the callee.

IMPORTANT

You need the information in this section only for machine-level debugging purposes, to understand the contents of the general-purpose and floating-point registers and the structure of the parameter area in a caller's stack frame. ▲

The compiler assigns parameters to registers and to the parameter area in the caller's stack frame according to this algorithm:

- The parameters are arranged in order as if they were fields of a record.
    - The leftmost parameter is the first field.
    - Each field is aligned on a 32-bit word boundary.
    - Integer parameters occupying less than 32 bits are extended to 32 bits.
- Some parameter values are passed in registers.
    - The first 8 words are passed in GPR3 through GPR10.
    - However, the first 13 floating-point parameters are passed in FPR1 through FPR13.
- Simple function results are returned in GPR3 or FPR1.
- Composite data (that is, custom data structures such as Pascal records or C structures) are passed intact, without expanding the fields to achieve word alignment. When composite data is returned, the caller leaves enough room to hold the result on the stack, puts the address of the result into GPR3, and starts the parameters in GPR4.
- Any parameters that do not fit into the available registers are passed in the parameter area of the caller's stack frame.

The compiler generates a parameter area in the caller's stack frame that is large enough to hold all parameters passed to the callee, regardless of how many of the parameters are actually passed in registers. There are several reasons for this scheme. First of all, it provides the callee with space to store a register-based parameter if it wants to use one of the parameter registers for some other purpose (for instance, to pass parameters to a subroutine). In addition, routines with variable-length parameter lists must access their parameters from RAM, not from registers. Finally, code that is built to allow debugging automatically writes parameters from the parameter registers into the parameter area in the stack frame; this allows you to see all the parameters by looking only at that parameter area.

Consider, for example, a function `MyFunction` with this declaration:

```
void MyFunction (int i1, float f1, double d1, short s1, double d2,
            unsigned char c1, unsigned short s2, float f2, int i2);
```

Note

On the PowerPC processor, integers and long integers are both 32 bits long and short integers are 16 bits long. Variables of type `float` are 32 bits long; variables of type `double` are 64 bits long. ◆

To see how the parameters of `MyFunction` are arranged in the parameter area on the stack, first convert the parameter list into a structure, as follows:

```
struct params {
    int         pi1;
    float       pf1;
    double      pd1;
    short       ps1;
```

```
double          pd2;
unsigned char   pc1;
unsigned short  ps2;
float           pf2;
int             pi2;
};
```

This structure serves as a template for constructing the parameter area on the stack. (Remember that, in actual practice, many of these variables are passed in registers; nonetheless, the compiler still allocates space for all of them on the stack, for the reasons just mentioned.)

The "top" position on the stack is for the field pi1 (the structure field corresponding to parameter i1). The floating-point field pf1 is assigned to the next word in the parameter area. The 64-bit double field pd1 is assigned to the next two words in the parameter area. Next, the short integer field ps1 is placed into the following 32-bit word; the original value of ps1 is in the lower half of the word, and the padding is in the upper half. The remaining fields of the param structure are assigned space on the stack in exactly the same way, with unsigned values being extended to fill each field to a 32-bit word. The final arrangement of the stack is illustrated in Figure 1-13. (Because the stack grows down, it looks as though the fields of the params structure are upside down.)

Figure 1-13   The organization of the parameter area on the stack

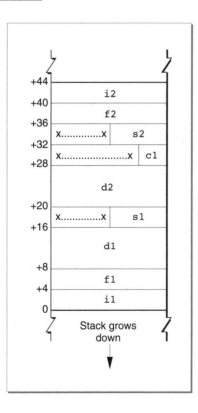

To see which parameters are passed in registers and which are passed on the stack, you need to map the stack, as illustrated in Figure 1-13, to the available general-purpose and floating-point registers. Registers GPR0 through GPR2, and register FPR0, are reserved for other uses. Therefore, the parameter i1 is passed in GPR3, the first available general-purpose register. The floating-point parameter f1 is passed in FPR1, the first available floating-point register.

Placing a floating-point parameter into a floating-point register also reserves one or two general-purpose registers, depending on whether the parameter is 32 or 64 bits long. This behavior is dictated in order to support the ability of a C function to call another function without knowing the number or types of the callee's parameters—that is, without knowing the callee's prototype. When no function prototype for the callee is available to the caller, the compiler cannot know whether to pass a given parameter in the general-purpose (that is, fixed-point) registers or in the floating-point registers. As a result, the compiler passes the parameter in both the floating-point and the general-purpose registers.

Even when the caller knows the function prototype of the callee, it still reserves one or two general-purpose registers for each floating-point register it fills. The only difference between cases in which the prototype is available and cases in which the prototype isn't available is that the floating-point parameters are copied into the general-purpose register(s) in the latter cases but not in the former.

The parameter d1 is placed into FPR2 and the corresponding general-purpose registers GPR5 and GPR6 are masked out. The parameter s1 is placed into the next available general-purpose register, GPR7. Parameter d2 is placed into FPR3, with GPR8 and GPR9 masked out. Parameter c1 is placed into GPR10, thereby exhausting all available general-purpose registers. However, parameter f2 is passed in FPR4, which is still available. Notice that there are no general-purpose registers that can be masked out for FPR4; as a result, the parameter f2 is passed both in FPR4 and on the stack. Finally, parameters s2 and i2 must be passed on the stack, because there are no more general-purpose registers to hold them.

Note

It would have been possible to pass all the fixed-point values in registers if the floating-point parameters had been grouped at the end of the parameter list. ◆

There is a special case that applies to routines that take a variable number of parameters (for example, the C language function printf). The callee doesn't know how many parameters are being passed to it on any given call. As a result, the callee saves registers GPR3 through GPR10 into the parameter area and then walks through the parameter area to access its parameters. This means that the parameter area must contain at least 8 words.

Import Libraries

You've already learned (in "Fragments" beginning on page 1-20) how a fragment can import code and data from some other fragment, which is always an import library.

Because the code or data that your application references from an import library is not actually contained in your application—but is only linked to it dynamically at application launch time—the executable code of your application is generally much smaller than it otherwise would be. This is one of the main advantages of using import libraries.

Of course, there's no particular advantage simply to moving code out of your application and into an import library, because the code in the import library, unless contained in ROM, must be loaded into RAM before it can be used. The real advantages accrue only when two or more applications use the same import library. The library's code is loaded into RAM only once, and all those applications reference that single code base. If you are developing several PowerPC applications that have parts of their source code in common, you should consider packaging all the shared code into an import library.

Another important advantage of using import libraries is that it's easy to update code contained in an import library. You can issue an updated version of your import library and have the changes propagate to all the applications that use that library. You don't need to update each individual application that uses the import library.

You can use shared libraries in other useful ways. You can, for instance, create a shared library that holds optional or infrequently executed code. For example, if you're writing a word-processing application, you might package its spell-checking module as a separate shared library. Because the Code Fragment Manager doesn't load the library at application launch time, your application uses less RAM and launches more quickly. When the user wants to execute the spelling checker, your application must explicitly load and prepare the shared library by calling Code Fragment Manager routines.

You can also use shared libraries as a way to allow other developers to add capabilities, such as optional tools, to your application. If you document the format of the parameters passed to an external routine and any other data that you expect to find in an optional tool, other developers can create shared libraries that conform to those specifications.

As you know, the principal advantage of using import libraries is that the code in the import library is loaded only once in memory, whence it is addressed by all applications (or other fragments) that import that code. The handling of an import library's data, however, is more complicated. The Code Fragment Manager supports two methods of allocating and using the static data (that is, global variables) in an import library:

- **Global instantiation.** The Code Fragment Manager allocates a single copy of the library's global data, no matter how many clients use that data.

- **Per-context instantiation.** The Code Fragment Manager allocates one copy of the library's global data for each separate application (and all other fragments in the application's context) that uses that data. Each application can access only its own copy of the data. The Operating System automatically keeps track of which copy of the library's global data is in use by which context. If a given application attempts to load the same import library more than once, it always accesses the same copy of the library's global data.

The method of allocating and handling a library's global data is determined at link time. The library developer can indicate either global or per-context data instantiation for each separate data section in a library. The method selected by the library developer for a particular data section is recorded by the linker in the library itself. In general, it's best to use one copy of the global data per application.

It's also possible to allocate one copy of an extension's global data for each request to load the extension, even if the same application issues multiple load requests. This type of data instantiation, called **per-load instantiation,** is available only when you explicitly load a shared library by calling a Code Fragment Manager routine (for example, the `GetSharedLibrary` function). For example, a communications application might use a shared library to implement a tool for connecting to a serial port. By requesting per-load data instantiation, you can ensure that your tool can connect to two or more serial ports simultaneously by maintaining separate copies of the tool's data. The tool itself can then be ignorant of how many connections it's handling.

The Code Fragment Manager honors the data allocation method recorded in the library for all import libraries that it loads automatically. This method must be either global or per context. To achieve a per-load instantiation of a library's data or to override the instantiation method recorded in the library, you must load and prepare the library programmatically by calling Code Fragment Manager routines.

The Organization of Memory

The organization of memory in the PowerPC run-time environment is reasonably similar to the organization of memory in the 680x0 run-time environment. The system partition occupies the lowest memory addresses, with most of the remaining space allocated to the Process Manager, which creates a partition for each opened application. Moreover, the organization of an application partition in the PowerPC run-time environment is reasonably similar to the organization of an application partition in the 680x0 run-time environment. In each application partition, there are a stack and a heap, as well as space for the application's global variables.

There are, however, a number of important differences between the PowerPC and 680x0 environments in regard to how memory is organized, both globally and in each application's partition. This section describes these differences. It also describes the different data alignment conventions used in each environment and the steps you might need to take to align data so that it can be exchanged between the two environments.

IMPORTANT

In general, you need the information in this section only for debugging purposes (for example, to understand where in memory your application's code section is loaded). You might also need this information to help you determine how large to make your application partition (as specified in your application's 'SIZE' resource). ▲

The two main differences between the 680x0 memory organization and the PowerPC memory organization concern the location of an application's code section and the location of an application's global variables. In addition, you need to pay attention to the differing data alignment rules in each environment.

File Mapping

As you know, a PowerPC application's executable code and global data are typically stored in a fragment container in the application's data fork. When the application is launched, the code and data sections of that fragment are loaded into memory. The data section is loaded into the application's heap, as described more fully in the following section. The location of the application's code section varies, depending on whether or not virtual memory is enabled.

If virtual memory is enabled, the Virtual Memory Manager uses a scheme called **file mapping** to map your application's fragment into memory: the Virtual Memory Manager uses the data fork of your application as the paging file for your application's code section. In the 680x0 environment, all unused pages of memory are written into a single systemwide backing-store file and reread from there when needed. This often results in a prolonged application launch, because an application's code is loaded into memory and then sometimes immediately written out to the backing-store file. In the PowerPC environment, this "thrashing" at application launch time is avoided; although the entire code fragment is mapped into the logical address space, only the needed portions of code are actually loaded into physical memory.

File mapping has additional benefits as well. The Operating System assumes that your application's code section is always read-only. This means that, when it's time to remove some of your application's code from memory (to page other code or data in), the Virtual Memory Manager doesn't need to write the pages back to the paging file. Instead, it simply purges the code from the needed pages, because it can always read the file-mapped code back from the paging file (your application's data fork).

IMPORTANT

Because your application's code section is marked read-only when virtual memory is enabled, it's not possible to write self-modifying code that will work on all PowerPC processor-based Macintosh computers. ▲

The virtual addresses occupied by the file-mapped pages of an application's (or an import library's) code are located outside both the system heap and the Process Manager's heap. As a result, an application's file-mapped code is never located in the application heap itself.

Figure 1-14 illustrates the general organization of memory when virtual memory is enabled. Application partitions (including the application's stack, heap, and global variables) are loaded into the Process Manager heap, which is paged to and from the systemwide backing-store file. Code sections of applications and import libraries are paged directly from the data fork of the application or import library file. Data sections of import libraries are put into an application's heap for any per-context instantiations and into the system heap for any global instantiations.

Figure 1-14   Organization of memory when virtual memory is enabled

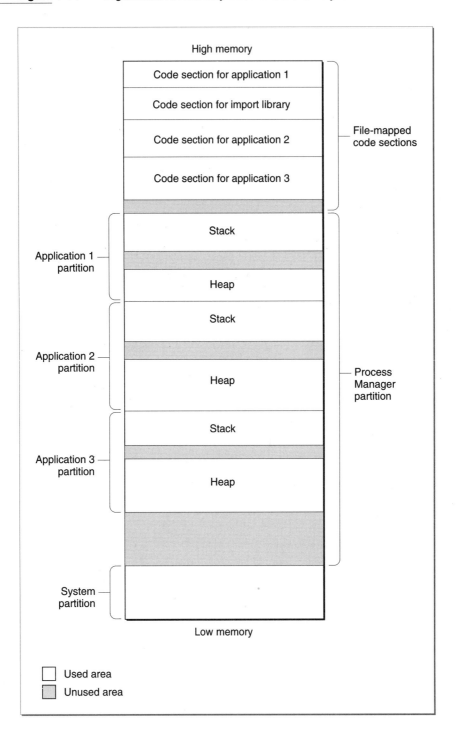

Sometimes, however, parts of your application's executable code are loaded into your application partition, not into the file-mapped space. This happens, for example, when you store an application extension (like a filter or a tool) as a resource in your application's resource fork. To make the code in that extension available, you need to call the Resource Manager to load it into your application heap. Then you need to call the Code Fragment Manager to prepare the extension for execution. (See the chapter "Code Fragment Manager" in this book for a more detailed description of this way of executing resource-based code.) Because that code is loaded into your application heap, it isn't eligible for file mapping (although it is still eligible for normal paging).

If virtual memory is not enabled, the code section of an application is loaded into the application heap. The Finder and Process Manager automatically expand your application partition as necessary to hold that code section. The code sections of other fragments are put into part of the Process Manager's heap known as **temporary memory.** If no temporary memory is available, code sections are loaded into the system heap.

IMPORTANT

It's possible for a fragment's code section to be loaded into the Process Manager's heap even when virtual memory is enabled. This happens whenever the fragment resides on a device that cannot be used as a paging device. For example, applications that are located on floppy disks, AppleShare servers, and compact discs cannot be file mapped. ▲

Figure 1-15 illustrates the general organization of memory when virtual memory is not enabled. Application partitions (including the application's stack, heap, and global variables) are loaded into the Process Manager heap. Code sections of applications and import libraries are loaded either into the Process Manager partition or (less commonly) into the system heap. No paging occurs.

Figure 1-15   Organization of memory when virtual memory is not enabled

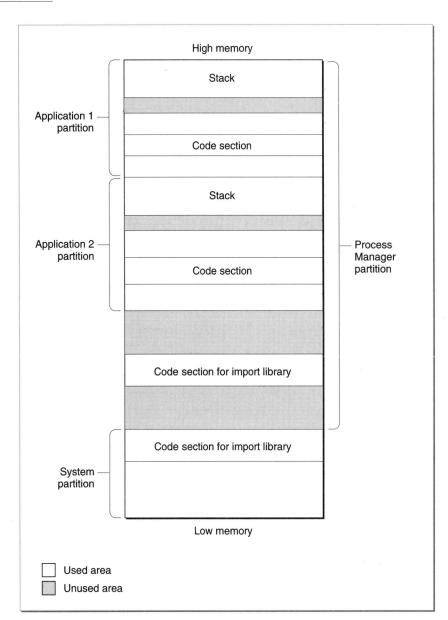

The System Partition

The system partition in PowerPC processor-based Macintosh computers is organized in essentially the same way as that in system software version 7.1 for 680x0-based computers. To support existing 680x0 applications and other software modules that access documented system global variables, the structure of much of the system partition remains unchanged. Both emulated 680x0 and native PowerPC system software components use and maintain the system global variables. However, some undocumented system global variables have moved, and some have been eliminated altogether.

The universal header files contain declarations for routines that you can use to access virtually all of the documented system global variables. For example, you can use the routines `LMGetCurDirStore` and `LMSetCurDirStore` to get and set the value of the system global variable `CurDirStore` (which contains the directory ID of the current directory). `LMGetCurDirStore` is declared essentially as follows:

```
#if USESCODEFRAGMENTS
extern long LMGetCurDirStore(void);
#else
#define LMGetCurDirStore() (* (long *) 0x0398)
#endif
```

In any environment that uses code fragments, the function `LMGetCurDirStore` is defined in the system software import library that is contained in ROM. In all other environments, the function `LMGetCurDirStore` is defined as a macro that reads the value of the appropriate low-memory address.

By using the routines provided by the system software, you can insulate your application or other software module from any future changes in the arrangement of low memory.

Note

See the MPW interface files for a complete listing of the routines you can use to access the system global variables. You should not use the compiler flag `USESCODEFRAGMENTS` in your source code; if you need to know whether the Code Fragment Manager is available, you can call the `Gestalt` function with the selector `gestaltCFMAttr`. ◆

The only other case in which your application might be affected by changes to the system partition concerns the method you use to install exception handlers. In the 680x0 environment, there is no programmatic way to install an exception handler; instead, you simply write the address of your exception handler into the appropriate location in memory (as determined jointly by the kind of exception you want to handle and the value in the microprocessor's vector base register). A PowerPC application cannot employ this method of installing exception handlers. Instead, the system software for PowerPC processor-based Macintosh computers includes the new Exception Manager, which you should use to install native PowerPC exception handlers. See the chapter "Exception Manager" in this book for details.

Application Partitions

The organization of an application partition in the PowerPC environment is substantially simpler than in the 680x0 environment. In particular, the application partition for a PowerPC application consists only of a stack and a heap. The A5 world that occupies part of a 680x0 application partition largely is absent from the PowerPC environment. The information that is maintained in the A5 world for 680x0 applications is either no longer needed by PowerPC applications or is maintained elsewhere (usually in the application heap).

IMPORTANT

Any software that makes assumptions about the organization of an application's A5 world will not work with PowerPC applications. For example, any 680x0 system extensions that modify an application's jump table will need to be rewritten to work with PowerPC applications. ▲

This section describes the new locations for the information in a 680x0 A5 world. Although in general the arrangement of your PowerPC application partition is transparent to your application, there are some instances (for example, while debugging) in which you might need to know where in your partition information is located. In addition, if your application previously depended on some information being in its A5 world (that is, accessed through the address in the A5 register), you will need to revise it to remove that dependence if you want to recompile your source code into a PowerPC application. More generally, you might need to rewrite any parts of your source code that depend on information being in any of the 680x0 registers.

Note

For a more complete explanation of a 680x0 application's A5 world, see *Inside Macintosh: Memory.* ◆

The A5 world of a 680x0 application contains four kinds of data:

- application global variables

- application QuickDraw global variables

- application parameters

- the application's jump table

Your 680x0 application's **jump table** contains an entry for each of the application's routines that is called by code in another segment. Because the executable code of a PowerPC application is not segmented, there is no need for a jump table in a PowerPC application partition.

IMPORTANT

The available PowerPC compilers ignore any segmentation directives in your source code. In addition, the Segment Manager treats the `UnloadSeg` procedure as nonoperative. ▲

In PowerPC applications, the application global variables are part of the fragment's data section, which the Code Fragment Manager loads into the application's heap. The application global variables are always allocated in a single nonrelocatable block and are addressed through a pointer in the fragment's table of contents.

The **application parameters** are 32 bytes of memory located above the application global variables that are reserved for use by the Operating System. The first 4 bytes of those parameters are a pointer to the application's **QuickDraw global variables,** which contain information about the application's drawing environment. For PowerPC applications, the application parameters are maintained privately by the Operating System. In addition, an application's QuickDraw global variables are stored as part of the application's global variables (in a nonrelocatable block in the application's heap).

Because the PowerPC run-time libraries don't implicitly define the QuickDraw global variable qd for native applications (as they do in the 680x0 environment), you'll need to reserve space for them globally in your application and then pass the address of that memory to the InitGraf routine. You can do this by using the code shown in Listing 1-11. The data type QDGlobals is defined in the QuickDraw header files.

Listing 1-11   Declaring an application's QuickDraw global variables

```
#ifndef MAC68K
#   define MAC68K 0            /*for PowerPC code*/
#else
#   define MAC68K 1            /*for 680x0 code*/
#endif
#if !MAC68K
QDGlobals        qd;
#endif

void DoInitManagers()          /*initialize Toolbox managers*/
{
    InitGraf(&qd.thePort);
    InitFonts();
    InitWindows();
    InitMenus();
    TEInit();
    InitDialogs(nil);
    InitCursor();
}
```

QuickDraw is one of the system software services that has been ported to native PowerPC code. It accesses the QuickDraw global variables of a 680x0 application by reading the application's A5 value that is stored in the 680x0 context block. That value points to the boundary between the application's global variables and the application parameters. As you've seen, the address of the QuickDraw global variables is the first 4 bytes of the application parameters.

Even for applications that have themselves been ported to native PowerPC code, there must be a minimal A5 world to support some nonported system software—as well as some system software patches that exist as 680x0 code—that accesses the QuickDraw global variables relative to the application's A5 value. This **mini-A5 world** contains only a pointer to the application's QuickDraw global variables, which reside in the application's global data section (in the application heap). The Process Manager creates a mini-A5 world for each native application at application launch time and installs its address in the 680x0 context block. As a result, the native QuickDraw can access the QuickDraw global variables of a native application in precisely the same way that it accesses the QuickDraw global variables of a 680x0 application (namely, by reading the value of the A5 register in the 680x0 context block and then finding the address of the QuickDraw global variables relative to the address of the A5 world).

The general structure of a PowerPC application partition is illustrated in Figure 1-16.

Figure 1-16 The structure of a PowerPC application partition

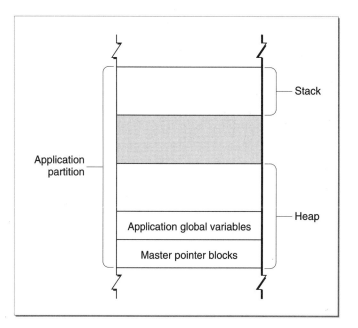

IMPORTANT

There is no guarantee that future versions of the run-time environment for PowerPC processor-based Macintosh computers will maintain this arrangement of the application partition. To modify the size of your application's stack, for example, you should use the techniques (described in the book *Inside Macintosh: Memory*) that use the `GetApplLimit` and `SetApplLimit` routines. You should not directly modify system global variables (for instance, `ApplLimit`). Note, however, that you can specify a minimum stack size in your PowerPC application's `'cfrg'` resource. The `GetApplLimit` and `SetApplLimit` techniques are still useful if you need to adjust that minimum size dynamically. A reasonable minimum stack size for PowerPC applications is 48 KB. ▲

Because a PowerPC application has no A5 world (apart from the mini-A5 world maintained privately by the Process Manager), you don't ever need to explicitly set up and restore your application's A5 world. In the 680x0 environment, there are two times when you need to manage your A5 value explicitly: (1) to gain access to your application's global variables or QuickDraw global variables from within some piece of "detached" code installed by your application (such as a Time Manager task or a VBL task) and (2) to create a 680x0 context for some other piece of code (such as a HyperCard XCMD).

In the first case, when you need to set up the A5 register for some piece of 680x0 code whose address you passed to the system software, there is no need for ported PowerPC code to set and restore the A5 register. The RTOC always points to the table of contents for the currently executing code, through which the application's global variables can be addressed. As a result, your application's global variables are transparently available to any code compiled into your application. To maintain a single source code base for both the 680x0 and the PowerPC environment, you can use conditional compilation. Consider the simple 680x0 VBL task defined in Listing 1-12.

Note
See the chapter "Vertical Retrace Manager" in *Inside Macintosh: Processes* for a complete explanation of the techniques used in Listing 1-12. ◆

Listing 1-12   A sample 680x0 VBL task definition

```
VBLRecPtr GetVBLRec (void)
        = 0x2008;                       /*MOVE.L A0,D0*/

void DoVBL (VBLRecPtr recPtr)
{
    gCounter++;                         /*modify a global variable*/
    /*Reset vblCount so that this procedure executes again.*/
    recPtr->myVBLTask.vblCount = kInterval;
}

void StartVBL (void)
{
    long        curA5;                  /*stored value of A5*/
    VBLRecPtr   recPtr;                 /*pointer to task record*/

    recPtr = GetVBLRec();               /*get address of task record*/

    /*Set our application's A5 and store old A5 in curA5.*/
    curA5 = SetA5(recPtr->vblA5);
    DoVBL(recPtr);

    recPtr->myVBLTask.vblCount = kInterval;
    (void) SetA5(curA5);                /*restore the old A5 value*/
}
```

The procedure StartVBL defined in Listing 1-12 installs the A5 value of the application by calling SetA5, passing in a value that it retrieves from an expanded VBL task record. In addition, StartVBL restores the previous A5 value immediately before exiting. For VBL tasks written as PowerPC code, both of these steps are unnecessary. You can rewrite the procedure DoVBL to include those steps only conditionally, as shown in Listing 1-13. Moreover, in the 680x0 environment, the address of the VBL task record is passed in register A0. If you need that address in a high-level language, you need to retrieve it immediately upon entry to your VBL task (as is done using the GetVBLRec function in Listing 1-12). In the PowerPC environment, however, the address of the VBL task record is passed to the task as an explicit parameter. Listing 1-13 illustrates how to conditionally select the appropriate task declaration.

Listing 1-13   A conditionalized VBL task definition

```
#if MAC68K
VBLRecPtr GetVBLRec (void) = 0x2008;        /*MOVE.L A0,D0*/
#endif

void DoVBL (VBLRecPtr recPtr)
{
   gCounter++;                              /*modify a global variable*/
   /*Reset vblCount so that this procedure executes again.*/
   recPtr->myVBLTask.vblCount = kInterval;
}

#if MAC68K
void StartVBL (void)
#else
void StartVBL (VBLTaskPtr recPtr)
#endif
{
#if MAC68K
   long        curA5;                   /*stored value of A5*/
   VBLRecPtr   recPtr;                   /*pointer to task record*/
   recPtr = GetVBLRec();                 /*get address of task record*/
   /*Set our application's A5 and store old A5 in curA5.*/
   curA5 = SetA5(recPtr->vblA5);
#endif
   DoVBL(recPtr);
#if MAC68K
   (void) SetA5(curA5);                  /*restore the old A5 value*/
#endif
}
```

Listing 1-13 also removes the dependence on the inline assembly-language code that retrieves a pointer to the VBL task record from register A0. In the PowerPC environment, information is passed to interrupt tasks as explicit parameters.

The second main case in which you need to set up and restore the A5 register is to create a 680x0 context for some existing 680x0 code (such as a stand-alone code module). To do this, you can call the `SetA5` and `SetCurrentA5` routines.

Note

See the book *Inside Macintosh: Memory* for more information on calling `SetA5` and `SetCurrentA5`. ◆

Data Alignment

The PowerPC and 680x0 compilers follow different conventions concerning the alignment of data in memory. Unless told to do otherwise, a compiler arranges a data structure in memory so as to minimize the amount of time required to access the fields of the structure. In general, this is what you'd like to have happen. In some cases, however, the processor's preferred method of aligning data might lead to problems. Suppose, for example, that a PowerPC version of your application writes some data from memory into a file. The data is arranged in the file in exactly the same order that it was arranged in memory, including any pad bytes that were required to achieve the desired data alignment in memory. It's likely, however, that the resulting file will not be readable by a 680x0 version of your application. That's because the data will be read from the file into a structure whose fields are very likely laid out slightly differently in memory. This section describes how this can happen, and provides some easy remedies for this kind of problem.

A 680x0 processor places very few restrictions on the alignment of data in memory. The processor can read or write a byte, word, or long word value at any even address in memory. In addition, the processor can read byte values at any address in memory. As a result, the only padding required might be a single byte to align 2-byte or larger fields to even boundaries or to make the size of an entire data structure an even number of bytes.

Note

Remember that a word on 680x0 processors is 2 bytes; on PowerPC processors, a word is 4 bytes. ◆

By contrast, the PowerPC processor prefers to access data in memory according to its natural alignment, which depends on the size of the data. A 1-byte value is always aligned in memory. A 2-byte value is aligned on any even address. A 4-byte value is aligned on any address that is divisible by 4, and so on. A PowerPC processor can access data that is not aligned on its natural boundary, but it performs aligned memory accesses more efficiently. As a result, PowerPC compilers usually insert pad bytes into data structures to enforce the preferred data alignment.

For example, consider the following data structure:

```
struct SampleStruct {
    short     version;
    long      address;
    short     count;
}
```

This structure occupies 8 bytes of memory in the 680x0 environment. To achieve the desired alignment of the `address` field in the PowerPC environment onto a 4-byte boundary, however, 2 bytes of padding are inserted after the `version` field. In addition, the structure itself is padded to a word boundary. As a result, the structure occupies 12 bytes of memory in the PowerPC environment.

In general, the different data alignment conventions of the 680x0 and PowerPC environments should be transparent to your application. You need to worry about the differences only when you need to transfer data between the two environments. This can happen in a number of ways:

- Your application creates files containing data structures and the user copies those files from a PowerPC processor-based Macintosh computer to a 680x0-based Macintosh computer (or vice versa).

- Your PowerPC application creates a data structure and passes it to some code running under the 68LC040 Emulator.

- Your application—running in either environment—customizes a Toolbox or Operating System data structure and passes it to the system software.

- Your PowerPC application sends data across a network connection to a 680x0-based Macintosh computer.

To ensure that data can be transferred successfully in all of these cases, it's sufficient simply to instruct the PowerPC compiler to use the 680x0 data alignment conventions. You can do this by using a compiler `pragma` statement, as follows:

```
#pragma option align=mac68k
struct SampleStruct {
    short     version;
    long      address;
    short     count;
}
#pragma option align=reset
```

You should make sure, however, that you use 680x0 alignment only when absolutely necessary. The PowerPC processor is less efficient when accessing misaligned data than when accessing aligned data.

Alternatively, instead of forcing the compiler to use 680x0 alignment in the PowerPC environment, you can try to rearrange your data structures to promote natural alignment in both environments. For example, you can change the declaration of the `SampleStruct` structure to be as follows:

```
struct SampleStruct {
    long        address;
    short       count;
    short       version;
}
```

A PowerPC compiler does not insert any pad bytes into the `SampleStruct` structure in this new arrangement, because the fields are already aligned along the desired memory boundaries.

Note

Your PowerPC compiler may use slightly different alignment methods than those described here. Consult your development system's documentation for complete information. For more details on specifying alignment methods with the PPCC compiler, see the book *Macintosh on PowerPC C Compiler*. ◆

You also need to be careful when passing floating-point data between the 680x0 and PowerPC environments. The most efficient floating-point data type in the 680x0 environment is the 80-bit (or 96-bit) `extended` data type. The most efficient data types in the PowerPC environment are `single`, `double`, and `long double`, which are 32, 64, and 128 bits, respectively. The PowerPC Numerics library includes routines you can use to convert among these various data types. See *Inside Macintosh: PowerPC Numerics* for complete details.

Compatibility and Performance

In general, it's relatively easy to modify existing ANSI-compliant C or C++ source code that successfully compiles and runs on 680x0-based Macintosh computers so that it can be compiled and run on PowerPC processor-based Macintosh computers. Most of the intricate work required to make your application compatible with the new PowerPC run-time environment is performed automatically by your development system's compiler and linker and by the Code Fragment Manager. As you've seen, the changes you need to make in your application's source code are fairly straightforward. You need to make these changes:

■ Create routine descriptors for any routines whose addresses you pass to code of an unknown type.

■ Minimize any dependencies on system global variables by using the new set of accessor routines defined in the MPW interface files.

■ Isolate and conditionalize any dependencies on specific features of the 680x0 A5 world or the 680x0 run-time environment.

■ Isolate and conditionalize any dependencies on information being passed in specific 680x0 registers.

■ Use 680x0 alignment for any data that is passed between environments, or declare your data structures so that their fields are aligned identically in both the 680x0 and PowerPC environments.

This section discusses several additional topics that relate more generally to the compatibility and performance of your PowerPC application.

Patches

Some applications or other kinds of software patch the Operating System's trap dispatch tables to augment or replace the capabilities of certain system software routines. In general, however, there is much less need to patch the system software now than there previously was, and you should avoid doing so if at all possible. One very good reason to avoid unnecessary patching is that you can incur a substantial performance reduction if your patch causes a mode switch. For example, when a PowerPC application calls a system software routine that is implemented as PowerPC code, the dispatching to the PowerPC code occurs fairly quickly. However, if you patch the PowerPC code with 680x0 code, the Mixed Mode Manager needs to intervene to switch the execution environments both when entering and when exiting your patch code. This switching results in a considerable overhead (approximately 15 microseconds on a 60 MHz PowerPC processor per round-trip mode switch, the equivalent of about fifty 680x0 instructions).

Note

The precise number of instructions or microseconds of overhead required to switch from one environment to the other and back is subject to change in future system software versions and on different hardware configurations. The important point to keep in mind is that switching modes is a reasonably expensive activity and you should avoid it whenever possible. ◆

The same situation occurs if you use PowerPC code to patch a system software routine that is implemented as 680x0 code. Once again, a mode switch is required before entering your patch code and after exiting it.

The ideal solution is simply to avoid patching the system software entirely. In the few cases in which you absolutely cannot avoid patching some system software routine, you can avoid the kind of mode switching just described by making sure to patch PowerPC code with a PowerPC patch and 680x0 code with a 680x0 patch. Because you cannot in general know what kind of code implements a particular system software routine, you should install a **fat patch,** which addresses both PowerPC and 680x0 versions of your code. To install a fat patch, you need to create a routine descriptor with two embedded routine records, one record describing the PowerPC routine and one record describing the 680x0 routine. Then you pass the address of that routine descriptor—that is, a universal procedure pointer—to an appropriate Trap Manager routine, which installs that universal procedure pointer into the trap dispatch table. When the patched routine is called, the Mixed Mode Manager inspects the routine descriptor addressed by the universal procedure pointer and selects the patch code that has the smallest impact on performance.

IMPORTANT

To install patches, you can use one of the Trap Manager routines `SetToolTrapAddress`, `SetOSTrapAddress`, and `NSetTrapAddress`. You should not use the obsolete routine `SetTrapAddress`. See the chapter "Trap Manager" in *Inside Macintosh: Operating System Utilities* for a more complete description of the recommended way to patch system software routines. You should never manipulate the trap dispatch tables directly. ▲

Your patch code should, of course, make sure to call through to the code originally addressed by the entry in the trap dispatch table. You can retrieve that address by calling `GetToolTrapAddress`, `GetOSTrapAddress`, or `NGetTrapAddress` before you install your patch. In the 680x0 patch code, you can simply jump to that address. In the PowerPC patch code, you execute the original code by calling the Mixed Mode Manager routine `CallUniversalProc` (for Toolbox traps) or `CallOSTrapUniversalProc` (for Operating System traps).

The `CallOSTrapUniversalProc` function behaves just like the `CallUniversalProc` function except that it preserves additional 680x0 registers around the execution of the called procedure. In addition, you need to pass it a value specifying the trap word. Operating System traps expect a 2-byte parameter in register D1; this parameter represents the actual A-trap word used to call the routine. (Some traps use bits in the trap word to dispatch to different code.) Any Operating System trap patches you install should accept that parameter in register D1 and pass it through when calling the original trap code. Listing 1-14 shows how to patch the `NewPtr` function using PowerPC code.

Listing 1-14 Patching an Operating System trap

```
enum {          /*procedure information for NewPtr function*/
   kNewPtrProcInfo = kRegisterBased |
      RESULT_SIZE(kFourByteCode) |
      REGISTER_RESULT_LOCATION(kRegisterA0) |
      REGISTER_ROUTINE_PARAMETER(1, kRegisterD1, kTwoByteCode) |
      REGISTER_ROUTINE_PARAMETER(2, kRegisterD0, kFourByteCode)
};

pascal Ptr MyNewPtrPatch(unsigned short trapWord, Size byteCount)
{
   /*Your patch code goes here.*/

   return (long) CallOSTrapUniversalProc(gOriginalNewPtr,
                     kNewPtrProcInfo, trapWord, byteCount);
}
```

Because `CallUniversalProc` and `CallOSTrapUniversalProc` are called as subroutines and return control to the calling code, all PowerPC patches are both

head patches and **tail patches** (that is, your patch has control both before and after the code originally pointed to by the trap dispatch table).

Notice that the address you call through to might be the address of someone else's patch. As a result, it's still possible for mode switches to occur, if at least one link in the patch daisy chain is not a fat patch. These mode switches are unavoidable.

Note also that the system software includes a small number of **split traps,** system software routines that are implemented with 680x0 code (usually in ROM) and as PowerPC code in an import library. Because the PowerPC code is contained directly in the import library, you cannot patch the PowerPC portion of a split trap. In general, however, only those routines are implemented as split traps that are not likely candidates for patching. For example, a number of very small utility routines like `AddPt` and `SetRect` are implemented as split traps.

The biggest restriction on patching is that you cannot patch any **selector-based traps** (system software routines that are dispatched through a selector code) with either pure PowerPC or fat patches. In the 680x0 environment, you can patch one or more selectors belonging to a dispatched trap and pass all others through to the original code. In the PowerPC environment, however, this is not possible. As a result, when patching with PowerPC code, you must patch all the routines selected by a single trap if you patch any of them. However, you cannot in general determine how many selectors are supported by a given selector-based trap. You cannot therefore safely patch selector-based traps in a way that is likely to remain compatible with future system software versions. For now, you should use 680x0 code if you need to patch selector-based traps.

The Memory Manager

As you've already learned, the Memory Manager has been rewritten for PowerPC processor-based Macintosh computers. The new Memory Manager, written in C and compiled into native PowerPC code, offers much better performance than the previous 680x0 assembly-language version, both because it runs in the native PowerPC environment and because it uses substantially improved algorithms to manage heaps. In general, however, the application programming interface has not changed. As a result, you'll benefit from the new version completely transparently, whether your application runs under the 68LC040 Emulator or in the native PowerPC environment.

The Memory control panel (shown in Figure 1-17) includes controls that allow the user to select whether applications and other software use the new Memory Manager or the original Memory Manager. By default, the new (or "Modern") Memory Manager is used.

Figure 1-17   The Memory control panel for PowerPC processor-based Macintosh computers

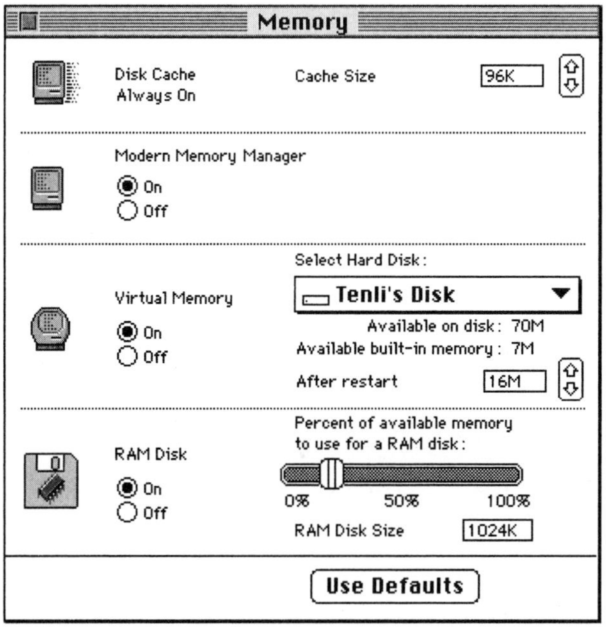

There are, however, several restrictions imposed by the new Memory Manager that might cause compatibility problems for your application. If you've followed the advice and warnings in the book *Inside Macintosh: Memory,* your application should run without problems. However, the new Memory Manager is generally much less forgiving toward code that fails to heed those warnings. Here are some areas to watch out for.

■ Don't dispose of blocks more than once. When you dispose of a block, whether relocatable or nonrelocatable, the Memory Manager immediately takes control of that block. Any future attempt to operate on the block (even simply to dispose of it) is likely to cause problems. Note that it's possible to dispose of a block twice in rather subtle ways. For example, you might call `GetPicture` to display a picture stored in a resource and then inadvertently call `KillPicture` or `DisposeHandle` to remove it. This way of disposing of the block of memory leaves the `'PICT'` resource in the resource map. When your application quits, the resource is disposed of once again. (The proper way to dispose of a picture loaded from a resource is to call `ReleaseResource`.)

■ Don't manipulate the Memory Manager's private data structures, including block headers for both relocatable and nonrelocatable blocks, zone headers, and any unused master pointers. The sizes and formats of some of these structures have changed.

■ Don't access any system global variables maintained by the Memory Manager. Whenever possible, use the documented application programming interface (such as the `SetApplLimit` and `SetGrowZone` procedures) to avoid manipulating those variables.

- Don't modify free blocks of data or rely on the integrity of any data in free blocks. The new Memory Manager assumes control of all unallocated memory in your heap and may overwrite any information in free blocks.

- Don't close a resource file without first detaching any resources in that file that you want to continue using. To detach a resource, call the `DetachResource` procedure.

- Don't use fake handles or pointers. You should call Memory Manager routines only on blocks that were created by the Memory Manager itself. Remember that the Memory Manager is fundamentally a heap managing tool. You should not, for example, call `DisposePtr` on data in your stack or in your application global variable space.

- Don't call Memory Manager routines at interrupt time. Except for the `BlockMove` procedure, all Memory Manager routines either move memory or manipulate system global variables. These operations must not occur at interrupt time.

- Make sure to flush the instruction cache whenever necessary. Because it's much harder to treat data as executable code in the PowerPC environment, the new Memory Manager flushes the instruction cache only when it moves blocks around in memory.

- Don't make assumptions about the relative positions of the stack and heap in your application partition. You should adjust the size of the stack, if necessary, by calling `GetApplLimit` and `SetApplLimit`.

To repeat, you shouldn't encounter any of these problems if you've used the routines and programming techniques documented in *Inside Macintosh: Memory*.

Performance Tuning

Once you've gotten your application or other software to execute correctly on a PowerPC processor-based Macintosh computer, you'll want to spend some time tuning it for maximum performance. Many factors affect the speed at which code executes, including

- how often you cause mode switches from one environment to another

- how you pass parameters to subroutines

- whether you use compiler-specific optimizations

The easiest way to increase the performance of your application is to use the compiler's optimization capabilities. It's not uncommon for compiler speed optimizations to improve your code's execution by as much as 50 percent. See the book *Macintosh on PowerPC C Compiler* for more information on compiler optimizations.

This section provides some preliminary discussion of the overhead associated with mode switches and parameter passing. In general, you'll need to combine the information presented here with empirical observations you obtain when using a performance-measurement tool, such as the Adaptive Sampling Profiler (ASP) built into the debugger. See the book *Macintosh Debugger Reference* for complete information about using the ASP.

Mode Switches

You've already learned (in "Patches" on page 1-66) that it's important to avoid mode switches whenever possible. The Mixed Mode Manager requires the equivalent of approximately fifty 680x0 instructions to switch from one environment to another. As a result, you might want to minimize the number of times your code invokes a mode switch.

Some mode switches are entirely avoidable. For example, if you need to patch a system software routine, you can avoid at least some mode switching by installing a fat patch (a patch that includes both 680x0 and PowerPC versions of the patching code). Similarly, if your application calls any resource-based code (for example, dynamically loadable filters), you can create **fat resources**: code resources that include both 680x0 and PowerPC versions of the executable code. Once again, the Mixed Mode Manager will select the code that minimizes mode switching.

Some mode switches, however, are entirely unavoidable. Any time your PowerPC application calls a system software routine that has not yet been ported to use the native PowerPC instruction set, the Mixed Mode Manager must switch to the 680x0 environment to execute the routine and then switch back to the PowerPC environment to allow your application to continue. This sometimes means that parts of your application might execute more slowly on a PowerPC processor-based Macintosh computer than on a 680x0-based Macintosh computer.

A good example of this behavior concerns calling Event Manager routines, which remain as 680x0 code in the first release of the system software for PowerPC processor-based Macintosh computers. Suppose that during a lengthy calculation your application calls `WaitNextEvent` or `EventAvail` to scan the event queue for a Command-period event (which typically indicates that the user wants to cancel the lengthy operation) and to give time to other applications. Each time you call the Event Manager, two mode switches occur (from your code to the emulated code and back). Moreover, because your code is native PowerPC code, it executes more quickly between Event Manager calls than it did in the 680x0 environment. The result is that your application is switching modes more often than it absolutely has to.

Although you cannot avoid the mode switches entirely when calling the Event Manager, you can lessen the overall impact of those switches on your application's performance by doing more work between successive Event Manager calls. One simple way to do this is to perform more than one iteration of a loop between calls to `WaitNextEvent`. Another simple way is to call `WaitNextEvent` only after a certain amount of time has elapsed. Listing 1-15 shows how you can rewrite a part of your main event loop to incorporate this feature.

_____ **Listing 1-15**   Waiting to call the `WaitNextEvent` function

```
static unsigned long    gWNEDelay = 5;    /*adjust this value as needed*/

void MainEventLoop(void)
{
    EventRecord        myEvent;
    unsigned long      nextTimeToCheckForEvents = 0;

    while (!gDone) {
        if ((gWNEDelay == 0) || (TickCount() > nextTimeToCheckForEvents)) {
            nextTimeToCheckForEvents = TickCount() + gWNEDelay;
            if (WaitNextEvent(everyEvent, &myEvent,
                                            MyGetSleep(), (RgnHandle) nil))
                HandleEvent(&myEvent);
        }
        DoIdle();
    }
}
```

As you can see, this code continues in the event loop only when a certain amount of time has elapsed. This method of adjusting the frequency of calls to `WaitNextEvent` works on any available Macintosh computer and doesn't require any conditional compilation.

Routine Parameters

You've already learned (in "Parameter Passing" beginning on page 1-47) that PowerPC compilers attempt to pass as many parameters as possible in the processor's registers, thereby minimizing the number of memory accesses that are required for a routine call. You can, however, help the compiler minimize memory accesses by following a few simple guidelines:

- Use function prototypes. A compiler can generate more efficient code if you include prototypes for any functions that accept floating-point parameters. The compiler then knows to use the floating-point registers to store those parameters. If no function prototype is available for a function taking floating-point parameters, the compiler needs to pass the same information in both general-purpose and floating-point parameters. (For more information, see the description of PowerPC calling conventions beginning on page 1-47.)

- Put floating-point parameters at the end of the parameter list. A PowerPC compiler reserves space for floating-point parameters not only in the floating-point registers but also either in the general-purpose registers or in a stack frame. (This is necessary to support passing floating-point parameters to a function for which no prototype is available.) It's best to let any non-floating-point parameters use the available general-purpose register, so you should move floating-point parameters to the end of the routine's parameter list.

- Minimize the use of variable parameter lists. For many reasons, it's inefficient to use variable parameter lists in the PowerPC environment. Use them only when absolutely necessary.

IMPORTANT

These floating-point parameter-passing optimizations are highly dependent on specific features of the PowerPC run-time environment. You should implement these guidelines only in those parts of your code where maximum efficiency is necessary. ▲

Mixed Mode Manager

Contents

About the Mixed Mode Manager   2-4
  External Code   2-4
  Procedure Pointers   2-5
  Mode Switches   2-7
    Calling PowerPC Code From 680x0 Code   2-8
    Calling 680x0 Code From PowerPC Code   2-12
Using the Mixed Mode Manager   2-14
  Specifying Procedure Information   2-14
  Using Universal Procedure Pointers   2-21
  Using Static Routine Descriptors   2-22
  Executing Resource-Based Code   2-24
Mixed Mode Manager Reference   2-26
  Constants   2-27
    Routine Descriptor Flags   2-27
    Procedure Information   2-27
    Routine Flags   2-34
    Instruction Set Architectures   2-35
  Data Structures   2-36
    Routine Records   2-36
    Routine Descriptors   2-37
  Mixed Mode Manager Routines   2-38
    Creating and Disposing of Routine Descriptors   2-39
    Calling Routines via Universal Procedure Pointers   2-42
    Determining Instruction Set Architectures   2-44
Summary of the Mixed Mode Manager   2-45
  C Summary   2-45
    Constants   2-45
    Data Types   2-48
    Mixed Mode Manager Routines   2-49

Mixed Mode Manager

This chapter describes the Mixed Mode Manager, the part of the Macintosh system software that manages the mixed-mode architecture of PowerPC processor-based computers running 680x0-based code (including system software, applications, and stand-alone code modules). The Mixed Mode Manager cooperates with the 68LC040 Emulator to provide a fast, efficient, and virtually transparent method for code in one instruction set architecture to call code in another architecture. The Mixed Mode Manager handles all the details of switching between architectures.

The Mixed Mode Manager is intended to operate transparently to most applications and other software. You need the information in this chapter only if

■ you want to recompile your application into PowerPC code and your application passes the address of some routine to the system software using a reference of type `ProcPtr`

■ your application—written in either PowerPC or 680x0 code—supports installable code modules that might be written in a different architecture

■ you are writing stand-alone code (for example, a VBL task or a component) that could be called from either the PowerPC native environment or the 680x0 emulated environment

■ you are writing a debugger or other software that needs to know about the structure of the stack at any time (for example, during a mode switch)

You do not need to read this chapter if you're simply writing 680x0 code that doesn't call external code modules of unknown type, or if you are writing PowerPC code that calls other PowerPC code using a procedure pointer. In these cases, any environment switching that might occur is handled completely transparently by the Mixed Mode Manager.

IMPORTANT

This chapter describes the operation and features of the Mixed Mode Manager and the 68LC040 Emulator as they exist in the first version of the system software for PowerPC processor-based Macintosh computers. ▲

To use this chapter, you should already be generally familiar with the Macintosh Operating System. See the books *Inside Macintosh: Processes* and *Inside Macintosh: Memory* for information about the run-time architecture of the 680x0 environment. You also need to be familiar with the run-time architecture of PowerPC processor-based Macintosh computers, as explained in the chapter "Introduction to PowerPC System Software."

This chapter begins by describing the mixed-mode architecture of PowerPC processor-based Macintosh computers and the operations of the Mixed Mode Manager. Then it shows how to use the Mixed Mode Manager to call external code.

About the Mixed Mode Manager

The Mixed Mode Manager is the part of the Macintosh Operating System that allows PowerPC processor-based Macintosh computers to cooperatively run 680x0 applications, PowerPC applications, 680x0 system software, and PowerPC system software. It provides a number of capabilities, including

- transparent access to 680x0-based system software from PowerPC applications
- transparent access to PowerPC processor-based system software from 680x0 applications
- a method—independent of the instruction set architecture—of calling an external piece of code. This includes
  - □ transparent access to PowerPC code by 680x0 applications
  - □ system support for calling 680x0 code from PowerPC code
  - □ system support for calling PowerPC code from 680x0 code
- support for patching PowerPC or 680x0 code with PowerPC or 680x0 code
- support for stand-alone code resources containing either 680x0 or PowerPC code

In short, the Mixed Mode Manager is intended to provide both PowerPC processor-based and 680x0-based code transparent access to code written in another instruction set (or in an instruction set whose type is unknown). It does this by keeping track of what kind of code is currently executing and, when necessary, switching modes. For example, if some PowerPC code calls a Macintosh Operating System routine that exists only in 680x0 form, the Mixed Mode Manager translates the routine's parameters from their PowerPC arrangement (for example, stored in registers GPR3 and GPR4) into the appropriate 680x0 arrangement (for example, stored in registers D0 and D1, with the result placed into register A0).

The Mixed Mode Manager is an integral part of the system software for PowerPC processor-based Macintosh computers. It is designed to hide, as much as possible, the dual nature of the operating environment supported on PowerPC processor-based Macintosh computers running the 68LC040 Emulator. Except in specific cases described later, your application or other software should not need to call the routines provided by the Mixed Mode Manager.

External Code

To appreciate when and why you might need to use the routines provided by the Mixed Mode Manager, you need to understand the circumstances in which you might directly or indirectly call code in an instruction set architecture different from that of the calling code. There are several ways to execute **external code** (code that is not directly contained in your application or software), including

- calling a trap
- calling a device driver (for example, by calling the driver's Open, Status, or Control routines)

- loading and then executing code contained in a resource

- using the address of a procedure or function obtained from an unknown source

In any of these four cases, the external code that you call might be in an instruction set architecture that is different from the instruction set architecture of the calling code. (For example, an application that uses the PowerPC instruction set might call a ROM-based Toolbox trap that uses the 680x0 instruction set.) As a result, in all these cases, the Mixed Mode Manager might have to switch environments to allow the called routine to execute and then switch back to allow your application or other software to continue execution.

In the first two of the four cases, the Mixed Mode Manager is able to handle all required mode switching virtually transparently to the calling software. In the two last cases, however, you might need to intervene in the otherwise automatic operations of the Mixed Mode Manager. This is because the Mixed Mode Manager cannot tell, from a given pointer to some executable code, what kind of code the pointer references.

The following section describes in greater detail the extent of this problem and the way you need to solve it, using universal procedure pointers in place of procedure pointers. See "Using the Mixed Mode Manager" beginning on page 2-14 for code samples that illustrate how to create and use universal procedure pointers.

Procedure Pointers

For present purposes, a **procedure pointer** is any reference generated by a compiler when taking the address of a routine. On 680x0-based Macintosh computers, a procedure pointer is simply the address of the routine's executable code (and is defined by the `ProcPtr` data type). On PowerPC processor-based Macintosh computers, a procedure pointer is the address of the routine's transition vector. Figure 2-1 illustrates the structure of procedure pointers in each environment.

Figure 2-1   680x0 and PowerPC procedure pointers

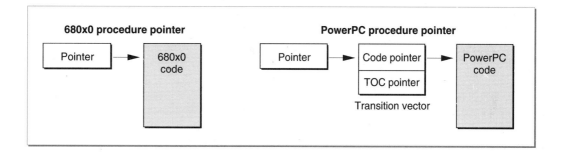

A **transition vector** is a set of two addresses: the address of the routine's executable code and the address of the fragment's table of contents (TOC).

The Macintosh programming interfaces allow you to use procedure pointers in several ways. A procedure pointer can be

■ passed as a parameter to a system software routine (for example, the growZone parameter to the SetGrowZone routine)

■ passed in a field of a parameter block or other data structure (for example, the gzProc field of a Zone parameter block)

■ stored in an application-specific global data structure (for example, the addresses stored in a grafProcs field of a graphics port)

■ installed into a vector accessed through system global variables (for example, the jGNEFilter global variable)

■ installed into the trap dispatch table or into a patch daisy chain using the SetToolTrapAddress or SetOSTrapAddress routine

As indicated previously, the Mixed Mode Manager cannot tell, from a given procedure pointer, what kind of code the pointer references (either directly through a pointer of type ProcPtr or indirectly through a transition vector). The Mixed Mode Manager solves this problem by requiring you to use generalized procedure pointers, known as universal procedure pointers, whenever you would previously have used a procedure pointer. A **universal procedure pointer** is either a normal 680x0 procedure pointer (that is, the address of a routine) or the address of a **routine descriptor,** a data structure that the Mixed Mode Manager uses to encapsulate information about an externally referenced routine. A routine descriptor describes the address of the routine, its parameters, and its calling conventions.

```
typedef RoutineDescriptor *UniversalProcPtr;
```

Note
See "Routine Descriptors" on page 2-37 for a description of the fields of a routine descriptor. ◆

The Macintosh application programming interfaces have been revised for the PowerPC platform to change all references to procedure pointers to references to universal procedure pointers. (The new interfaces are called the universal interface files.) For example, the SetGrowZone function was previously declared in the interface file Memory.h like this:

```
typedef ProcPtr GrowZoneProcPtr;
pascal void SetGrowZone (GrowZoneProcPtr growZone);
```

In the updated interface file Memory.h, SetGrowZone is declared like this:

```
typedef UniversalProcPtr GrowZoneUPP;
extern pascal void SetGrowZone (GrowZoneUPP growZone);
```

This redefinition of all procedure pointers as universal procedure pointers ensures that at the time a procedure is to be executed, the Operating System has enough information to determine the routine's instruction set architecture and hence to determine whether a mode switch is necessary. In addition, if a mode switch is necessary, the universal procedure pointer (if it is a pointer to a routine descriptor) provides information about the routine's calling conventions, the number and sizes of its parameters, and so forth.

It's important to understand exactly when you need to be concerned about routine descriptors and when you need to use the new programming interfaces when writing your application. The following cases cover most of the relevant possibilities:

■ If your application uses the 680x0 instruction set (and therefore executes under the 68LC040 Emulator on PowerPC processor-based Macintosh computers) and does not support external code modules, you do not need to use routine descriptors or the new programming interfaces.

■ If your application uses the PowerPC instruction set, you must use the new programming interfaces.

■ If your application uses either the 680x0 instruction set or the PowerPC instruction set and makes calls only to code of the same type, you do not need to create routine descriptors.

■ If your code uses the PowerPC instruction set and passes a routine's address to code that might be in the 680x0 instruction set, then you need instead to pass the address of a routine descriptor. This applies to all the methods of passing a routine address listed earlier in this section (as a parameter to a system software routine, in a field of a parameter block, and so forth).

■ If you create a resource containing PowerPC code that might be called either by 680x0 code or by PowerPC code, that code must be preceded by a routine descriptor. It's possible that the calling code simply loads the resource and jumps to its beginning; if the resource does not begin with a routine descriptor, the Mixed Mode Manager will not be called to determine whether a mode switch is necessary. See "Executing Resource-Based Code" on page 2-24 for more details.

IMPORTANT

In short, you need to convert procedure pointers to universal procedure pointers only if you pass a routine's address to code that is external to your application. See "Using Universal Procedure Pointers" beginning on page 2-21 for details on making the appropriate modifications to your application. ▲

Mode Switches

This section describes the operations of the Mixed Mode Manager in switching modes (from PowerPC native mode to 680x0 emulation mode, or vice versa). It describes the circumstances under which mode switches are performed and the mechanism that the Mixed Mode Manager uses to switch modes.

IMPORTANT

The information in this section is provided for debugging purposes only. Your application (or other code) should not rely on the details of mode switching presented here. ▲

Every mode switch occurs as a result of either an explicit or an implicit cross-mode call. An **explicit cross-mode call** occurs when the calling software itself calls the CallUniversalProc function and passes a universal procedure pointer of a routine that exists in an instruction set architecture other than that of the caller. An **implicit cross-mode call** occurs when the calling software executes a routine descriptor for a routine that exists in an instruction set architecture other than that of the caller.

The mixed-mode architecture of PowerPC processor-based computers running 680x0-based code gives rise to four possible situations when a piece of code calls a system software routine:

- When 680x0 code calls a system software routine that exists as 680x0 code, the routine is called directly, using the trap dispatch mechanism provided in the 68LC040 Emulator.

- When 680x0 code calls a system software routine that exists as PowerPC code, the routine is called indirectly, using the address—contained in the trap dispatch table—of a routine descriptor, which invokes a mode switch to the PowerPC environment. When the PowerPC code returns, the executing environment is switched back to the 68LC040 Emulator. See the next section, "Calling PowerPC Code From 680x0 Code," for more details.

- When PowerPC code calls a system software routine that exists as PowerPC code, the routine is called through glue in the system software import library. The glue code calls CallUniversalProc, which determines that the routine is PowerPC code and then calls it directly.

- When PowerPC code calls a system software routine that exists as 680x0 code, the routine is called through glue code contained in the system software import library. The glue code sets up a 680x0 universal procedure pointer (which is simply a 680x0 procedure pointer) and executes the 680x0 code by calling the CallUniversalProc function. See "Calling 680x0 Code From PowerPC Code" on page 2-12 for more details.

IMPORTANT

Only 680x0 code can make implicit cross-mode calls. Native PowerPC code must always make explicit cross-mode calls. The Mixed Mode Manager determines whether a mode switch is necessary. ▲

Calling PowerPC Code From 680x0 Code

This section describes how the Mixed Mode Manager switches modes from the 680x0 emulated environment to the PowerPC native environment. This usually happens when 680x0 code calls a system software routine that is implemented in the PowerPC instruction set.

Suppose that a 680x0 application calls some system software routine. The application is not aware that it is running under the 68LC040 Emulator, so it just pushes the routine's parameters onto the stack (or stores them into registers) and then jumps to the routine or calls a trap that internally jumps to the routine. If the routine exists as 680x0 code, no mode switch is required and the routine is called as usual. If, however, the routine exists as PowerPC code, the calling application must implicitly invoke the Mixed Mode Manager.

If the calling application merely jumps to the PowerPC code, the code must begin with a routine descriptor, as explained in "Executing Resource-Based Code" on page 2-24. If the calling application calls a trap, the trap dispatch table must contain—instead of the address of the routine's executable code—the address of a routine descriptor for that routine. This routine descriptor is created at system startup time.

Figure 2-2 shows the path followed when a 680x0 application calls a system software routine implemented as PowerPC code. The trap dispatch table contains the address of the native routine's routine descriptor. The routine descriptor contains the address of the routine's transition vector, which in turn contains the routine's entry point and TOC value.

Figure 2-2   Calling PowerPC code from a 680x0 application

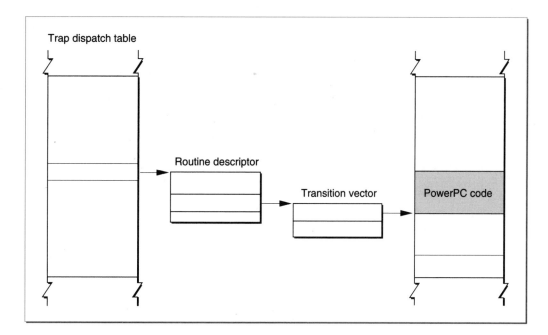

For example, suppose that your application calls the `CountResources` function, as follows:

```
myResCount = CountResources('PROC');
```

Suppose further that `CountResources` has been ported to the PowerPC instruction set. When your application calls `CountResources`, the stack looks like the one shown in Figure 2-3.

Figure 2-3　　The stack before a mode switch

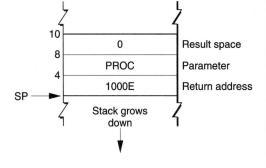

The trap dispatcher executes the `CountResources` routine descriptor, which begins with an executable instruction that invokes the Mixed Mode Manager. The Mixed Mode Manager retrieves the transition vector and creates a switch frame on the stack. A **switch frame** is a stack frame that contains information about the routine to be executed, the state of various registers, and the address of the previous frame. Figure 2-4 shows the structure of a 680x0-to-PowerPC switch frame.

IMPORTANT

Notice in Figure 2-4 that the low-order bit in the back chain pointer to the saved A6 value is set. The Mixed Mode Manager uses that bit internally as a signal that a switch frame is on the stack. The Mixed Mode Manager will fail if the stack pointer has an odd value. ▲

Figure 2-4   A 680x0-to-PowerPC switch frame

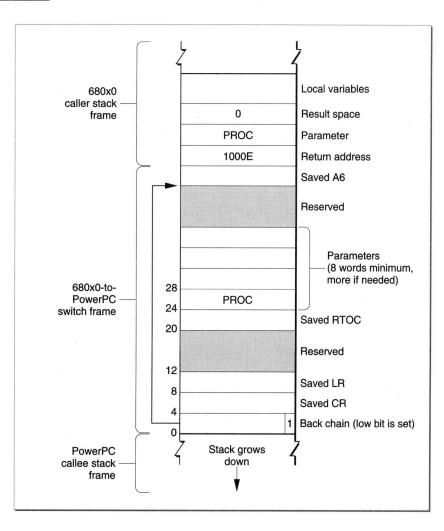

In addition to creating a switch frame, the Mixed Mode Manager also sets up several CPU registers:

■ The Table of Contents Register (RTOC) must be set to the TOC address of the fragment containing the `CountResources` routine. This value is obtained from the transition vector whose address is extracted from the routine descriptor.

■ The Link Register (LR) must be set to point to code that cleans up the stack and restarts the emulator.

At this point, it's safe to execute the native `CountResources` code. When `CountResources` completes, the Mixed Mode Manager copies the return value from R3 into its proper location (in a register or on the stack). The RTOC, LR, and CR are restored to their saved values, and the switch frame is popped off the stack. The Mixed Mode Manager also pops the return address off the stack, as well as the parameters of routines of type `pascal`. Finally, the Mixed Mode Manager jumps back into the 68LC040 Emulator and the application continues execution.

Calling 680x0 Code From PowerPC Code

This section describes how the Mixed Mode Manager switches modes from the PowerPC native environment to the 680x0 emulated environment. This usually happens when PowerPC code calls a system software routine that is implemented in the 680x0 instruction set.

For example, suppose that a PowerPC application calls a system software routine that exists only as 680x0 code. In the system software import library must exist a small piece of glue code that

- allocates space on the stack for the routine's result, if any
- determines the address of the 680x0 routine from the trap dispatch table
- provides the procedure information for the routine
- calls the `CallUniversalProc` function

Listing 2-1 illustrates a sample glue routine for the QuickDraw text-measuring routine `TextWidth`.

IMPORTANT

Glue routines like the one illustrated in Listing 2-1 are part of the system software import library. You do not need to write glue routines like this. ▲

Listing 2-1   Sample glue code for a 680x0 routine

```
enum {
   uppTextWidthProcInfo =  kPascalStackBased
                     | RESULT_SIZE(kTwoByteCode)
                     | STACK_ROUTINE_PARAMETER(1, kFourByteCode)
                     | STACK_ROUTINE_PARAMETER(2, kTwoByteCode)
                     | STACK_ROUTINE_PARAMETER(3, kTwoByteCode)
};

short TextWidth (Ptr textBuf, short firstByte, short byteCount)
{
   ProcPtr        textWidth_68K;

   textWidth_68K = NGetTrapAddress(_TextWidth, ToolTrap);
   return CallUniversalProc((UniversalProcPtr)textWidth_68K,
            uppTextWidthProcInfo, textBuf, firstByte, byteCount);
}
```

See "Specifying Procedure Information" beginning on page 2-14 for a description of the constants and macros used to define the procedure information (that is, the `myProcInfo` parameter).

Note

For Operating System traps (that is, traps of type `OSTrap`), the trap dispatcher copies the trap number into register D1. As a result, the glue code illustrated in Listing 2-1 would need to call the function `CallOSTrapUniversalProc`. ◆

The call to `CallUniversalProc` invokes the Mixed Mode Manager, which verifies that a mode switch is necessary. At that point, the Mixed Mode Manager saves all nonvolatile registers and other necessary information on the stack in a switch frame. Figure 2-5 shows the structure of a PowerPC-to-680x0 switch frame.

Figure 2-5   A PowerPC-to-680x0 switch frame

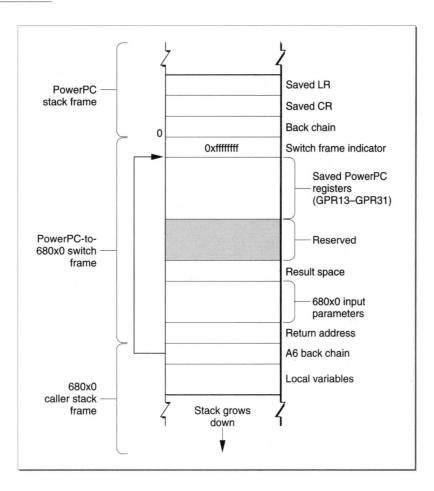

Once the switch frame is set up, the Mixed Mode Manager sets up the 68LC040 Emulator's context block and then jumps into the emulator. When the routine has finished executing, it attempts to jump to the return address pushed onto the stack. That return address points to a mode-switching structure contained in the Reserved area in the switch frame. The emulator encounters the instruction in the `goMixedModeTrap` field of the routine descriptor and then saves the current 680x0 state in its context block. Once this is done, the Mixed Mode Manager restores native registers that were previously saved and deallocates the switch frame. Control then returns to the caller of `CallUniversalProc`.

IMPORTANT

As currently implemented, the instruction that causes a return from the 68LC040 Emulator to the native PowerPC environment clears the low-order 5 bits of the Condition Code Register (CCR). This prevents 680x0 callback procedures from returning information in the CCR. If you want to port 680x0 code that calls an external routine that returns results in the CCR, you must instead call a 680x0 stub that saves that information in some other place. ▲

Using the Mixed Mode Manager

You can use the Mixed Mode Manager to specify the procedure information for a routine, create routine descriptors, and execute the code referenced by a universal procedure pointer. Typically, you'll call `NewRoutineDescriptor` to create a routine descriptor and `CallUniversalProc` to execute the code described by a routine descriptor. You can dispose of routine descriptors you no longer need by calling the `DisposeRoutineDescriptor` function.

Remember that if you are compiling code for the 680x0 environment, you don't need to worry about creating, calling, or disposing of routine descriptors. For 680x0 code, the compiler variable `USESROUTINEDESCRIPTORS` is set to `false` (the default setting). Any calls in your source code to the `NewRoutineDescriptor` function are replaced by the code address passed as a parameter to `NewRoutineDescriptor`. Similarly, any calls to `DisposeRoutineDescriptor` are simply removed.

Note

Your development environment sets the `USESROUTINEDESCRIPTOR` variable to the value appropriate for the kind of code you are compiling, You don't need to set or reset this variable. ◆

Specifying Procedure Information

The primary task of the Mixed Mode Manager is to convert routine parameters between the 680x0 and PowerPC environments. The parameter passing conventions in the PowerPC environment are identical for all routines, so you'll need to specify the calling conventions only for 680x0 routines.

In the Macintosh Operating System, there are five basic kinds of calling conventions:

■ Pascal routines with the parameters passed on the stack

■ C routines with the parameters passed on the stack

■ routines with the parameters passed in registers

■ dispatched Pascal or C routines with the selector in a register and the parameters on the stack

■ dispatched Pascal routines with the selector and the parameters on the stack

In addition to these five basic kinds of calling conventions, there exist a number of cases that the Mixed Mode Manager treats specially. For example, an ADB service routine is passed information in registers A0, A1, A2, and D0.

The Mixed Mode Manager uses a long word of type `ProcInfoType` to encode a routine's **procedure information,** which contains essential information about the calling conventions and other features of a routine. You need to specify procedure information when you create a new routine descriptor by calling the `NewRoutineDescriptor` function.

```
typedef unsigned long ProcInfoType;
```

IMPORTANT

In all likelihood, you do not need to read the remainder of this section, which explains in detail the structure of the `ProcInfoType` long word and shows how to create custom procedure information. The universal interface files define procedure information for each universal procedure pointer used by the system. For example, the interfaces define the constant `uppGrowZoneProcInfo` for you to use when specifying the procedure information for a grow-zone function. You need to create procedure information only for routines not defined in the programming interfaces. You can probably skip to the section "Using Universal Procedure Pointers" on page 2-21. ▲

The lower-order 4 bits of the procedure information encode the routine's calling conventions. You specify calling conventions using these constants:

```
enum {
    /*calling conventions*/
    kPascalStackBased                   = (CallingConventionType)0,
    kCStackBased                        = (CallingConventionType)1,
    kRegisterBased                      = (CallingConventionType)2,
    kThinkCStackBased                   = (CallingConventionType)5,
    kD0DispatchedPascalStackBased       = (CallingConventionType)8,
    kD0DispatchedCStackBased            = (CallingConventionType)9,
    kD1DispatchedPascalStackBased       = (CallingConventionType)12,
    kStackDispatchedPascalStackBased    = (CallingConventionType)14,
    kSpecialCase                        = (CallingConventionType)15
};
```

For example, a routine that passes its parameters on the stack according to normal C language conventions would have the rightmost 4 bits of the procedure information set to 0001 (hexadecimal 0x00000001).

Except for routines having calling conventions of type kSpecialCase, the 2 bits to the left of the calling convention bits encode the size of the result returned by the routine. You can access those bits using a constant:

```
#define kResultSizePhase            4
```

The Mixed Mode Manager provides four constants and a macro that you can use to set a routine's result size in its procedure information.

```
enum {
    kNoByteCode                 = 0,
    kOneByteCode                = 1,
    kTwoByteCode                = 2,
    kFourByteCode               = 3
};

#define RESULT_SIZE(sizeCode) \
            ((ProcInfoType)(sizeCode) << kResultSizePhase)
```

Except as already noted, every set of procedure information uses its rightmost 6 bits to specify the calling conventions and result size information. The calling conventions, which take up the rightmost 4 bits, determine how the remaining bits of a routine's procedure information are interpreted. For example, if the rightmost 4 bits contain the value kCStackBased or the value kPascalStackBased, then the remaining bits encode the sizes and number of the parameters passed on the stack. Figure 2-6 shows how the Mixed Mode Manager interprets the procedure information for a stack-based routine.

Figure 2-6   Procedure information for a stack-based routine

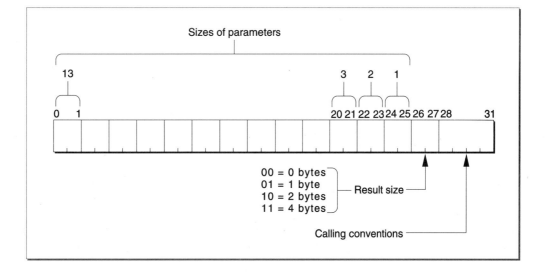

Once again, the Mixed Mode Manager provides a set of constants and macros that you can use to specify a stack-based routine's procedure information.

```
#define kStackParameterPhase 6
#define kStackParameterWidth 2

#define STACK_ROUTINE_PARAMETER(whichParam, sizeCode) \
   ((ProcInfoType)(sizeCode) << (kStackParameterPhase + \
                   (((whichParam) - 1) * kStackParameterWidth)))
```

As you can see, the maximum number of stack-based parameters whose sizes you can specify using a variable of type `ProcInfoType` is 13. The procedure information encoding used by the Mixed Mode Manager places limits on the number of specifiable register-based parameters as well. See Table 2-1 at the end of this section (page 2-20) for a complete list of these limits.

The new application programming interface files described earlier (on page 2-6) include constants that define procedure information for each type of routine to which you might need to create a universal procedure pointer. For example, the interface file `Memory.h` includes these definitions:

```
enum {
   uppGrowZoneProcInfo = kPascalStackBased
      | RESULT_SIZE(SIZE_CODE(sizeof(long)))
      | STACK_ROUTINE_PARAMETER(1, SIZE_CODE(sizeof(Size))),
   uppPurgeProcProcInfo = kPascalStackBased
      | STACK_ROUTINE_PARAMETER(1, SIZE_CODE(sizeof(Handle)))
};
```

A grow-zone function follows normal Pascal calling conventions, returns a value that is 4 bytes long, and takes a single 4-byte parameter on the stack. A purge-warning procedure follows normal Pascal calling conventions, returns no value, and takes a single 4-byte parameter on the stack.

The Mixed Mode Manager provides similar constants and macros for specifying procedure information for register-based routines.

```
#define kRegisterResultLocationPhase                       \
                        (kCallingConventionWidth + kResultSizeWidth)
#define kRegisterResultLocationWidth                5
#define kRegisterParameterPhase                            \
                        (kCallingConventionWidth + kResultSizeWidth + \
                            kRegisterResultLocationWidth)
#define kRegisterParameterWidth                     5
#define kRegisterParameterWhichPhase                2
#define kRegisterParameterSizePhase                 0
#define kDispatchedSelectorSizeWidth                2

#define kDispatchedSelectorSizePhase                       \
                        (kCallingConventionWidth + kResultSizeWidth)
#define kDispatchedParameterPhase                          \
                        (kCallingConventionWidth + kResultSizeWidth + \
                            kDispatchedSelectorSizeWidth)
#define REGISTER_RESULT_LOCATION(whichReg) \
    ((ProcInfoType)(whichReg) << kRegisterResultLocationPhase)
#define REGISTER_ROUTINE_PARAMETER(whichParam, whichReg, sizeCode) \
    ((((ProcInfoType)(sizeCode) << kRegisterParameterSizePhase) | \
    ((ProcInfoType)(whichReg) << kRegisterParameterWhichPhase)) << \
    (kRegisterParameterPhase + (((whichParam)- 1) * kRegisterParameterWidth)))
```

For example, Figure 2-7 shows the arrangement of the procedure information for a register-based routine.

Figure 2-7 Procedure information for a register-based routine

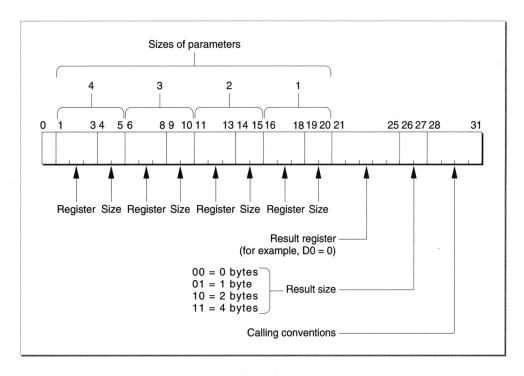

The register fields use the following constants to encode 680x0 register information:

```
enum {
    /*680x0 registers*/
    kRegisterD0                 = 0,
    kRegisterD1                 = 1,
    kRegisterD2                 = 2,
    kRegisterD3                 = 3,
    kRegisterD4                 = 8,
    kRegisterD5                 = 9,
    kRegisterD6                 = 10,
    kRegisterD7                 = 11,
    kRegisterA0                 = 4,
    kRegisterA1                 = 5,
    kRegisterA2                 = 6,
    kRegisterA3                 = 7,
    kRegisterA4                 = 12,
    kRegisterA5                 = 13,
    kRegisterA6                 = 14,
    kCCRegisterCBit             = 16,
    kCCRegisterVBit             = 17,
    kCCRegisterZBit             = 18,
```

```
    kCCRegisterNBit              = 19,
    kCCRegisterXBit              = 20
};
```

Note
The result size should be specified as 0 for results returned
in any of the CCR registers. ◆

The Mixed Mode Manager also provides constants and macros to specify the procedure
information for stack-based routines that take a register-based selector and for stack-
based routines that take a stack-based selector.

Note
See "Procedure Information" beginning on page 2-27 for a complete
description of the constants you can use to specify a routine's procedure
information. See "C Language Macros for Defining Procedure
Information" on page 2-50 for a complete list of the Mixed Mode
Manager macros you can use to create procedure information. ◆

As noted earlier, there are limits on the number of parameters that a procedure
information can describe. Table 2-1 lists the available calling conventions and the
maximum number of specifiable parameters and selectors for each convention.

IMPORTANT
The input parameters can be passed in any of the registers D0–D3 and
A0–A3; the output parameter can be returned in any register. ▲

Table 2-1   Limits on the number of specifiable parameters in a procedure information

Calling convention	Maximum number of parameters	Number of selectors
kPascalStackBased	13	0
kCStackBased	13	0
kRegisterBased	4 input, 1 output	0
kThinkCStackBased	13	0
kD0DispatchedPascalStackBased	12	1
kD0DispatchedCStackBased	12	1
kD1DispatchedPascalStackBased	12	1
kStackDispatchedPascalStackBased	12	1

In general, these limitations should not affect you. There are, however, a very few cases
in which the documented behavior of a routine prevents it from being implemented in
native PowerPC code. For example, the low-level .ENET driver routines `ReadRest`
and `ReadPacket` return information in several registers. As a result, they cannot be
implemented natively. (Because these routines are typically called only in code where

speed of execution is critical, it's not likely that you would want to incur the overhead of a mode switch by writing native callbacks to the .ENET driver.)

Using Universal Procedure Pointers

When you call the `NewRoutineDescriptor` or `NewFatRoutineDescriptor` function to create a routine descriptor, the Mixed Mode Manager calls the Memory Manager to allocate a nonrelocatable block in the current heap in which to store the new routine descriptor. Eventually, you might want to dispose of the space occupied by the routine descriptor; you can do this by calling the `DisposeRoutineDescriptor` function.

In general, there are two ways you'll probably handle this allocation and deallocation. By far the easiest method is to allocate in your application's heap, at application initialization time, a routine descriptor for each routine whose address you'll need to pass elsewhere. For example, if your application calls `TrackControl` with a custom action procedure, you can create a routine descriptor in the application heap when your application starts up, as shown in Listing 2-2.

Listing 2-2 Creating global routine descriptors

```
UniversalProcPtr myActionProc;
myActionProc = NewRoutineDescriptor((ProcPtr)MyAction,
                                    uppControlActionProcInfo,
                                    GetCurrentISA());
```

Later you would call `TrackControl` like this:

```
TrackControl(myControl, myPoint, myActionProc);
```

The routine descriptor pointed to by the global variable `myActionProc` remains allocated until your application quits, at which time the Process Manager reclaims all the memory in your application heap.

Note
If you don't want `TrackControl` to call an application-defined action procedure, you must pass NULL in place of `myActionProc`. In that case, you don't need to call `NewRoutineDescriptor`. ◆

The other way to handle routine descriptors is to create them as you need them and then dispose of them as soon as you're finished with them. This practice would be useful for routines you don't call very often. Listing 2-3 shows a way to call the `ModalDialog` function to display a rarely used modal dialog box.

Listing 2-3   Creating local routine descriptors

```
void DoAboutBox (void)
{
    short               myItem = 0;
    DialogPtr           myDialog;
    UniversalProcPtr    myModalProc;

    myDialog = GetNewDialog(kAboutBoxID, NULL, (WindowPtr) -1L);
    myModalProc = NewRoutineDescriptor((ProcPtr)MyEventFilter,
                                    uppModalFilterProcInfo,
                                    GetCurrentISA());
    while (myItem != iOK)
        ModalDialog(myModalProc, &myItem);
    DisposeDialog(myDialog);
    DisposeRoutineDescriptor(myModalProc);
}
```

If you decide to allocate and dispose of routine descriptors locally, make sure that you don't dispose of a routine descriptor before it's actually used by the Operating System. (This could happen, for instance, if you pass a universal procedure pointer for a completion routine and then exit the local procedure before the completion routine is called.)

Note
You should call `DisposeRoutineDescriptor` only to dispose routine descriptors that you created using either `NewRoutineDescriptor` or `NewFatRoutineDescriptor`. ◆

Using Static Routine Descriptors

Instead of allocating space for routine descriptors in your application heap (as described in the previous section), you can also create routine descriptors on the stack or in your global variable space by using macros supplied by the Mixed Mode Manager. Most likely, you'll create a descriptor on the stack when you need to use a routine descriptor for a very short time. For example, you could use the function defined in Listing 2-4 instead of the one defined in Listing 2-3.

Listing 2-4   Creating static routine descriptors

```
void DoAboutBox (void)
{
    short               myItem = 0;
    DialogPtr           myDialog;
    RoutineDescriptor   myRD =
                            BUILD_ROUTINE_DESCRIPTOR(uppModalFilterProcInfo,
                                                     (ProcPtr)MyEventFilter);
    UniversalProcPtr    myModalProc;

    myDialog = GetNewDialog(kAboutBoxID, NULL, (WindowPtr) -1L);
    myModalProc = @myRD;
    while (myItem != iOK)
        ModalDialog(myModalProc, &myItem);
    DisposeDialog(myDialog);
}
```

As you can see, the `DoAboutBox` function defined in Listing 2-4 uses the macro `BUILD_ROUTINE_DESCRIPTOR` to create a routine descriptor on the stack and then passes the address of that routine descriptor to the `ModalDialog` procedure. Because the routine descriptor is created on the stack, there is no need to dispose of it before exiting the `DoAboutBox` function.

You can create a routine descriptor in your application's global data area by using the `BUILD_ROUTINE_DESCRIPTOR` macro as follows:

```
static RoutineDescriptor    myRD =
                                BUILD_ROUTINE_DESCRIPTOR(uppModalFilterProcInfo,
                                                         (ProcPtr)MyEventFilter);
```

This line of code creates a routine descriptor as part of the application global variables. The advantage of this method is that you don't have to call `NewRoutineDescriptor` to allocate a routine descriptor in your heap.

The C language macro `BUILD_ROUTINE_DESCRIPTOR` is defined in Listing 2-5.

Listing 2-5   Building a static routine descriptor

```
#define BUILD_ROUTINE_DESCRIPTOR(procInfo, procedure)                       \
{                                                                           \
    _MixedModeMagic,                    /*mixed-mode A-trap*/               \
    kRoutineDescriptorVersion,          /*version*/                         \
    kSelectorsAreNotIndexable,          /*RD flags: not dispatched*/        \
    0,                                  /*reserved1*/                       \
    0,                                  /*reserved2*/                       \
```

```
0,                                     /*selector info*/              \
0,                                     /*number of routines*/         \
{                                      /*it's an array*/              \
    {                                  /*it's a structure*/           \
    (procInfo),                        /*the procedure info*/         \
    0,                                 /*reserved*/                   \
    kPowerPCISA,                       /*ISA*/                        \
    kProcDescriptorIsAbsolute |        /*flags: absolute address*/    \
    kFragmentIsPrepared |              /*it's prepared*/              \
    kUseNativeISA,                     /*always use native ISA*/      \
    (ProcPtr)(procedure),              /*the procedure*/              \
    0,                                 /*reserved*/                   \
    0,                                 /*not dispatched*/             \
    },                                                                \
    },                                                                \
}
```

IMPORTANT

You should use the BUILD_ROUTINE_DESCRIPTOR macro only to create a routine descriptor that describes a nondispatched routine that exists as PowerPC code. ▲

The Mixed Mode Manager also defines a C language macro that you can use to create static fat routine descriptors. See the Mixed Mode Manager interface file for the definition of the BUILD_FAT_ROUTINE_DESCRIPTOR macro.

Executing Resource-Based Code

As you've seen earlier in this book (in the section "Executable Resources" on page 1-34), you can create executable resources that contain PowerPC code to serve as accelerated versions of 680x0 code resources. The accelerated resource is simply a PowerPC version of the 680x0 code resource, prefixed with a routine descriptor for the code contained in the resource. The routine descriptor is necessary for the Mixed Mode Manager to know whether it needs to change modes in order to execute the code. The routine descriptor also lets the Mixed Mode Manager know whether it needs to call the Code Fragment Manager to prepare the fragment. Figure 2-8 shows the structure your code-containing resources should have.

Figure 2-8   General structure of an executable code resource

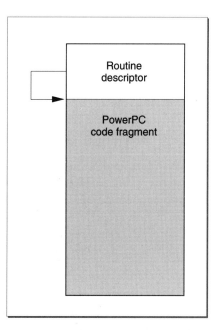

The `procDescriptor` field of the routine record—contained in the `routineRecords` field of the routine descriptor—should contain the offset from the beginning of the resource (that is, the beginning of the routine descriptor) to the beginning of the executable code fragment. In addition, the routine flags for the specified code should have the `kProcDescriptorIsRelative` bit set, indicating that the address is relative, not absolute. If the code contained in the resource is PowerPC code, you should also set the `kFragmentNeedsPreparing` bit.

It's also possible to create "fat" code-bearing resources, that is, resources containing both 680x0 and PowerPC versions of some routine. Figure 2-9 shows the general structure of such a resource.

Figure 2-9   General structure of a fat resource

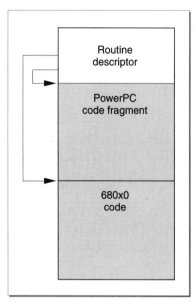

In this case, the routine descriptor contains two routine records in its `routineRecords` field, one describing the 680x0 code and one describing the PowerPC code. As with any code-bearing resource, the `procDescriptor` field of each routine record should contain the offset from the beginning of the resource to the beginning of the appropriate code. The flags for both routine records should have the `kProcDescriptorIsRelative` flag set, and the routine flags for the PowerPC routine record should have the `kFragmentNeedsPreparing` flag set.

The MPW interface file `MixedMode.r` provides Rez templates that you can use to create the accelerated resource shown in Figure 2-8 or the fat resource shown in Figure 2-9.

▲ **WARNING**
Do not call accelerated resources at interrupt time unless you are certain that the resource has already been loaded into memory, locked, and prepared for execution. If the resource containing the code hasn't been prepared, the Code Fragment Manager will attempt to do so, and thereby allocate memory. (Memory allocation is not allowed at interrupt time.) ▲

Mixed Mode Manager Reference

This section describes the constants, data structures, and routines provided by the Mixed Mode Manager. See "Using the Mixed Mode Manager" beginning on page 2-14 for detailed instructions on using these routines.

Constants

This section describes the constants provided by the Mixed Mode Manager. You use these constants to specify routine descriptor flags and a routine's procedure information. Because the universal interface files define procedure information for the most common callback routines, it's likely that you won't need to use the procedure information constants listed here.

Routine Descriptor Flags

The `routineDescriptorFlags` field of a routine descriptor contains a set of routine descriptor flags that specify attributes of the described routine. You can use constants to specify the routine descriptor flags. In general, you should use the constant `kSelectorsAreNotIndexable` when constructing your own routine descriptors; the value `kSelectorsAreIndexable` is reserved for use by Apple.

```
enum {
    kSelectorsAreNotIndexable       = (RDFlagsType)0x00,
    kSelectorsAreIndexable          = (RDFlagsType)0x01
};
```

Constant descriptions

`kSelectorsAreNotIndexable`
> For dispatched routines, the recognized routine selectors are not contiguous.

`kSelectorsAreIndexable`
> For dispatched routines, the recognized routine selectors are contiguous and therefore indexable.

Procedure Information

The Mixed Mode Manager uses a long word of type `ProcInfoType` to encode a routine's procedure information, which contains essential information about the calling conventions and other features of a routine. These values specify

■ the routine's calling conventions

■ the sizes and locations of the routine's parameters, if any

■ the size and location of the routine's result, if any

See "Specifying Procedure Information" beginning on page 2-14 for a description of the general structure of a routine's procedure information. The Mixed Mode Manager provides a number of constants that you can use to specify the procedure information.

The following constants are used to specify the size (in bytes) of a value encoded in a routine's procedure information.

```
enum {
    /*size codes*/
    kNoByteCode                     = 0,
    kOneByteCode                    = 1,
    kTwoByteCode                    = 2,
    kFourByteCode                   = 3
};
```

Constant descriptions

kNoByteCode   The value occupies no bytes.

kOneByteCode   The value occupies 1 byte.

kTwoByteCode   The value occupies 2 bytes.

kFourByteCode   The value occupies 4 bytes.

The offsets to fields and the widths of the fields within a value of type `ProcInfoType` are defined by constants:

```
/*offsets to and widths of procedure information fields*/
#define kCallingConventionPhase             0
#define kCallingConventionWidth             4
#define kResultSizePhase                    kCallingConventionWidth
#define kResultSizeWidth                    2
#define kResultSizeMask                     0x30
#define kStackParameterPhase                6
#define kStackParameterWidth                2
#define kRegisterResultLocationPhase        \
                    (kCallingConventionWidth + kResultSizeWidth)
#define kRegisterResultLocationWidth        5
#define kRegisterParameterPhase             \
                    (kCallingConventionWidth + kResultSizeWidth + \
                        kRegisterResultLocationWidth)
#define kRegisterParameterWidth                 5
#define kRegisterParameterWhichPhase            2
#define kRegisterParameterSizePhase             0
#define kDispatchedSelectorSizeWidth            2
#define kDispatchedSelectorSizePhase        \
                    (kCallingConventionWidth + kResultSizeWidth)
#define kDispatchedParameterPhase           \
                    (kCallingConventionWidth + kResultSizeWidth + \
                        kDispatchedSelectorSizeWidth)
```

Constant descriptions

kCallingConventionPhase

The offset from the least significant bit in the procedure information to the calling convention information.

kCallingConventionWidth

> The number of bits in the procedure information that encode the calling convention information.

kResultSizePhase

> The offset from the least significant bit in the procedure information to the function result size information.

kResultSizeWidth

> The number of bits in the procedure information that encode the function result size information.

kResultSizeMask

> A mask for the bits in the procedure information that encode the function result size information.

kStackParameterPhase

> The offset from the least significant bit in the procedure information to the stack parameter information.

kStackParameterWidth

> The number of bits in the procedure information that encode the size of a stack-based parameter.

kRegisterResultLocationPhase

> The offset from the least significant bit in the procedure information to the result register information.

kRegisterResultLocationWidth

> The number of bits in the procedure information that encode which register the result will be stored in.

kRegisterParameterPhase

> The offset from the least significant bit in the procedure information to the register parameter information.

kRegisterParameterWidth

> The number of bits in the procedure information that encode the information about a register-based parameter.

kRegisterParameterWhichPhase

> The offset from the beginning of a register parameter information field to the encoded register.

kRegisterParameterSizePhase

> The offset from the beginning of a register parameter information field to the encoded size of the parameter.

kDispatchedSelectorSizeWidth

> The number of bits in the procedure information that encode the size of a routine-dispatching selector.

kDispatchedSelectorSizePhase

> The offset from the least significant bit in the procedure information to the selector size information of a routine that is dispatched though a selector.

kDispatchedParameterPhase

> The offset from the least significant bit in the procedure information to the parameter information of a routine that is dispatched though a selector.

The following constants are used to specify a routine's calling conventions:

```
enum {
    /*calling conventions*/
    kPascalStackBased                    = (CallingConventionType)0,
    kCStackBased                         = (CallingConventionType)1,
    kRegisterBased                       = (CallingConventionType)2,
    kThinkCStackBased                    = (CallingConventionType)5,
    kD0DispatchedPascalStackBased        = (CallingConventionType)8,
    kD0DispatchedCStackBased             = (CallingConventionType)9,
    kD1DispatchedPascalStackBased        = (CallingConventionType)12,
    kStackDispatchedPascalStackBased     = (CallingConventionType)14,
    kSpecialCase                         = (CallingConventionType)15
};
```

Constant descriptions

kPascalStackBased
: The routine follows normal Pascal calling conventions.

kCStackBased
: The routine follows the C calling conventions employed by the MPW development environment.

kRegisterBased
: The parameters are passed in registers.

kThinkCStackBased
: The routine follows the C calling conventions employed by the THINK C software development environment. Arguments are passed on the stack from right to left, and a result is returned in register D0. All arguments occupy an even number of bytes on the stack. An argument having the size of a char is passed in the high-order byte. You should always provide function prototypes; failure to do so may cause THINK C to generate code that is incompatible with this parameter-passing convention.

kD0DispatchedPascalStackBased
: The parameters are passed on the stack according to Pascal conventions, and the routine selector is passed in register D0.

kD0DispatchedCStackBased
: The parameters are passed on the stack according to C conventions, and the routine selector is passed in register D0.

kD1DispatchedPascalStackBased
: The parameters are passed on the stack according to Pascal conventions, and the routine selector is passed in register D1.

kStackDispatchedPascalStackBased
: The routine selector and the parameters are passed on the stack.

kSpecialCase
: The routine is a special case. You can use the following constants to specify a special case.

```
enum {
    /*special cases*/
    kSpecialCaseHighHook            = 0,
    kSpecialCaseCaretHook           = kSpecialCaseHighHook,
    kSpecialCaseEOLHook             = 1,
    kSpecialCaseWidthHook           = 2,
    kSpecialCaseNWidthHook          = 3,
    kSpecialCaseTextWidthHook       = kSpecialCaseWidthHook,
    kSpecialCaseDrawHook            = 4,
    kSpecialCaseHitTestHook         = 5,
    kSpecialCaseTEFindWord          = 6,
    kSpecialCaseProtocolHandler     = 7,
    kSpecialCaseSocketListener      = 8,
    kSpecialCaseTERecalc            = 9,
    kSpecialCaseTEDoText            = 10,
    kSpecialCaseGNEFilterProc       = 11,
    kSpecialCaseMBarHook            = 12
};
```

Constant descriptions

kSpecialCaseHighHook

> The routine follows the calling conventions documented in *Inside Macintosh: Text;* a rectangle is on the stack and a pointer is in register A3; no result is returned.

kSpecialCaseCaretHook

> The routine follows the calling conventions documented in *Inside Macintosh: Text;* a rectangle is on the stack and a pointer is in register A3; no result is returned.

kSpecialCaseEOLHook

> Parameters are passed to the routine in registers A3, A4, and D0, and output is returned in the Z flag of the Status Register. An EOLHook routine has these calling conventions.

kSpecialCaseWidthHook

> Parameters are passed to the routine in registers A0, A3, A4, D0, and D1, and output is returned in register D1. A WIDTHHook routine has these calling conventions.

kSpecialCaseNWidthHook

> Parameters are passed to the routine in registers A0, A2, A3, A4, D0, and D1, and output is returned in register D1. An nWIDTHHook routine has these calling conventions.

kSpecialCaseTextWidthHook

> Parameters are passed to the routine in registers A0, A3, A4, D0, and D1, and output is returned in register D1. A TextWidthHook routine has these calling conventions.

kSpecialCaseDrawHook

> Parameters are passed to the routine in registers A0, A3, A4, D0, and

D1, and no result is returned. A DRAWHook routine has these calling conventions.

kSpecialCaseHitTestHook

Parameters are passed to the routine in registers A0, A3, A4, D0, D1, and D2, and output is returned in registers D0, D1, and D2. A HITTESTHook routine has these calling conventions.

kSpecialCaseTEFindWord

Parameters are passed to the routine in registers A3, A4, D0, and D2, and output is returned in registers D0 and D1. A TEFindWord hook has these calling conventions.

kSpecialCaseProtocolHandler

Parameters are passed to the routine in registers A0, A1, A2, A3, A4, and in the low-order word of register D1; output is returned in the Z flag of the Status Register. A protocol handler has these calling conventions.

kSpecialCaseSocketListener

Parameters are passed to the routine in registers A0, A1, A2, A3, A4, in the low-order byte of register D0, and in the low-order word of register D1; output is returned in the Z flag of the Status Register. A socket listener has these calling conventions.

kSpecialCaseTERecalc

Parameters are passed to the routine in registers A3 and D7, and output is returned in registers D2, D3, and D4. A TextEdit line-start recalculation routine has these calling conventions.

kSpecialCaseTEDoText

Parameters are passed to the routine in registers A3, D3, D4, and D7, and output is returned in registers A0 and D0. A TextEdit text-display, hit-test, and caret-positioning routine has these calling conventions.

kSpecialCaseGNEFilterProc

Parameters are passed to the routine in registers A1 and D0 and on the stack, and output is returned on the stack. A GetNextEvent filter procedure has these calling conventions.

kSpecialCaseMBarHook

Parameters are passed to the routine on the stack, and output is returned in register D0. A menu bar hook routine has these calling conventions.

For register-based routines, the registers are encoded in the routine's procedure information using these constants:

```
enum {
    /*680x0 registers*/
    kRegisterD0                     = 0,
    kRegisterD1                     = 1,
    kRegisterD2                     = 2,
    kRegisterD3                     = 3,
    kRegisterD4                     = 8,
```

```
        kRegisterD5                 = 9,
        kRegisterD6                 = 10,
        kRegisterD7                 = 11,
        kRegisterA0                 = 4,
        kRegisterA1                 = 5,
        kRegisterA2                 = 6,
        kRegisterA3                 = 7,
        kRegisterA4                 = 12,
        kRegisterA5                 = 13,
        kRegisterA6                 = 14,
        kCCRegisterCBit             = 16,
        kCCRegisterVBit             = 17,
        kCCRegisterZBit             = 18,
        kCCRegisterNBit             = 19,
        kCCRegisterXBit             = 20
};
```

Constant descriptions

kRegisterD0   Register D0.

kRegisterD1   Register D1.

kRegisterD2   Register D2.

kRegisterD3   Register D3.

kRegisterD4   Register D4.

kRegisterD5   Register D5.

kRegisterD6   Register D6.

kRegisterD7   Register D7.

kRegisterA0   Register A0.

kRegisterA1   Register A1.

kRegisterA2   Register A2.

kRegisterA3   Register A3.

kRegisterA4   Register A4.

kRegisterA5   Register A5.

kRegisterA6   Register A6.

kCCRegisterCBit
                The C (carry) flag of the Status Register.

kCCRegisterVBit
                The V (overflow) flag of the Status Register.

kCCRegisterZBit
                The Z (zero) flag of the Status Register.

kCCRegisterNBit
                The N (negative) flag of the Status Register.

kCCRegisterXBit
                The X (extend) flag of the Status Register.

Routine Flags

The `routineFlags` field of a routine record contains a set of flags that specify information about a routine. You can use constants to specify the desired routine flags. Currently, only 5 of the 16 bits in a routine flags word are defined. You should set all the other bits to 0.

```
enum {
    kProcDescriptorIsAbsolute      = (RoutineFlagsType)0x00,
    kProcDescriptorIsRelative      = (RoutineFlagsType)0x01
};
```

Constant descriptions

`kProcDescriptorIsAbsolute`

The address of the routine's entry point specified in the `procDescriptor` field of a routine record is an absolute address.

`kProcDescriptorIsRelative`

The address of the routine's entry point specified in the `procDescriptor` field of a routine record is relative to the beginning of the routine descriptor. If the code is contained in a resource and its absolute location is not known until run time, you should set this flag.

```
enum {
    kFragmentIsPrepared            = (RoutineFlagsType)0x00,
    kFragmentNeedsPreparing        = (RoutineFlagsType)0x02
};
```

Constant descriptions

`kFragmentIsPrepared`

The fragment containing the code to be executed is already loaded into memory and prepared by the Code Fragment Manager.

`kFragmentNeedsPreparing`

The fragment containing the code to be executed needs to be loaded into memory and prepared by the Code Fragment Manager. If this flag is set, the `kPowerPCISA` and `kProcDescriptorIsRelative` flags should also be set.

```
enum {
    kUseCurrentISA                 = (RoutineFlagsType)0x00,
    kUseNativeISA                  = (RoutineFlagsType)0x04
};
```

Constant descriptions

`kUseCurrentISA`   If possible, use the current instruction set architecture when executing a routine.

`kUseNativeISA`   Use the native instruction set architecture when executing a routine.

```
enum {
   kPassSelector                    = (RoutineFlagsType)0x00,
   kDontPassSelector                = (RoutineFlagsType)0x08
};
```

Constant descriptions

kPassSelector   Pass the routine selector to the target routine as a parameter.

kDontPassSelector

Do not pass the routine selector to the target routine as a parameter. You should not use this flag for 680x0 routines.

```
enum {
   kRoutineIsNotDispatchedDefaultRoutine
                                    = (RoutineFlagsType)0x00,
   kRoutineIsDispatchedDefaultRoutine
                                    = (RoutineFlagsType)0x10
};
```

Constant descriptions

kRoutineIsNotDispatchedDefaultRoutine

This routine is not the default routine for a set of routines that is dispatched using a routine selector.

kRoutineIsDispatchedDefaultRoutine

This routine is the default routine for a set of routines that is dispatched using a routine selector. If a set of routines is dispatched using a routine selector and the routine corresponding to a specified selector cannot be found, this default routine is called. This routine must be able to accept the same procedure information for all routines. If possible, it is passed the procedure information passed in a call to CallUniversalProc.

IMPORTANT

In general, you should use the constants kPassSelector and kRoutineIsNotDispatchedDefaultRoutine. The constants kDontPassSelector and kRoutineIsDispatchedDefaultRoutine are reserved for use with selector-based system software routines. ▲

Instruction Set Architectures

The ISA field of a routine record contains a flag that specifies the instruction set architecture of a routine. You can use constants to specify the instruction set architecture.

```
enum {
   kM68kISA                      = (ISAType)0,     /*MC680x0 architecture*/
   kPowerPCISA                   = (ISAType)1      /*PowerPC architecture*/
};
```

Constant descriptions

kM68kISA   The routine consists of 680x0 code.

kPowerPCISA   The routine consists of PowerPC code.

Data Structures

This section describes the two data structures provided by the Mixed Mode Manager:

■ the routine record, which contains information about a routine's calling conventions, the sizes and locations of its parameters, and its location in memory

■ the routine descriptor, which provides a generalization of procedure pointers (variables of type ProcPtr) common in the 680x0 environment

Routine Records

A routine record is a data structure that contains information about a particular routine. The routine descriptor specifies, among other things, the instruction set architecture of the routine, the number and size of the routine's parameters, the routine's calling conventions, and the routine's location in memory. At least one routine record is contained in the routineRecords field of a routine descriptor. A routine record is defined by the RoutineRecord data type.

```
struct RoutineRecord {
   ProcInfoType         procInfo;           /*calling conventions*/
   unsigned char        reserved1;          /*reserved*/
   ISAType              ISA;                /*instruction set architecture*/
   RoutineFlagsType     routineFlags;       /*flags for each routine*/
   ProcPtr              procDescriptor;     /*the thing we're calling*/
   unsigned long        reserved2;          /*reserved*/
   unsigned long        selector;           /*selector for dispatched calls*/
};
typedef struct RoutineRecord RoutineRecord;
typedef RoutineRecord *RoutineRecordPtr, **RoutineRecordHandle;
```

Field descriptions

procInfo   A value of type ProcInfoType that encodes essential information about the routine's calling conventions and parameters. See "Procedure Information" beginning on page 2-27 for a complete list of the constants you can use to set this field.

reserved1   Reserved. This field must be 0.

ISA   The instruction set architecture of the routine. See "Instruction Set Architectures" beginning on page 2-35 for a complete listing of the constants you can use to set this field.

routineFlags   A value of type RoutineFlagsType that contains a set of flags describing the routine. See "Routine Flags" beginning on page 2-34 for a complete listing of the constants you can use to set this field.

procDescriptor

A pointer to the routine's code. If the routine consists of 680x0 code and the kProcDescriptorIsAbsolute flag is set in the routineFlags field, then this field contains the address of the routine's entry point. If the routine consists of 680x0 code and the kProcDescriptorIsRelative flag is set, then this field contains the offset from the beginning of the routine descriptor to the routine's entry point. If the routine consists of PowerPC code, the kFragmentIsPrepared flag is set, and the kProcDescriptorIsAbsolute flag is set, then this field contains the address of the routine's transition vector. If the routine consists of PowerPC code, the kFragmentNeedsPreparing flag is set, and the kProcDescriptorIsRelative flag is set, then this field contains the offset from the beginning of the routine descriptor to the routine's entry point.

reserved2   Reserved. This field must be 0.

selector   Reserved. This field must be 0. For routines that are dispatched, this field contains the routine selector.

Routine Descriptors

A routine descriptor is a data structure used by the Mixed Mode Manager to execute a routine. The external interface to a routine descriptor is through a universal procedure pointer, of type UniversalProcPtr, which is defined as a procedure pointer (if the code is 680x0 code) or as a pointer to a routine descriptor (if the code is PowerPC code). A routine descriptor is defined by the RoutineDescriptor data type.

```
struct RoutineDescriptor {
    unsigned short        goMixedModeTrap;    /*mixed-mode A-trap*/
    char                  version;            /*routine descriptor version*/
    RDFlagsType           routineDescriptorFlags;
                                              /*routine descriptor flags*/
    unsigned long         reserved1;          /*reserved*/
    unsigned char         reserved2;          /*reserved*/
    unsigned char         selectorInfo;       /*selector information*/
    short                 routineCount;       /*index of last RR in this RD*/
    RoutineRecord         routineRecords[1];/*the individual routines*/
};
typedef struct RoutineDescriptor RoutineDescriptor;
```

Field descriptions

`goMixedModeTrap`

An A-line instruction that is used privately by the Mixed Mode Manager. When the emulator encounters this instruction, it transfers control to the Mixed Mode Manager. This field contains the value $AAFE.

`version`

The version number of the `RoutineDescriptor` data type. The current version number is defined by the constant `kRoutineDescriptorVersion`:

```
enum {kRoutineDescriptorVersion = 7};
```

`routineDescriptorFlags`

A set of routine descriptor flags. Currently, all the bits in this field should be set to 0, unless you are specifying a routine descriptor for a dispatched routine. See "Routine Descriptor Flags" on page 2-27 for a complete description of these flags.

`reserved1`   Reserved. This field must initially be 0.

`reserved2`   Reserved. This field must be 0.

`selectorInfo`   Reserved. This field must be 0.

`routineCount`

The index of the final routine record in the following array, `routineRecords`. Because the `routineRecords` array is zero-based, this field does not contain an actual count of the routine records contained in that array. Often, you'll use a routine descriptor to describe a single procedure, in which case this field should contain the value 0. You can, however, construct a routine descriptor that contains pointers to both 680x0 and PowerPC code (known as a "fat" routine descriptor). In that case, this field should contain the value 1.

`routineRecords`

An array of routine records for the routines described by this routine descriptor. See "Routine Records" on page 2-36 for the structure of a routine record. This array is zero-based.

IMPORTANT

Your application (or other software) should never attempt to guide its execution by inspecting the value in the `ISA` field of a routine record and jumping to the address in the `procDescriptor` field. ▲

Mixed Mode Manager Routines

This section describes the routines provided by the Mixed Mode Manager. You can use these routines to

■ create and dispose of routine descriptors

■ execute routines described by routine descriptors

In general, you need to call these routines only from PowerPC code. To maintain a single source code base for your software, however, you can call Mixed Mode Manager routines from 680x0 code, as long as you set the USESROUTINEDESCRIPTORS compiler flag to `false` (its default setting). To compile code for the PowerPC environment, you should set the USESROUTINEDESCRIPTORS flag to `true`.

See "Using the Mixed Mode Manager" beginning on page 2-14 for detailed instructions on using these routines.

Creating and Disposing of Routine Descriptors

The Mixed Mode Manager provides routines that you can use to create and dispose of routine descriptors. In general, you need to create routine descriptors only for routines whose addresses are exported to the system software (for example, a completion procedure). You don't need to create a routine descriptor for a routine that is called by code of the same type.

NewRoutineDescriptor

You can call the `NewRoutineDescriptor` function to create a new routine descriptor.

```
pascal UniversalProcPtr NewRoutineDescriptor
                    (ProcPtr theProc, ProcInfoType theProcInfo,
                        ISAType theISA);
```

theProc   The address of the routine.

theProcInfo
             The procedure information to be associated with the routine.

theISA   The instruction set architecture of the routine being described.

DESCRIPTION

The `NewRoutineDescriptor` function creates a new routine descriptor and returns a pointer (of type `UniversalProcPtr`) to it. If the value of the `theProc` parameter is `NULL`, `NewRoutineDescriptor` returns the value `NULL`.

The memory occupied by the new routine descriptor is allocated in the current heap. If you want the memory to be allocated in some other heap, you'll need to set the current heap to that heap and then restore the current heap before exiting.

SPECIAL CONSIDERATIONS

The `NewRoutineDescriptor` function allocates memory; you should not call it at interrupt time or from any code that might be executed when memory is low. In addition, the block of memory allocated by `NewRoutineDescriptor` is nonrelocatable.

To help minimize heap fragmentation, you should try to allocate any routine descriptors you will need early in your application's execution.

When the USESROUTINEDESCRIPTORS compile flag is false, the NewRoutineDescriptor function simply returns the address passed in the theProc parameter and does not allocate memory for a routine descriptor.

SEE ALSO

See "Using Universal Procedure Pointers" beginning on page 2-21 for a more complete description of when and how to create routine descriptors. See "Specifying Procedure Information" beginning on page 2-14 for information on creating procedure information.

NewFatRoutineDescriptor

You can call the NewFatRoutineDescriptor function to create a new fat routine descriptor.

```
pascal UniversalProcPtr NewFatRoutineDescriptor
                    (ProcPtr theM68kProc, ProcPtr thePowerPCProc,
                     ProcInfoType theProcInfo);
```

theM68kProc
> The address of a 680x0 routine.

thePowerPCProc
> The address of a PowerPC routine.

theProcInfo
> The procedure information to be associated with the routine.

DESCRIPTION

The NewFatRoutineDescriptor function creates a new fat routine descriptor and returns a pointer (of type UniversalProcPtr) to it. The routine descriptor contains routine records for both 680x0 and PowerPC versions of a routine. If the value of either the theM68kProc parameter or the thePowerPCProc parameter is NULL, NewFatRoutineDescriptor returns the value NULL.

The memory occupied by the new routine descriptor is allocated in the current heap. If you want the memory to be allocated in some other heap, you'll need to set the current heap to that heap and then restore the original heap before exiting.

SPECIAL CONSIDERATIONS

The NewFatRoutineDescriptor function allocates memory; you should not call it at interrupt time or from any code that might be executed when memory is low. In addition, the block of memory allocated by NewFatRoutineDescriptor is nonrelocatable. To help minimize heap fragmentation, you should try to allocate any routine descriptors you will need early in your application's execution.

When the USESROUTINEDESCRIPTORS compile flag is `false`, the `NewFatRoutineDescriptor` function is undefined.

SEE ALSO

See "Using Universal Procedure Pointers" beginning on page 2-21 for a more complete description of when and how to create routine descriptors. See "Specifying Procedure Information" beginning on page 2-14 for information on creating procedure information.

DisposeRoutineDescriptor

You can call the `DisposeRoutineDescriptor` function to dispose of a routine descriptor.

```
pascal void DisposeRoutineDescriptor
                              (UniversalProcPtr theProcPtr);
```

theProcPtr
          A universal procedure pointer.

DESCRIPTION

The `DisposeRoutineDescriptor` function disposes of the routine descriptor pointed to by the `theProcPtr` parameter. You should call this function to release any memory allocated by a previous call to `NewRoutineDescriptor`.

The Operating System automatically disposes of any remaining routine descriptors held by your application when `ExitToShell` is executed on its behalf. As a result, you don't need to explicitly dispose of any routine descriptors that you have allocated in your application heap.

SPECIAL CONSIDERATIONS

Be careful not to dispose of a routine descriptor that is still in use by the Operating System. Code that installs completion routines or other routines called asynchronously may complete before the completion routine is actually called.

When the USESROUTINEDESCRIPTORS compile flag is `false`, the `DisposeRoutineDescriptor` function does nothing.

Calling Routines via Universal Procedure Pointers

The Mixed Mode Manager provides a function that allows you to execute the routine associated with a universal procedure pointer. It also provides a function that allows you to call the routine associated with a universal procedure pointer, following Operating System register saving and restoring conventions.

CallUniversalProc

You can use the `CallUniversalProc` function to call the routine associated with a universal procedure pointer.

```
long CallUniversalProc (UniversalProcPtr theProcPtr,
                             ProcInfoType theProcInfo, ...);
```

theProcPtr
        A universal procedure pointer.

theProcInfo
        The procedure information associated with the routine specified by the
        theProcPtr parameter.

DESCRIPTION

The `CallUniversalProc` function executes the routine associated with the specified universal procedure pointer. You pass `CallUniversalProc` a universal procedure pointer (which may be either a 680x0 procedure pointer or the address of the routine descriptor), a set of procedure information, and a variable number of parameters that are passed to the routine. `CallUniversalProc` returns a result of type `long` that contains the result (if any) returned by the called routine.

SPECIAL CONSIDERATIONS

If the universal procedure pointer passed to `CallUniversalProc` is the address of the routine descriptor, that routine descriptor must already exist before you call `CallUniversalProc`. If you pass the address of an invalid routine descriptor to `CallUniversalProc`, a system error will occur.

CallOSTrapUniversalProc

You can call the `CallOSTrapUniversalProc` function to call the routine associated with a universal procedure pointer, following Operating System register saving and restoring conventions. You're likely to need to use this function only if you need to patch an Operating System trap.

```
long CallOSTrapUniversalProc (UniversalProcPtr theProcPtr,
                              ProcInfoType theProcInfo, ...);
```

theProcPtr
> A universal procedure pointer.

theProcInfo
> The procedure information associated with the routine specified by the theProcPtr parameter.

DESCRIPTION

The CallOSTrapUniversalProc function executes the routine associated with the specified universal procedure pointer, following standard conventions for executing Operating System traps. Registers A1, A2, D1, and D2 are saved before the routine is executed and restored after its completion; in addition, register A0 is saved and restored, depending on the setting of the appropriate flag bit in the trap word. The trap number is put into register D1; you should make certain to record that fact in any procedure information you build yourself.

You pass CallOSTrapUniversalProc a universal procedure pointer (which may be either a 680x0 procedure pointer or the address of a routine descriptor), a set of procedure information, and a variable number of parameters that are passed to the routine. CallOSTrapUniversalProc returns a result of type long that contains the result (if any) returned by the called routine.

SPECIAL CONSIDERATIONS

If the universal procedure pointer passed to CallOSTrapUniversalProc is the address of the routine descriptor, that routine descriptor must already exist before you call CallOSTrapUniversalProc. If you pass the address of an invalid routine descriptor to CallOSTrapUniversalProc, a system error will occur.

The CallOSTrapUniversalProc function is defined only for register-based Operating System traps. Make sure that the procedure information specified in the theProcInfo parameter correctly specifies the calling conventions of the trap. In particular, do not specify either C or Pascal calling conventions.

Determining Instruction Set Architectures

The Mixed Mode Manager contains a function that you can use to determine the current instruction set architecture.

GetCurrentISA

You can use the GetCurrentISA function to get the current instruction set architecture.

```
ISAType GetCurrentISA (void);
```

DESCRIPTION

The GetCurrentISA function returns the current instruction set architecture. See "Instruction Set Architectures" on page 2-35 for a list of the values GetCurrentISA can return.

SPECIAL CONSIDERATIONS

Currently, the GetCurrentISA function is defined as a compiler macro.

```
#if defined(powerc) || defined(__powerc)
#define GetCurrentISA()         ((ISAType) kPowerPCISA)
#else
#define GetCurrentISA()         ((ISAType) kM68kISA)
#endif
```

The implementation details are subject to change.

Summary of the Mixed Mode Manager

C Summary

Constants

```
/*Gestalt selector and response bits*/
#define gestaltMixedModeAttr       'mixd'    /*Mixed Mode Mgr attributes*/
enum {
    gestaltPowerPCAware            = 0        /*true if MMMgr supports PowerPC*/
};

enum {
    /*current version of RoutineDescriptor data type*/
    kRoutineDescriptorVersion      = 7
};
```

Routine Flags

```
enum {
    kProcDescriptorIsAbsolute      = (RoutineFlagsType)0x00,
    kProcDescriptorIsRelative      = (RoutineFlagsType)0x01
};

enum {
    kFragmentIsPrepared            = (RoutineFlagsType)0x00,
    kFragmentNeedsPreparing        = (RoutineFlagsType)0x02
};

enum {
    kUseCurrentISA                 = (RoutineFlagsType)0x00,
    kUseNativeISA                  = (RoutineFlagsType)0x04
};

enum {
    kPassSelector                  = (RoutineFlagsType)0x00,
    kDontPassSelector              = (RoutineFlagsType)0x08
};
```

```
enum {
   kRoutineIsNotDispatchedDefaultRoutine
                              = (RoutineFlagsType)0x00,
   kRoutineIsDispatchedDefaultRoutine
                              = (RoutineFlagsType)0x10
};
```

Instruction Set Architectures

```
enum {
   kM68kISA                   = (ISAType)0,     /*MC680x0 architecture*/
   kPowerPCISA                = (ISAType)1      /*PowerPC architecture*/
};
```

Routine Descriptor Flags

```
enum {
   kSelectorsAreNotIndexable  = (RDFlagsType)0x00,
   kSelectorsAreIndexable     = (RDFlagsType)0x01
};
```

Procedure Information

```
enum {
   /*size codes*/
   kNoByteCode                = 0,
   kOneByteCode               = 1,
   kTwoByteCode               = 2,
   kFourByteCode              = 3
};
```

```
/*offsets to and widths of procedure information fields*/
#define kCallingConventionPhase                 0
#define kCallingConventionWidth                 4
#define kResultSizePhase                        kCallingConventionWidth
#define kResultSizeWidth                        2
#define kResultSizeMask                         0x30
#define kStackParameterPhase                    6
#define kStackParameterWidth                    2
#define kRegisterResultLocationPhase            \
                     (kCallingConventionWidth + kResultSizeWidth)
#define kRegisterResultLocationWidth            5
```

```
#define kRegisterParameterPhase                          \
                        (kCallingConventionWidth + kResultSizeWidth + \
                            kRegisterResultLocationWidth)
#define kRegisterParameterWidth                   5
#define kRegisterParameterWhichPhase              2
#define kRegisterParameterSizePhase               0
#define kDispatchedSelectorSizeWidth              2
#define kDispatchedSelectorSizePhase                     \
                        (kCallingConventionWidth + kResultSizeWidth)
#define kDispatchedParameterPhase                        \
                        (kCallingConventionWidth + kResultSizeWidth + \
                            kDispatchedSelectorSizeWidth)

enum {
    /*calling conventions*/
    kPascalStackBased                = (CallingConventionType)0,
    kCStackBased                     = (CallingConventionType)1,
    kRegisterBased                   = (CallingConventionType)2,
    kThinkCStackBased                = (CallingConventionType)5,
    kD0DispatchedPascalStackBased    = (CallingConventionType)8,
    kD0DispatchedCStackBased         = (CallingConventionType)9,
    kD1DispatchedPascalStackBased    = (CallingConventionType)12,
    kStackDispatchedPascalStackBased = (CallingConventionType)14,
    kSpecialCase                     = (CallingConventionType)15
};

enum {
    /*special cases*/
    kSpecialCaseHighHook        = 0,
    kSpecialCaseCaretHook       = kSpecialCaseHighHook,
    kSpecialCaseEOLHook         = 1,
    kSpecialCaseWidthHook       = 2,
    kSpecialCaseNWidthHook      = 3,
    kSpecialCaseTextWidthHook   = kSpecialCaseWidthHook,
    kSpecialCaseDrawHook        = 4,
    kSpecialCaseHitTestHook     = 5,
    kSpecialCaseTEFindWord      = 6,
    kSpecialCaseProtocolHandler = 7,
    kSpecialCaseSocketListener  = 8,
    kSpecialCaseTERecalc        = 9,
    kSpecialCaseTEDoText        = 10,
    kSpecialCaseGNEFilterProc   = 11,
    kSpecialCaseMBarHook        = 12
};
```

```
enum {
    /*680x0 registers*/
    kRegisterD0                = 0,
    kRegisterD1                = 1,
    kRegisterD2                = 2,
    kRegisterD3                = 3,
    kRegisterD4                = 8,
    kRegisterD5                = 9,
    kRegisterD6                = 10,
    kRegisterD7                = 11,
    kRegisterA0                = 4,
    kRegisterA1                = 5,
    kRegisterA2                = 6,
    kRegisterA3                = 7,
    kRegisterA4                = 12,
    kRegisterA5                = 13,
    kRegisterA6                = 14,
    kCCRegisterCBit            = 16,
    kCCRegisterVBit            = 17,
    kCCRegisterZBit            = 18,
    kCCRegisterNBit            = 19,
    kCCRegisterXBit            = 20
};
```

Data Types

```
typedef unsigned char ISAType;                  /*instruction set architecture*/

typedef unsigned short CallingConventionType;   /*calling convention*/

typedef unsigned long ProcInfoType;             /*procedure information*/

typedef unsigned short RegisterSelectorType;

typedef unsigned short RoutineFlagsType;

struct RoutineRecord {
    ProcInfoType        procInfo;        /*calling conventions*/
    unsigned char       reserved1;       /*reserved*/
    ISAType             ISA;             /*instruction set architecture*/
    RoutineFlagsType    routineFlags;    /*flags for each routine*/
    ProcPtr             procDescriptor;  /*the thing we're calling*/
    unsigned long       reserved2;       /*reserved*/
    unsigned long       selector;        /*selector for dispatched calls*/
```

```
};
typedef struct RoutineRecord RoutineRecord;
typedef RoutineRecord *RoutineRecordPtr, **RoutineRecordHandle;

typedef unsigned char RDFlagsType;         /*routine descriptor flags*/

struct RoutineDescriptor {
    unsigned short      goMixedModeTrap;    /*mixed-mode A-trap*/
    char                version;            /*routine descriptor version*/
    RDFlagsType         routineDescriptorFlags;
                                            /*routine descriptor flags*/
    unsigned long       reserved1;          /*reserved*/
    unsigned char       reserved2;          /*reserved*/
    unsigned char       selectorInfo;       /*selector information*/
    short               routineCount;       /*index of last RR in this RD*/
    RoutineRecord       routineRecords[1];  /*the individual routines*/
};
typedef struct RoutineDescriptor RoutineDescriptor;
typedef RoutineDescriptor *UniversalProcPtr, **UniversalProcHandle;
typedef RoutineDescriptor *RoutineDescriptorPtr, **RoutineDescriptorHandle;
```

Mixed Mode Manager Routines

Creating and Disposing of Routine Descriptors

```
pascal UniversalProcPtr NewRoutineDescriptor
                        (ProcPtr theProc, ProcInfoType theProcInfo,
                         ISAType theISA);
pascal UniversalProcPtr NewFatRoutineDescriptor
                        (ProcPtr theM68kProc, ProcPtr thePowerPCProc,
                         ProcInfoType theProcInfo);
pascal void DisposeRoutineDescriptor
                        (UniversalProcPtr theProcPtr);
```

Calling Routines via Universal Procedure Pointers

```
long CallUniversalProc    (UniversalProcPtr theProcPtr,
                           ProcInfoType theProcInfo, ...);
long CallOSTrapUniversalProc
                          (UniversalProcPtr theProcPtr,
                           ProcInfoType theProcInfo, ...);
```

Determining Instruction Set Architectures

```
ISAType GetCurrentISA     (void);
```

C Language Macros for Defining Procedure Information

```
#define SIZE_CODE(size) (((size) == 4) ? kFourByteCode : \
   (((size) == 2) ? kTwoByteCode : (((size) == 1) ? kOneByteCode : 0)))

#define RESULT_SIZE(sizeCode) ((ProcInfoType)(sizeCode) << kResultSizePhase)

#define STACK_ROUTINE_PARAMETER(whichParam, sizeCode) \
   ((ProcInfoType)(sizeCode) << (kStackParameterPhase + \
              (((whichParam) - 1) * kStackParameterWidth)))

#define DISPATCHED_STACK_ROUTINE_PARAMETER(whichParam, sizeCode) \
   ((ProcInfoType)(sizeCode) << (kDispatchedParameterPhase + \
              (((whichParam) - 1) * kStackParameterWidth)))

#define DISPATCHED_STACK_ROUTINE_SELECTOR_SIZE(sizeCode) \
   ((ProcInfoType)(sizeCode) << kDispatchedSelectorSizePhase)

#define REGISTER_RESULT_LOCATION(whichReg) \
   ((ProcInfoType)(whichReg) << kRegisterResultLocationPhase)

#define REGISTER_ROUTINE_PARAMETER(whichParam, whichReg, sizeCode) \
   ((((ProcInfoType)(sizeCode) << kRegisterParameterSizePhase) | \
   ((ProcInfoType)(whichReg) << kRegisterParameterWhichPhase)) << \
   (kRegisterParameterPhase + (((whichParam)- 1) * kRegisterParameterWidth)))

#define SPECIAL_CASE_PROCINFO(specialCaseCode) \
   (kSpecialCase | ((ProcInfoType)(specialCaseCode) << 4))
```

Code Fragment Manager

Contents

About the Code Fragment Manager   3-3
    Fragments   3-4
    Import Library Searching   3-5
    Version Checking   3-7
Using the Code Fragment Manager   3-10
    Loading Code Fragments   3-10
    Creating a Code Fragment Resource   3-12
    Getting Information About Exported Symbols   3-14
Code Fragment Manager Reference   3-15
    Data Structures   3-15
        Fragment Initialization Block   3-15
        Fragment Location Record   3-16
        Memory Location Record   3-17
        Disk Location Record   3-17
        Segment Location Record   3-18
    Code Fragment Manager Routines   3-18
        Loading Fragments   3-19
        Unloading Fragments   3-23
        Finding Symbols   3-24
    Fragment-Defined Routines   3-26
    Resources   3-28
        The Code Fragment Resource   3-28
Summary of the Code Fragment Manager   3-32
    C Summary   3-32
        Constants   3-32
        Data Types   3-33
        Code Fragment Manager Routines   3-34
        Fragment-Defined Routines   3-35
    Result Codes   3-35

This chapter describes the Code Fragment Manager, the part of the Macintosh system software that loads fragments into memory and prepares them for execution. A fragment can be an application, an import library, a system extension, or any other block of executable code and its associated data.

The Code Fragment Manager is intended to operate transparently to most applications and other software. You need to use the Code Fragment Manager explicitly only if

- you need to load code modules dynamically during the execution of your application or other software

- you want to unload code modules before the termination of your application

- you want to obtain information about the symbols exported by a fragment

For example, if your application supports dynamic loading of tools, filters, or other software modules contained in fragments, you'll need to use the Code Fragment Manager to load and prepare them for execution.

This chapter also describes the format of the code fragment resource, which defines information about a fragment. You need to create a code fragment resource (a resource of type 'cfrg') for each application or import library you create. For information on doing this, see "Creating a Code Fragment Resource" on page 3-12.

To use this chapter, you should already be generally familiar with the Macintosh Operating System. See the books *Inside Macintosh: Processes* and *Inside Macintosh: Memory* for information about the run-time architecture of the 680x0 environment. You also need to be familiar with the run-time architecture of PowerPC processor-based Macintosh computers, as explained in the chapter "Introduction to PowerPC System Software." That chapter describes the general nature and structure of fragments.

This chapter begins by describing the capabilities of the Code Fragment Manager. Then it describes how the Code Fragment Manager searches for the appropriate versions of import libraries. In general, you need to know these details about searching and version checking only if you are creating updated versions of an existing import library. The section "Using the Code Fragment Manager" beginning on page 3-10 provides code samples illustrating how to use some of the routines provided by the Code Fragment Manager. The section "Code Fragment Manager Reference" beginning on page 3-15 is a complete reference to the Code Fragment Manager.

About the Code Fragment Manager

The Code Fragment Manager is the Operating System loader for executable code and data that are contained in fragments. Its operations are loosely analogous to those of the Segment Manager in previous versions of the Macintosh system software. The Code Fragment Manager, however, provides a much richer set of services than the Segment Manager, including

- loading and preparation of fragments for execution

- automatic resolution of imported symbols by locating and loading import libraries used by a fragment

■ automatic execution of a fragment's initialization and termination routines

■ support for updated versions of import libraries

The following sections describe how fragments are structured, how the Code Fragment Manager searches fragments for unresolved symbols, and how it manages different versions of import libraries.

Fragments

The Code Fragment Manager operates primarily on fragments. A **fragment** is a block of executable code and its associated data. Fragments can be loosely differentiated into three categories, based on how they are used:

■ applications

■ import libraries

■ extensions

Fragments contain symbols, some or all of which may be referenced by code or data in other fragments; these kinds of symbols are called **exported symbols** (or, for brevity, **exports**). An import library is a fragment that consists primarily of exported symbols and their associated code and data. Other kinds of fragments can contain references to the exported symbols of an import library; these references are called **imported symbols** (or, for brevity, **imports**).

During the linking phase of building a fragment, the linker creates an import for each external symbol that is resolved to an export from some import library. The code or data referenced by that import is not copied into the fragment. Instead, as part of the process of loading the fragment into memory and preparing it for execution, the Code Fragment Manager replaces the imported symbol with the address of the exported code or data.

Note
Both code and data may be exported by name. However, routines are usually exported indirectly, via a transition vector to the routine. A routine's transition vector is stored in the fragment's data area. See "The Table of Contents" on page 1-26 for more details. ◆

A fragment is stored in a **container**, which can be any logically contiguous object accessible by the Operating System. For example, the executable code and global variables of a PowerPC application are typically stored in a fragment in the application's data fork. The Macintosh ROM is itself a container for the import library that exports the Macintosh system software and for several other import libraries. Application extensions, such as dynamically loadable filters or other code modules, can be stored in resources in the application's resource fork. It's better, however, to use the data fork of some file as the container of an application extension fragment. The extension can be put into the application's data fork (either before or after the application's code fragment) or into the data fork of some other file.

Note

A single data fork can contain multiple containers. The `'cfrg'` resource in the file's resource fork allows the Operating System to find each individual container in a data fork. ◆

The Code Fragment Manager is responsible for loading fragments (by calling the Code Fragment Loader) and preparing them for execution. It resolves the imported symbols in a fragment, loading and preparing any additional fragments whose exports are referenced by that fragment. Loading a given fragment, such as an application, usually involves loading and preparing additional fragments.

An import library can have its exported symbols imported by any number of other fragments. When the Code Fragment Manager resolves the imports in a particular fragment, it establishes a **connection** to each individual fragment whose code or data that fragment references. In general, the connections are transparent to the importing fragment. If you call the Code Fragment Manager directly, however, it returns a **connection ID** to you that uniquely identifies the connection. You can use the connection ID to perform various actions on the exporting fragment (for example, to break the connection and unload the fragment or to get information about its exported symbols).

Note

There is no practical limit on the size of a fragment. ◆

Import Library Searching

When searching for an import library to find code or data that is imported by some other fragment, the Code Fragment Manager follows a standard search path. It looks in various files and folders in a specific order until it finds an import library that exports the code or data imported by the fragment being loaded. Once the Code Fragment Manager finds a library that it deems compatible with the fragment it's loading, it stops searching and resolves imports in the fragment to code or data in that library. In general, the exact order in which the Code Fragment Manager searches for import libraries is transparent to your software. However, you might need the information in this section to ensure that a particular import library is found before some other import library, which might also be compatible with your fragment.

Note

See the next section, "Version Checking" beginning on page 3-7, for information on how the Code Fragment Manager determines whether some import library is compatible with a fragment. ◆

When loading and preparing an application that imports code or data from an import library, the Code Fragment Manager searches first in the application file itself, by looking for import libraries indicated in the application's `'cfrg'` resource. Typically, any import libraries contained in your application are located in your application's data fork, either before or after the container that holds your application's code and data. Less commonly, you can put an import library into a resource in your application's resource fork. The `'cfrg'` resource specifies the location of any import libraries that you've included with your application, whether in the data or the resource fork.

If an import library used by your application is not found in the application file itself, the Code Fragment Manager next searches in any directory designated as the application's **library directory,** a directory used by the application to store import libraries or aliases to import libraries. You specify a library directory by including in the appropriate field of your `'cfrg'` resource the ID of an alias resource that picks out the library directory. See "The Code Fragment Resource" beginning on page 3-28 for details.

The Code Fragment Manager searches a directory by looking for files of type `'shlb'` that contain a resource of type `'cfrg'`. The `'cfrg'` resource identifies the logical name of the import library, which is needed to match the library's name generated at link time. There can be more than one logical name listed in a single `'cfrg'` resource. This might happen if there are multiple import libraries contained in the data fork of a single `'shlb'` file. This might also happen if a single import library or application is to be identified by more than one name. Within a directory, the Code Fragment Manager also looks for aliases to files of type `'shlb'` and resolves them to their targets. The alias file must itself be of type `'shlb'`.

If no suitable import library has been found yet, the Code Fragment Manager searches next in the directory that contains the application. If any import libraries—whether located in the application's directory or targeted by an alias in the application's directory—are determined to be compatible with the fragment whose imports are being resolved, the Code Fragment Manager chooses the most compatible library and stops searching.

IMPORTANT

The Code Fragment Manager looks only in the top level of the application's directory, not in any subdirectories contained in it. ▲

If no suitable import library has been found yet, the Code Fragment Manager searches next in the Extensions folder in the System Folder and in all the subdirectories of the Extensions folder, including any directories that are targets of directory aliases in the Extensions folder. Once again, both files of type `'shlb'` and targets of aliases of type `'shlb'` are candidates for compatibility checking. This scheme allows you to store your import libraries in a vendor-specific location in the Extensions folder.

If the Code Fragment Manager still hasn't found a compatible import library that exports the imported symbols in the fragment it's trying to prepare, it continues by looking in a **ROM registry,** which keeps track of all import libraries that are stored in the ROM of a Macintosh computer. The Code Fragment Manager registers all ROM-based import libraries in this registry at system startup time.

The final stage of the search path is a **file and directory registry** that it maintains internally. This registry is a list of files and directories that, for various reasons, cannot be put into the normal search path followed by the Code Fragment Manager or would not be recognized as import libraries even if they were in that path. For example, to be registered automatically by the Component Manager, a component must be stored in a file of type `'thng'`. To inform the Code Fragment Manager that the file also contains one or more import libraries in its data fork, it can be registered in the file and directory registry.

Note

The Code Fragment Manager routine to register a file or directory is currently private. ◆

If your application or other software loads a fragment explicitly from disk by calling the `GetDiskFragment` routine, the Code Fragment Manager first looks for any needed import libraries in the **load directory,** the directory that contains the fragment being loaded. (This directory is the one specified in the `fileSpec` parameter you pass to `GetDiskFragment`.) If no suitable import library is found there, the search continues along the path followed when loading and preparing an application. However, the Code Fragment Manager looks in the load directory first only if it is different from the application's directory. Otherwise, the load directory is searched in its normal sequence, after the application file itself and the library directory.

In summary, the Code Fragment Manager looks in the following places when searching for an import library to resolve one or more imports in a fragment being loaded:

1. The load directory (the directory containing the fragment being loaded). The load directory, however, is searched only when a fragment is loaded in response to a call to `GetDiskFragment` or `GetSharedLibrary`, and only when it's different from the application's directory.

2. The application file, if the application's `'cfrg'` resource indicates that the application file contains import libraries. The application fragment is implicitly treated here as an import library.

3. The application's library directory (as specified in the application's `'cfrg'` resource).

4. The application's directory. Only the top level of this directory is searched.

5. The Extensions folder in the System Folder. The Extensions folder and all directories in the Extensions folder are searched.

6. The ROM registry maintained internally by the Code Fragment Manager.

7. The file and directory registry maintained internally by the Code Fragment Manager.

At any stage, the Code Fragment Manager selects the one import library of all those available to it that best satisfies its compatibility version checking. If an import library meets the relevant criteria, the library search stops. Otherwise, the search continues to the next stage. If the final stage (the file and directory registry) is reached and no suitable library can be found, the Code Fragment Manager gives up and does not load the original fragment.

Version Checking

One of the principal benefits of import libraries, aside from their ability to reduce the size of applications and other fragments, is the ease with which a library developer can make improvements in portions of the import library without requiring developers to modify or rebuild any applications that use the import library. The library developer needs only to ensure that the updated version is compatible with the version expected by the applications using the library. In general, this means that the external programming interface provided by the import library remains unchanged throughout changes in the underlying implementation.

The Code Fragment Manager provides a simple but powerful version-checking scheme intended to prevent incompatibilities between import libraries and the fragments that use them. This checking is always performed automatically as part of the normal fragment loading and preparation process. In general, your application does not need to concern itself with checking the version of an import library whose code or data it uses.

To take a simple example, suppose that an application uses a single import library. When the application is created, it is linked with some version of that library. Unresolved external symbols in the application are resolved, by the linker, to exported code or data in the import library. The version of the import library used at link time is called the **definition version** of the library (because it supplies the definitions of exported symbols, not the actual implementation of routines and initialization of variables).

When the application is loaded and prepared for execution, it must be connected to a version of that import library. The version of the import library used at load time is called the **implementation version** of the library (because it supplies the implementations of routines and initializations of variables exported by the library). The essential requirement is that the implementation version of an import library used at run time be compatible with the definition version used at link time. The two versions do not need to be identical, but they must satisfy the same programming interface. (The implementation can be a superset of the definition library.)

To allow the Code Fragment Manager to check the implementation version of an import library against the definition version used when linking the application, the linker copies version information from the definition library into the application. When the application is launched, the version information in the application is compared with the version information stored in the implementation library. If the version of the import library is identical to that expected by the application, the library and the application are deemed compatible. If, however, the two versions are not identical, the Code Fragment Manager inspects additional information in whichever of the two fragments (the application and the import library) is the newer fragment. The idea is to allow the newer fragment to decide whether it is compatible with the older fragment.

Every import library contains three version numbers: the current version number, the oldest supported definition version number, and the oldest supported implementation version number. The two latter version numbers are included to provide a way for the Code Fragment Manager to determine whether a given definition version is compatible with a given implementation version, if the current versions of the library and the definition version used to link the application are not identical.

IMPORTANT

The current version number must always be greater than or equal to both the oldest supported definition version number and the oldest supported implementation version number. ▲

The linker copies into the application both the current version number of the definition library and the oldest supported implementation version number. When the application is launched, the Code Fragment Manager checks those numbers with the version numbers in the implementation libraries according to the algorithm shown in Listing 3-1.

Listing 3-1   Pseudocode for the version-checking algorithm

```
if (Definition.Current == Implementation.Current)
   return(kLibAndAppAreCompatible);
else if (Definition.Current > Implementation.Current)
   /*definition version is newer than implementation version*/
   if (Definition.OldestImp <= Implementation.Current)
      return(kImplAndDefAreCompatible);
   else
      return(kImplIsTooOld);
else
   /*definition version is older than implementation version*/
   if (Implementation.OldestDef <= Definition.Current)
      return(kImplAndDefAreCompatible);
   else
      return(kDefIsTooOld);
```

If the current version number copied into the application from the definition library at link time is the same as the current version number of the candidate version of the implementation import library, then the Code Fragment Manager accepts that version of the implementation import library and continues with the loading and preparation of the application. Otherwise, the Code Fragment Manager determines which of the two fragments is newer and then applies a further check.

If the current version number copied into the application from the definition library at link time is greater than the current version number of the candidate version of the implementation import library, the Code Fragment Manager compares the oldest supported implementation version number in the application with the current version number of the implementation library. If the definition library's oldest supported implementation version number is less than or equal to the library's current version number, the application and library are deemed compatible. Otherwise, the library is too old for the application.

If the current version number copied into the application from the definition library at link time is less than the current version number of the most recent version of the implementation import library, the Code Fragment Manager compares the oldest supported definition library version number (stored in the implementation library) with the current definition library version number (stored in the application). If the oldest supported definition library version number is less than or equal to the application's current version number, the application and library are deemed compatible. Otherwise, the application is too old for the library.

Note

In general, of course, the Code Fragment Manager checks the
compatibility of a fragment being loaded and *all* of the import
libraries from which it imports code and data. ◆

The version numbers in both the definition and implementation versions of an import
library should have the same format as the first 4 bytes of a version resource (that is,
a resource of type `'vers'`). See the chapter "Finder Interface" in *Inside Macintosh:
Macintosh Toolbox Essentials* for complete information on version resources. When
comparing version numbers, however, the Code Fragment Manager treats those 4 bytes
simply as an unsigned long quantity. As a result, the value 0x00000000 is interpreted as
a valid version number.

Using the Code Fragment Manager

The Code Fragment Manager provides routines that you can use to explicitly load code
fragments and to get information about symbols exported by a particular fragment. This
section illustrates how to use those routines.

IMPORTANT

In general, the Code Fragment Manager automatically loads all import
libraries required by your application at the time your application is
launched. You need to use the routines described in this section only if
your application supports dynamically loaded application tools, filters,
or other code modules. ▲

This section also describes how to create a code fragment resource. Every application
and import library must have a code fragment resource to describe basic information
about the application or import library.

Loading Code Fragments

You can use the Code Fragment Manager to load fragments from the containers in which
they are stored. You need to do this only for code fragments that are dynamically added
to your application's context during execution. This might happen, for instance, if your
application supports dynamically loadable filters or tools.

The executable code you want to bind to your application context can be stored in any
kind of container. If the container is an import library (a file of type `'shlb'`), you can
use the Code Fragment Manager's `GetSharedLibrary` function. If the container is a
disk file, you call the `GetDiskFragment` function. If the container is a resource, you
need to load the resource into memory (using normal Resource Manager routines)
and then call the `GetMemFragment` function. See "Loading Fragments" beginning on
page 3-19 for complete details on each of these functions.

Code Fragment Manager

Listing 3-2 and Listing 3-3 illustrate how to load application-specific tools into memory using the Code Fragment Manager. Listing 3-2 shows how to load a resource-based fragment.

Listing 3-2   Loading a resource-based fragment

```
Handle        myHandle;
OSErr         myErr;
ConnectionID  myConnID;
Ptr           myMainAddr;
Str255        myErrName;

myHandle = GetResource('tool', 128);
HLock(myHandle);
myErr = GetMemFragment(*myHandle, GetHandleSize(myHandle),
            myToolName, kLoadNewCopy, &myConnID,
            (Ptr*)&myMainAddr, myErrName);
if (myErr) {
   AlertUser(myErr);
   goto noLoad;
}
```

As you can see, Listing 3-2 loads the resource into memory by calling the Resource Manager function GetResource and locks it by calling the Memory Manager procedure HLock. Then it calls GetMemFragment to prepare the fragment. The first parameter passed to GetMemFragment specifies the address in memory of the fragment. Because GetResource returns a handle to the resource data, Listing 3-2 dereferences the handle to obtain a pointer to the resource data. To avoid dangling pointers, you need to lock the block of memory before calling GetMemFragment. The constant kLoadNewCopy passed as the fourth parameter requests that the Code Fragment Manager allocate a new copy of the fragment's global data section.

Listing 3-3 shows how to load a disk-based fragment.

Listing 3-3   Loading a disk-based fragment

```
myErr = GetDiskFragment(&myFSSpec, 0, kWholeFork, myToolName,
            kLoadNewCopy, &myConnID, (Ptr*)&myMainAddr,
            myErrName);
if (myErr) {
   AlertUser(myErr);
   goto noLoad;
}
```

All import libraries and other fragments that are loaded on behalf of your application (either as part of its normal startup or programmatically by your application) are unloaded by the Process Manager at application termination; therefore, a library can be loaded and does not have to be unloaded by the application before it terminates.

Creating a Code Fragment Resource

You need to create a **code fragment resource** (a resource of type 'cfrg') for each native application or import library you create. This resource identifies the instruction set architecture, location, size, and logical name of the application or import library, as well as version information for import libraries.

In PowerPC or fat applications, the code fragment resource is read by the Process Manager at application launch time. The Process Manager needs to know whether the application contains PowerPC code and, if so, where that code is located. If the Process Manager cannot find a 'cfrg' resource in the application's resource fork, it assumes that the application is a 680x0 application, where the executable code is contained within 'CODE' resources in the application's resource fork.

IMPORTANT

A code fragment resource must have resource ID 0. ▲

For an application, the code fragment resource typically indicates that the application's executable code fragment begins at offset 0 within the application's data fork and extends for the entire length of the data fork. Listing 3-4 shows the Rez input for a typical application's code fragment resource.

Listing 3-4   The Rez input for a typical application's 'cfrg' resource

```
#include "CodeFragmentTypes.r"
resource 'cfrg' (0) {
    {
        kPowerPC,               /*instruction set architecture*/
        kFullLib,               /*no update level for apps*/
        kNoVersionNum,          /*no current version number*/
        kNoVersionNum,          /*no oldest def'n version number*/
        kDefaultStackSize,      /*use default stack size*/
        kNoAppSubFolder,        /*no library directory*/
        kIsApp,                 /*fragment is an application*/
        kOnDiskFlat,            /*fragment is on disk*/
        kZeroOffset,            /*fragment starts at fork start*/
        kWholeFork,             /*fragment occupies entire fork*/
        "SurfWriter"            /*name of the application*/
    }
};
```

Note

See "The Code Fragment Resource" on page 3-28 for complete information about the structure of a code fragment resource. ◆

For import libraries, the code fragment resource is read by the Code Fragment Manager as part of the process of searching for symbols imported by some fragment that is currently being loaded and prepared for execution. (See the section "Import Library Searching" on page 3-5 for details on how the Code Fragment Manager searches for import libraries.) The information in the `'cfrg'` resource is also used to ensure that the Code Fragment Manager finds an implementation version of an import library that is compatible with the definition version used to link the fragment being loaded and prepared for execution. Listing 3-5 shows the Rez input for a typical code fragment resource for an import library.

Listing 3-5   The Rez input for a typical import library's `'cfrg'` resource

```
#define kOldDefVers    0x01008000    /*version 1.0*/
#define kCurrVers      0x02008000    /*version 2.0*/

#include "CodeFragmentTypes.r"
resource 'cfrg' (0) {
    {
        kPowerPC,              /*instruction set architecture*/
        kFullLib,              /*base library*/
        kCurrVers,             /*current version number*/
        kOldDefVers,           /*oldest definition version number*/
        kDefaultStackSize,     /*ignored for import library*/
        kNoAppSubFolder,       /*ignored for import library*/
        kIsLib,                /*fragment is a library*/
        kOnDiskFlat,           /*fragment is on disk*/
        kZeroOffset,           /*fragment starts at fork start*/
        kWholeFork,            /*fragment occupies entire fork*/
        "SurfTools"            /*name of the library*/
    }
};
```

An import library's code fragment resource also specifies the logical name of the import library. This is the name used by the Code Fragment Manager to resolve imports in some other fragment. The logical name can be different from the name of the file containing the import library.

Note that code fragment resources are required only for fragments that are either applications or import libraries. If you need similar version-checking or name-binding capabilities for fragments that are application extensions, you will need to provide your own code to do this.

Getting Information About Exported Symbols

In cases in which you load a fragment programmatically (that is, by calling Code Fragment Manager routines), you can get information about the symbols exported by that fragment by calling the CountSymbols and GetIndSymbol functions. The CountSymbols function returns the total number of symbols exported by a fragment. CountSymbols takes as one of its parameters a connection ID; accordingly, you must already have established a connection to a fragment before you can determine how many symbols it exports.

Given an index ranging from 1 to the total number of symbols in a fragment, the GetIndSymbol function returns the name, address, and class of a symbol in that fragment. You can use CountSymbols in combination with GetIndSymbol to get information about all the symbols in a fragment. For example, the code in Listing 3-6 prints the names of all the symbols in a particular fragment.

Listing 3-6   Finding symbol names

```
void MyGetSymbolNames (ConnectionID myConnID);
{
    long            myIndex;
    long            myCount;        /*number of exported symbols in fragment*/
    OSErr           myErr;
    Str255          myName;         /*symbol name*/
    Ptr             myAddr;         /*symbol address*/
    SymClass        myClass;        /*symbol class*/

    myErr = CountSymbols(myConnID, &myCount);
    if (!myErr)
        for (myIndex = 1; myIndex <= myCount; myIndex++)
            {
                myErr = GetIndSymbol(myConnID, myIndex, myName,
                                    &myAddr, &myClass);
                if (!myErr)
                    printf("%P", myName);
            }
}
```

If you already know the name of a particular symbol whose address and class you want to determine, you can use the FindSymbol function. See page 3-24 for details on calling FindSymbol.

Code Fragment Manager Reference

This section describes the data structures and routines provided by the Code Fragment Manager. See "Using the Code Fragment Manager" beginning on page 3-10 for detailed instructions on using these routines. This section also describes the format of the optional initialization and termination routines you can include in a fragment, as well as the structure of the code fragment resource.

Data Structures

This section describes the data structures that define the format of the data passed to a fragment's initialization routine.

IMPORTANT

You need the information in this section only if your fragment (application, import library, or extension) contains an initialization routine. In addition, much of the information passed to an initialization routine is intended for use by language implementors. Most other developers are likely to need only the pointer to a file specification record passed to disk-based fragments. (This information allows the initialization routine to access its own resource fork.) ▲

Fragment Initialization Block

The Code Fragment Manager passes to your fragment's initialization routine a pointer to a **fragment initialization block,** which contains information about the fragment. A fragment initialization block is defined by the InitBlock data type.

```
struct InitBlock {
    long                    contextID;       /*context ID*/
    long                    closureID;       /*closure ID*/
    long                    connectionID;    /*connection ID*/
    FragmentLocator         fragLocator;     /*fragment location*/
    Ptr                     libName;         /*pointer to fragment name*/
    long                    reserved4a;      /*reserved*/
    long                    reserved4b;      /*reserved*/
    long                    reserved4c;      /*reserved*/
    long                    reserved4d;      /*reserved*/
};
typedef struct InitBlock InitBlock, *InitBlockPtr;
```

Field descriptions

contextID   A context ID.

closureID   A closure ID.

connectionID   A connection ID.

fragLocator   A fragment location record that specifies the location of the
                   fragment. See the following section for details about the structure
                   of a fragment location record.

libName   A pointer to the name of the fragment being initialized. The name is
                   a Pascal string (a length byte followed by the name itself).

reserved4a   Reserved for use by Apple Computer.

reserved4b   Reserved for use by Apple Computer.

reserved4c   Reserved for use by Apple Computer.

reserved4d   Reserved for use by Apple Computer.

IMPORTANT

The fields of a fragment initialization block are aligned in memory in
accordance with 680x0 alignment conventions. ▲

Fragment Location Record

The `fragLocator` field of an initialization block contains a **fragment location record**
that provides information about the location of a fragment. A fragment location record is
defined by the `FragmentLocator` data type.

```
struct FragmentLocator {
    long                    where;          /*location selector*/
    union {
        MemFragment         inMem;          /*memory location record*/
        DiskFragment        onDisk;         /*disk location record*/
        SegmentedFragment   inSegs;         /*segment location record*/
    } u;
};
typedef struct FragmentLocator FragmentLocator, *FragmentLocatorPtr;
```

Field descriptions

where   A selector that determines which member of the following union is
                   relevant. This field can contain one of these constants:

```
enum {
    kInMem,              /*container in memory*/
    kOnDiskFlat,         /*container in a data fork*/
    kOnDiskSegmented     /*container in a resource*/
};
```

inMem   A memory location record.

onDisk   A disk location record.

inSegs   A segment location record.

IMPORTANT

The fields of a fragment location record are aligned in memory in accordance with 680x0 alignment conventions. ▲

Memory Location Record

For fragments located in memory, the `inMem` field of a fragment location record contains a **memory location record,** which specifies the location of the fragment in memory. A memory location record is defined by the `MemFragment` data type.

```
struct MemFragment {
    Ptr                     address;    /*pointer to start of fragment*/
    long                    length;     /*length of fragment*/
    Boolean                 inPlace;    /*is data section in place?*/
};
typedef struct MemFragment MemFragment;
```

Field descriptions

address   A pointer to the beginning of the fragment in memory.

length   The length, in bytes, of the fragment.

inPlace   A Boolean value that specifies whether the container's data section is instantiated in place (`true`) or elsewhere (`false`).

IMPORTANT

The fields of a memory location record are aligned in memory in accordance with 680x0 alignment conventions. ▲

Disk Location Record

For fragments located in the data fork of a file on disk, the `onDisk` field of a fragment location record contains a **disk location record,** which specifies the location of the fragment. A disk location record is defined by the `DiskFragment` data type.

```
struct DiskFragment {
    FSSpecPtr               fileSpec;   /*pointer to FSSpec*/
    long                    offset;     /*offset to start of fragment*/
    long                    length;     /*length of fragment*/
};
typedef struct DiskFragment DiskFragment;
```

Field descriptions

fileSpec   A pointer to a file specification record (a data structure of type `FSSpec`) for the data fork of a file. This pointer is valid only while the initialization routine is executing. If you need to access the information in the file specification record at any later time, you must make a copy of that record.

offset   The offset, in bytes, from the beginning of the file's data fork to the
                    beginning of the fragment.

length   The length, in bytes, of the fragment. If this field contains the value
                    0, the fragment extends to the end-of-file.

IMPORTANT

The fields of a disk location record are aligned in memory in accordance
with 680x0 alignment conventions. ▲

Segment Location Record

For fragments located in the resource fork of a file on disk, the inSegs field of a fragment
location record contains a **segment location record,** which specifies the location of the
fragment. A segment location record is defined by the SegmentedFragment data type.

```
struct SegmentedFragment {
    FSSpecPtr               fileSpec;       /*pointer to FSSpec*/
    OSType                  rsrcType;       /*resource type*/
    short                   rsrcID;         /*resource ID*/
};
typedef struct SegmentedFragment SegmentedFragment;
```

Field descriptions

fileSpec   A pointer to a file specification record (a data structure of type
                    FSSpec) for the resource fork of a file. This pointer is valid only
                    while the initialization routine is executing. If you need to access
                    the information in the file specification record at any later time, you
                    must make a copy of that record.

rsrcType   The resource type of the resource containing the fragment.

rsrcID   The resource ID of the resource containing the fragment.

IMPORTANT

The fields of a segment location record are aligned in memory in
accordance with 680x0 alignment conventions. ▲

Code Fragment Manager Routines

You can use the routines provided by the Code Fragment Manager to

- load a fragment by filename or library name

- identify an import library that is already loaded

- unload a fragment

- find a symbol by name in a fragment

- find all the symbols in a fragment

Loading Fragments

The Code Fragment Manager provides three functions that you can use to load various kinds of fragments: GetDiskFragment, GetMemFragment, and GetSharedLibrary. Loading involves finding the specified fragment, reading it into memory (if it isn't already in memory), and preparing it for execution. The Code Fragment Manager attempts to resolve all symbols imported by the fragment; to do so may involve loading import libraries.

If the fragment loading fails, the Code Fragment Manager returns an error code. Note, however, that the error encountered is not always in the fragment you asked to load. Rather, the error might have occurred while attempting to load an import library that the fragment you want to load depends on. For this reason, the Code Fragment Manager also returns, in the errName parameter, the name of the fragment that caused the load to fail. Although fragment names are restricted to 63 characters, the errName parameter is declared as type Str255; doing this allows future versions of the Code Fragment Manager to return a more informative message in the errName parameter.

GetDiskFragment

You can use the GetDiskFragment function to locate and possibly also load a fragment contained in a file's data fork into your application's context.

```
OSErr GetDiskFragment (FSSpecPtr fileSpec, long offset,
                       long length, Str63 fragName,
                       LoadFlags findFlags, ConnectionID *connID,
                       Ptr *mainAddr, Str255 errName);
```

fileSpec   A file system specification that identifies the disk-based fragment to load.

offset   The number of bytes from the beginning of the file's data fork at which the beginning of the fragment is located.

length   The length (in bytes) of the fragment. Specify the constant kWholeFork for this parameter if the fragment extends to the end-of-file of the data fork. Specify a nonzero value for the exact length of the fragment.

fragName   An optional name of the fragment. (This information is used primarily to allow you to identify the fragment during debugging.)

findFlags   A flag that specifies the operation to perform on the fragment. See the description below for the values you can pass in this parameter.

connID   On exit, the connection ID that identifies the connection to the fragment. You can pass this ID to other Code Fragment Manager routines.

mainAddr   On exit, the main address of the fragment. The value returned is specific to the fragment itself. Your application can use this parameter for its own purposes.

errName   On exit, the name of the fragment that could not successfully be loaded. This parameter is meaningful only if the call to GetDiskFragment fails.

DESCRIPTION

The GetDiskFragment function locates and possibly also loads a disk-based fragment into your application's context. The actions of GetDiskFragment depend on the action flag you pass in the findFlags parameter. The Code Fragment Manager recognizes these constants:

```
enum {
    kLoadLib          = 1,  /*load fragment*/
    kFindLib          = 2,  /*find fragment*/
    kLoadNewCopy      = 5   /*load fragment with new copy of data*/
};
```

The kFindLib constant specifies that the Code Fragment Manager search for the specified fragment. If the fragment is already prepared and connected to your application, GetDiskFragment returns fragNoErr as its function result and the existing connection ID in the connID parameter. If the specified fragment is not found, GetDiskFragment returns the result code fragLibNotFound. If the specified fragment is found but could not be connected to your application, GetDiskFragment returns the result code fragLibConnErr.

The kLoadLib constant specifies that the Code Fragment Manager search for the specified fragment and, if it finds it, load it into memory. If the fragment has already been loaded, it's not loaded again. The Code Fragment Manager uses the data-instantiation method specified in the fragment's container (which is either global or per-connection instantiation).

The kLoadNewCopy constant specifies that the Code Fragment Manager load the specified fragment, creating a new copy of any writable data maintained by the fragment. You specify kLoadNewCopy to obtain one instance per load of the fragment's data and to override the data-instantiation method specified in the container itself. This is most useful for application extensions (for example, drop-in tools).

RESULT CODES

fragNoErr	0	No error
paramErr	−50	Parameter error
fragLibNotFound	−2804	Specified fragment not found
fragHadUnresolveds	−2807	Loaded fragment has unacceptable unresolved symbols
fragNoMem	−2809	Not enough memory for internal bookkeeping
fragNoAddrSpace	−2810	Not enough memory in user's address space for section
fragObjectInitSeqErr	−2812	Order error during user initialization function
fragImportTooOld	−2813	Import library is too old
fragImportTooNew	−2814	Import library is too new
fragInitLoop	−2815	Circularity in required initialization order
fragLibConnErr	−2817	Error connecting to fragment
fragUserInitProcErr	−2821	Initialization procedure did not return noErr

See "Loading Code Fragments" on page 3-10 for more details on the fragment-loading process.

GetMemFragment

You can use the GetMemFragment function to prepare a memory-based fragment.

```
OSErr GetMemFragment (Ptr memAddr, long length, Str63 fragName,
                      LoadFlags findFlags, ConnectionID *connID,
                      Ptr *mainAddr, Str255 errName);
```

memAddr	The address of the fragment.
length	The size, in bytes, of the fragment.
fragName	The name of the fragment. (This information is used primarily to allow you to identify the fragment during debugging.)
findFlags	A flag that specifies the operation to perform on the fragment. See the description of the GetDiskFragment function on page 3-19 for the values you can pass in this parameter.
connID	On exit, the connection ID that identifies the connection to the fragment. You can pass this ID to other Code Fragment Manager routines (for example, CloseConnection).
mainAddr	On exit, the main address of the fragment. The value returned is specific to the fragment itself.
errName	On exit, the name of the fragment that could not successfully be loaded. This parameter is meaningful only if the call to GetMemFragment fails.

DESCRIPTION

The GetMemFragment function prepares for subsequent execution a fragment that is already loaded into memory. This function is most useful for handling code that is contained in a resource. You can read the resource data into memory using normal Resource Manager routines (for example, Get1Resource) and then call GetMemFragment to complete the processing required to prepare it for use (for example, to resolve any imports and execute the fragment's initialization routine).

▲ **WARNING**
You must lock the resource-based fragment into memory (for example, by calling HLock) before calling GetMemFragment. You must not unlock the memory until you've closed the connection to the fragment (by calling CloseConnection). ▲

RESULT CODES

fragNoErr	0	No error
paramErr	–50	Parameter error
fragLibNotFound	–2804	Specified fragment not found
fragHadUnresolveds	–2807	Loaded fragment has unacceptable unresolved symbols
fragNoMem	–2809	Not enough memory for internal bookkeeping
fragNoAddrSpace	–2810	Not enough memory in user's address space for section
fragObjectInitSeqErr	–2812	Order error during user initialization function
fragImportTooOld	–2813	Import library is too old
fragImportTooNew	–2814	Import library is too new
fragInitLoop	–2815	Circularity in required initialization order
fragLibConnErr	–2817	Error connecting to fragment
fragUserInitProcErr	–2821	Initialization procedure did not return noErr

SEE ALSO

See "Loading Code Fragments" on page 3-10 for more details on the fragment-loading process.

GetSharedLibrary

You can use the GetSharedLibrary function to locate and possibly also load an import library into your application's context.

```
OSErr GetSharedLibrary (Str63 libName, OSType archType,
                        LoadFlags findFlags,
                        ConnectionID *connID, Ptr *mainAddr,
                        Str255 errName);
```

libName   The name of an import library.

archType   The instruction set architecture of the import library. For the PowerPC architecture, use the constant kPowerPCArch. For the 680x0 architecture, use the constant kMotorola68KArch.

findFlags   A flag that specifies the operation to perform on the import library. See the description of the GetDiskFragment function on page 3-19 for the values you can pass in this parameter.

connID   On exit, the connection ID that identifies the connection to the import library. You can pass this ID to other Code Fragment Manager routines.

mainAddr   On exit, the main address of the import library. The value returned is specific to the import library itself and is not used by the Code Fragment Manager.

errName   On exit, the name of the fragment that could not successfully be loaded. This parameter is meaningful only if the call to GetSharedLibrary fails.

DESCRIPTION

The GetSharedLibrary function locates the import library named by the libName parameter and possibly also loads that import library into your application's context. The actions of GetSharedLibrary depend on the action flag you pass in the findFlags parameter; pass kFindLib to get the connection ID of an existing connection to the specified fragment, kLoadLib to load the specified fragment, or kLoadNewCopy to load the fragment with a new copy of the fragment's data section.

The GetSharedLibrary function does not resolve any unresolved imports in your application. In particular, you cannot use it to resolve any weak imports in your code fragment.

RESULT CODES

fragNoErr	0	No error
paramErr	−50	Parameter error
fragLibNotFound	−2804	Specified fragment not found
fragHadUnresolveds	−2807	Loaded fragment has unacceptable unresolved symbols
fragNoMem	−2809	Not enough memory for internal bookkeeping
fragNoAddrSpace	−2810	Not enough memory in user's address space for section
fragObjectInitSeqErr	−2812	Order error during user initialization function
fragImportTooOld	−2813	Import library is too old
fragImportTooNew	−2814	Import library is too new
fragInitLoop	−2815	Circularity in required initialization order
fragLibConnErr	−2817	Error connecting to fragment
fragUserInitProcErr	−2821	Initialization procedure did not return noErr

SEE ALSO

See "Loading Code Fragments" on page 3-10 for more details on the fragment-loading process.

Unloading Fragments

The Code Fragment Manager provides one function that you can use to close an existing connection to a fragment.

CloseConnection

You can use the CloseConnection function to close a connection to a fragment.

```
OSErr CloseConnection (ConnectionID *connID);
```

connID   A connection ID.

DESCRIPTION

The `CloseConnection` function closes the connection to a fragment indicated by the `connID` parameter. `CloseConnection` decrements the count of existing connections to the specified fragment and, if the resulting count is 0, calls the fragment's termination routine and releases the memory occupied by the code and data sections of the fragment. If the resulting count is not 0, any per-connection data is released but the code section remains in memory.

When a fragment is unloaded as a result of its final connection having been closed, all libraries that depend on that fragment are also released, provided that their usage counts are also 0.

The Code Fragment Manager automatically closes any connections that remain open at the time `ExitToShell` is called for your application, so you need to call `CloseConnection` only for fragments you wish to unload before your application terminates.

SPECIAL CONSIDERATIONS

You can close a connection only to the root of a loading sequence (that is, the fragment whose loading triggered the entire load chain).

RESULT CODES

fragNoErr	0	No error
fragConnectionIDNotFound	–2801	Connection ID is not valid

Finding Symbols

The Code Fragment Manager provides three functions that you can use to find the symbols exported by a fragment and get information about them: `FindSymbol`, `CountSymbols`, and `GetIndSymbol`.

FindSymbol

You can use the `FindSymbol` function to search for a specific exported symbol.

```
OSErr FindSymbol (ConnectionID connID, Str255 symName,
                    Ptr *symAddr, SymClass *symClass);
```

connID   A connection ID.

symName   A symbol name.

symAddr   On exit, the address of the symbol whose name is `symName`.

symClass   On exit, the class of the symbol whose name is `symName`. See the description below for a list of the recognized symbol classes.

DESCRIPTION

The FindSymbol function searches the code fragment identified by the connID parameter for the symbol whose name is specified by the symName parameter. If that symbol is found, FindSymbol returns the address of the symbol in the symAddr parameter and class of the symbol in the symClass parameter. The currently recognized symbol classes are defined by constants.

```
enum {
    kCodeSymbol      = 0,  /*a code symbol*/
    kDataSymbol      = 1,  /*a data symbol*/
    kTVectSymbol     = 2   /*a transition vector symbol*/
};
```

Because a fragment's code is normally exported through transition vectors to that code, the value kCodeSymbol is not returned in the PowerPC environment. You can use the other two constants to distinguish exports that represent code (of class kTVectSymbol) from those that represent general data (of class kDataSymbol).

RESULT CODES

fragNoErr	0	No error
fragConnectionIDNotFound	–2801	Connection ID is not valid
fragSymbolNotFound	–2802	Symbol was not found in connection

CountSymbols

You can use the CountSymbols function to determine how many symbols are exported from a specified fragment.

```
OSErr CountSymbols (ConnectionID connID, long *symCount);
```

connID   A connection ID.

symCount   On exit, the number of exported symbols in the fragment whose connection ID is connID.

DESCRIPTION

The CountSymbols function returns, in the symCount parameter, the number of symbols exported by the fragment whose connection ID is connID. You can use the value returned in symCount to index through all the exported symbols in a particular fragment (using the GetIndSymbol function).

Code Fragment Manager

RESULT CODES

fragNoErr	0	No error
fragConnectionIDNotFound	–2801	Connection ID is not valid

GetIndSymbol

You can use the GetIndSymbol function to get information about the exported symbols in a fragment.

```
OSErr GetIndSymbol (ConnectionID connID, long symIndex,
                    Str255 symName, Ptr *symAddr,
                    SymClass *symClass);
```

connID   A connection ID.

symIndex   A symbol index. The value of this parameter should be greater than or equal to 1 and less than or equal to the value returned by the CountSymbols function.

symName   On exit, the name of the indicated symbol.

symAddr   On exit, the address of the indicated symbol.

symClass   On exit, the class of the indicated symbol.

DESCRIPTION

The GetIndSymbol function returns information about a particular symbol exported by the fragment whose connection ID is connID. If GetIndSymbol executes successfully, it returns the symbol's name, starting address, and class in the symName, symAddr, and symClass parameters, respectively. See the description of the FindSymbol function (page 3-24) for a list of the values that can be returned in the symClass parameter.

A fragment's exported symbols are retrieved in no predetermined order.

RESULT CODES

fragNoErr	0	No error
fragConnectionIDNotFound	–2801	Connection ID is not valid
fragSymbolNotFound	–2802	Symbol was not found in connection

Fragment-Defined Routines

This section describes the initialization and termination routines that you can define for a fragment.

ConnectionInitializationRoutine

You can define a fragment initialization routine that is executed by the Code Fragment Manager when the fragment is first loaded into memory and prepared for execution. An initialization routine has the following type definition:

```
typedef OSErr ConnectionInitializationRoutine
                                    (InitBlockPtr initBlkPtr);
```

initBlkPtr

A pointer to a fragment initialization block specifying information about the fragment.

Parameter block

→	contextID	long	A context ID.
→	closureID	long	A closure ID.
→	connectionID	long	A connection ID.
→	fragLocator	FragmentLocator	A fragment location block.
→	libName	Ptr	A pointer to fragment's name.
→	reserved4a	long	Reserved.
→	reserved4b	long	Reserved.
→	reserved4c	long	Reserved.
→	reserved4d	long	Reserved.

DESCRIPTION

A fragment's initialization routine is executed immediately after the fragment has been loaded into memory (if necessary) and prepared for execution, and immediately before the fragment's main routine (if it has one) is executed. The initialization routine is passed a pointer to an initialization block, which contains information about the fragment, such as its location and connection ID. See "Fragment Initialization Block" on page 3-15 for a description of the fields of the initialization block.

You can use the initialization routine to perform any tasks that need to be performed before any of the code or data in the fragment is accessed. For example, you might want to open the fragment's resource fork (if it has one). You can determine the location of the fragment's container from the `FragmentLocator` field of the fragment initialization block whose address is passed to your initialization routine.

RESULT CODES

Your initialization routine should return `noErr` if it executes successfully, and some other result code if it does not. If your initialization routine returns any result code other than `noErr`, the entire load fails and the error `fragUserInitProcErr` is returned to the code that requested the root load.

ConnectionTerminationRoutine

You can define a fragment termination routine that is executed by the Code Fragment Manager when a fragment is unloaded from memory. A termination routine has the following type definition:

```
typedef void ConnectionTerminationRoutine (void);
```

DESCRIPTION

A fragment's termination routine is executed immediately before the fragment is unloaded from memory. You can use the termination routine to perform any necessary clean-up tasks, such as closing open resource files or disposing of any memory allocated by the fragment.

Note that a termination routine is not passed any parameters and does not return any result. You are expected to maintain any information about the fragment (such as file reference numbers of any open files) in its static data area.

Resources

This section describes the code fragment resource, a resource of type 'cfrg' that is used by the Code Fragment Manager when loading fragments such as applications and import libraries.

This section describes the structure of this resource after it is compiled by the Rez resource compiler, available from APDA. If you are interested in creating the Rez input file for this resource, see "Creating a Code Fragment Resource" on page 3-12 for detailed information.

The Code Fragment Resource

You use a code fragment resource to specify some characteristics of a code fragment. For an application, the code fragment resource indicates to the Process Manager that the application's data fork contains an executable code fragment. For an import library, the code fragment resource specifies the library's name and version information.

IMPORTANT

A code fragment resource must have resource ID 0. ▲

Figure 3-1 shows the structure of a compiled code fragment resource.

Figure 3-1   Structure of a compiled code fragment ('cfrg') resource

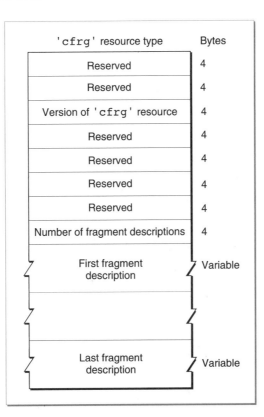

The compiled version of a code fragment resource contains the following elements:

- Reserved. The first two long integers are reserved and should be set to 0.

- Version information. This field specifies the current version of the 'cfrg' resource. The current version is 0x00000001.

- Reserved. The next four long integers are reserved and should be set to 0.

- Number of fragment descriptions. This field specifies the number of code fragment information records that follow this field in the resource. (The value in this field should be the actual number of information records that follow, beginning with 1.)

Following the array count is an array of **code fragment information records.** A single file can include one or more containers. Similarly, it might occasionally be useful to assign more than one name to a single import library or application. Typically, however, both applications and import libraries include just a single code fragment information record in their 'cfrg' resources. Each record has the format illustrated in Figure 3-2.

Figure 3-2   The format of a code fragment information record

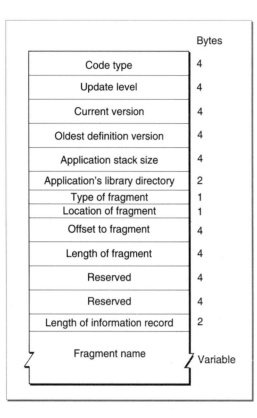

A code fragment information record contains the following elements:

- The instruction set architecture. You can use the Rez constant kPowerPC ('pwpc') to specify the PowerPC instruction set architecture.

- The update level. For an import library, you can specify either the value kFullLib (0), to indicate that the library is a base library (not an update of some other library), or the value kUpdateLib (1), to indicate that the library updates only part of some other library. Applications should specify the value kFullLib in this field.

- The current version number. For an import library, this field specifies the implementation version. This field has the same format as the first 4 bytes of a resource of type 'vers'. See the chapter "Finder Interface" in *Inside Macintosh: Macintosh Toolbox Essentials* for details on the structure of a 'vers' resource.

- The oldest definition version number. For an import library, this field specifies the oldest version of the definition library with which the implementation import library is compatible. This field has the same format as the first 4 bytes of a resource of type 'vers'.

- The application stack size. For an application, this field specifies the minimum size, in bytes, of the application stack. You can use the Rez constant kDefaultStackSize (0) to indicate that the stack should be given the default size for the current software and hardware configuration. If you determine at run time that your application needs a larger or smaller stack, you can use the standard stack-adjusting techniques that call `GetApplLimit` and `SetApplLimit`.

- The application's library directory. For an application, this field specifies the resource ID of an alias resource (a resource of type `'alis'`) in the application's resource fork that describes the application's load directory. See "Import Library Searching" on page 3-5 for more information about load directories. For information about alias resources, see the chapter "Alias Manager" in *Inside Macintosh: Files*.

- A usage field. This field specifies the type of fragment that this record describes. The value `kIsLib` (0) indicates that the fragment is an import library. The value `kIsApp` (1) indicates that the fragment is an application. The value `kIsDropIn` (2) indicates that the fragment is an extension. The Code Fragment Manager recognizes only the values `kIsLib` and `kIsApp`. The value `kIsDropIn` is provided to allow you to put private application extensions in a file and not have the Code Fragment Manager recognize them as shared libraries.

- A location field. This field specifies the location of the fragment's container. The value `kInMem` (0) indicates that the container is in memory (usually in ROM). This value is intended for use by the Operating System; in general, you should not use it. The value `kOnDiskFlat` (1) indicates that the container is in the data fork of some file. The value `kOnDiskSegmented` (2) indicates that the container is in a resource in the resource fork of some file.

- The offset to the beginning of the fragment. The interpretation of this field depends on the value specified in the location field immediately preceding this field. If the location field has the value `kInMem`, this field is the address in memory of the beginning of the fragment. If the location field has the value `kOnDiskFlat`, this field is the number of bytes from the beginning of the data fork to the beginning of the fragment itself. You can use the Rez constant `kZeroOffset` (0) to specify an offset of 0 bytes. If the location field has the value `kOnDiskSegmented`, this field is the resource type (of type `OSType`) of the resource that contains the fragment.

- The length of the fragment. The interpretation of this field depends on the value specified in the location field immediately preceding the offset field. If the location field has the value `kInMem`, this field is the address in memory of the end of the fragment. If the location field has the value `kOnDiskFlat`, this field is the length, in bytes, of the fragment. You can use the Rez constant `kWholeFork` (0) to indicate that the fragment occupies the entire fork. If the location field has the value `kOnDiskSegmented`, this field is the sign-extended resource ID of the resource that contains the fragment.

- Reserved. The next two long integers are reserved and should be set to 0.

- The total length of the code fragment information record. This field specifies the length, in bytes, of this code fragment information record, including the fragment name and any pad bytes added to the name field.

- The fragment's name. This field is a Pascal string that indicates the name of the application or import library. This is the default name used by the debugger for this fragment. This field is padded with null bytes, if necessary, so that the information record extends to a 4-byte boundary.

Summary of the Code Fragment Manager

C Summary

Constants

```
/*Gestalt selector and response bits*/
#define gestaltCFMAttr      'cfrg'    /*Code Fragment Manager attributes*/
enum {
   gestaltCFMPresent = 0              /*set if Code Fragment Mgr is present*/
};


#define kPowerPCArch        'pwpc'    /*PowerPC instruction set architecture*/
#define kMotorola68KArch    'm68k'    /*680x0 instruction set architecture*/

#define kNoLibName                    ((unsigned char *) 0)
#define kNoConnectionID               ((ConnectionID) 0)
#define kUnresolvedSymbolAddress      ((Ptr) 0x0)

enum {
   kLoadLib        = 1,               /*load fragment*/
   kFindLib        = 2,               /*find fragment*/
   kLoadNewCopy    = 5               /*load fragment with new copy of data*/
};

enum {
   kCodeSymbol     = 0,               /*a code symbol*/
   kDataSymbol     = 1,               /*a data symbol*/
   kTVectSymbol    = 2               /*a transition vector symbol*/
};

enum {
   /*selectors for fragment location record*/
   kInMem,                            /*container in memory*/
   kOnDiskFlat,                       /*container in a data fork*/
   kOnDiskSegmented                   /*container in a resource*/
};
```

Data Types

```
typedef long                    ConnectionID;   /*connection ID number*/

typedef unsigned long           LoadFlags;      /*a flag long word*/

typedef unsigned char           SymClass;       /*symbol class*/
```

Fragment Initialization Block

```
struct InitBlock {
    long                contextID;      /*context ID*/
    long                closureID;      /*closure ID*/
    long                connectionID;   /*connection ID*/
    FragmentLocator     fragLocator;    /*fragment location*/
    Ptr                 libName;        /*pointer to fragment name*/
    long                reserved4a;     /*reserved*/
    long                reserved4b;     /*reserved*/
    long                reserved4c;     /*reserved*/
    long                reserved4d;     /*reserved*/
};
typedef struct InitBlock InitBlock, *InitBlockPtr;
```

Fragment Location Record

```
struct FragmentLocator {
    long                where;          /*location selector*/
    union {
       MemFragment      inMem;          /*memory location record*/
       DiskFragment     onDisk;         /*disk location record*/
       SegmentedFragment inSegs;        /*segment location record*/
    } u;
};
typedef struct FragmentLocator FragmentLocator, *FragmentLocatorPtr;
```

Memory Location Record

```
struct MemFragment {
    Ptr                 address;        /*pointer to start of fragment*/
    long                length;         /*length of fragment*/
    Boolean             inPlace;        /*is data section in place?*/
};
typedef struct MemFragment MemFragment;
```

Disk Location Record

```
struct DiskFragment {
   FSSpecPtr                    fileSpec;      /*pointer to FSSpec*/
   long                         offset;        /*offset to start of fragment*/
   long                         length;        /*length of fragment*/
};
typedef struct DiskFragment DiskFragment;
```

Segment Location Record

```
struct SegmentedFragment {
   FSSpecPtr                    fileSpec;      /*pointer to FSSpec*/
   OSType                       rsrcType;      /*resource type*/
   short                        rsrcID;        /*resource ID*/
};
typedef struct SegmentedFragment SegmentedFragment;
```

Code Fragment Manager Routines

Loading Fragments

```
OSErr GetDiskFragment      (FSSpecPtr fileSpec, long offset, long length,
                            Str63 fragName, LoadFlags findFlags,
                            ConnectionID *connID, Ptr *mainAddr,
                            Str255 errName);

OSErr GetMemFragment       (Ptr memAddr, long length, Str63 fragName,
                            LoadFlags findFlags, ConnectionID *connID,
                            Ptr *mainAddr, Str255 errName);

OSErr GetSharedLibrary     (Str63 libName, OSType archType,
                            LoadFlags findFlags, ConnectionID *connID,
                            Ptr *mainAddr, Str255 errName);
```

Unloading Fragments

```
OSErr CloseConnection      (ConnectionID *connID);
```

Finding Symbols

```
OSErr FindSymbol           (ConnectionID connID, Str255 symName,
                            Ptr *symAddr, SymClass *symClass);

OSErr CountSymbols         (ConnectionID connID, long *symCount);

OSErr GetIndSymbol         (ConnectionID connID, long symIndex,
                            Str255 symName, Ptr *symAddr,
                            SymClass *symClass);
```

Fragment-Defined Routines

Initializing Fragments

```
typedef OSErr ConnectionInitializationRoutine
                        (InitBlockPtr initBlkPtr);
```

Terminating Fragments

```
typedef void ConnectionTerminationRoutine
                        (void);
```

Result Codes

fragNoErr	0	No error
paramErr	−50	Parameter error
fragContextNotFound	−2800	Context ID is not valid
fragConnectionIDNotFound	−2801	Connection ID is not valid
fragSymbolNotFound	−2802	Symbol was not found in connection
fragSectionNotFound	−2803	Section was not found
fragLibNotFound	−2804	Library name not found in fragment registry
fragDupRegLibName	−2805	Registered name already in use
fragFormatUnknown	−2806	Fragment container format unknown
fragHadUnresolveds	−2807	Loaded fragment has unacceptable unresolved symbols
fragNoMem	−2809	Not enough memory for internal bookkeeping
fragNoAddrSpace	−2810	Not enough memory in user's address space for section
fragNoContextIDs	−2811	No more context IDs available
fragObjectInitSeqErr	−2812	Order error during user initialization function
fragImportTooOld	−2813	Import library is too old
fragImportTooNew	−2814	Import library is too new
fragInitLoop	−2815	Circularity in required initialization order
fragInitRtnUsageErr	−2816	Boot library has initialization routine
fragLibConnErr	−2817	Error connecting to library
fragMgrInitErr	−2818	Error during Code Fragment Manager initialization
fragConstErr	−2819	Internal inconsistency discovered
fragCorruptErr	−2820	Fragment container is corrupted
fragUserInitProcErr	−2821	Initialization procedure did not return noErr
fragAppNotFound	−2822	No application found in 'cfrg' resource
fragArchErr	−2823	Fragment targeted for unacceptable architecture
fragInvalidFragmentUsage	−2824	Fragment is used invalidly

Exception Manager

Contents

About the Exception Manager   4-3
  Exception Contexts   4-4
  Types of Exceptions   4-5
Using the Exception Manager   4-6
  Installing an Exception Handler   4-6
  Writing an Exception Handler   4-7
Exception Manager Reference   4-9
  Constants   4-9
    Exception Kinds   4-9
    Memory Reference Kinds   4-11
  Data Structures   4-12
    Machine Information Records   4-12
    Register Information Records   4-12
    Floating-Point Information Records   4-14
    Memory Exception Records   4-15
    Exception Information Records   4-16
  Exception Manager Routines   4-17
  Application-Defined Routines   4-17
Summary of the Exception Manager   4-19
  C Summary   4-19
    Constants   4-19
    Data Types   4-19
    Exception Manager Routines   4-22
    Application-Defined Routines   4-22

This chapter describes the Exception Manager, the part of the Macintosh system software that handles exceptions that occur during the execution of PowerPC applications or other software. The Exception Manager provides a simple way for your application to handle exceptions that occur in its context.

You need the information in this chapter if you need to handle exceptions that occur in native PowerPC code. If your application or other software is written in 680x0 code and therefore executes under the 68LC040 Emulator on PowerPC processor-based Macintosh computers, you do not in general need to read this chapter, because the existing 680x0 mechanism for handling exceptions is fully supported by the emulator.

IMPORTANT

The Exception Manager is available only in the system software for PowerPC processor-based Macintosh computers. In addition, not all features described here are available in the first version. For example, the Exception Manager in the first version does not return exceptions that arise during floating-point calculations. If your application performs floating-point operations and needs to handle any exceptions that arise during those operations, you should use the exception-handling mechanisms provided by the PowerPC Numerics library. See *Inside Macintosh: PowerPC Numerics* for complete information. ▲

To use this chapter, you should already be generally familiar with the Macintosh Operating System. See the books *Inside Macintosh: Processes* and *Inside Macintosh: Memory* for information about the run-time architecture of the 680x0 environment. You also need to be familiar with the run-time architecture of PowerPC processor-based Macintosh computers, as explained in the chapter "Introduction to PowerPC System Software."

This chapter begins with a description of exceptions and their handling in the PowerPC native environment. Then it shows how to use the Exception Manager to install your own exception handler.

About the Exception Manager

An **exception** is an error or other special condition detected by the microprocessor in the course of program execution. When an exception occurs, the Operating System transfers control synchronously to the relevant **exception handler,** which attempts to recover gracefully from the error or special condition. The kinds of errors or other conditions that give rise to exceptions differ from one processor to another. On 680x0 processors, for example, an exception is generated if the currently executing program attempts to divide by zero. By contrast, the PowerPC processor does not generate an exception under that condition.

In general, applications or other types of software (including much of the Macintosh Operating System and the Macintosh Toolbox) cannot tolerate the occurrence of exceptions. To provide some measure of protection from potentially fatal exceptions, the Operating System installs its own set of exception handlers. You can, if necessary, use the

Exception Manager to install application-specific exception handlers. Any exception handlers that you install apply only to your current context and only to exceptions that are not first intercepted and handled by the Operating System.

IMPORTANT

Not all exceptions that occur in your application's context are passed to your exception handler. Certain exceptions (for example, page faults) are handled completely by the Operating System's exception handlers. As a result, those exceptions do not affect the normal execution of your application or other software. ▲

When your exception handler is called, the Exception Manager passes it a parameter that contains information about the state of the machine at the time the exception occurred. On PowerPC processor-based Macintosh computers, this information includes

- the kind of exception that occurred

- the contents of the 32 general-purpose registers

- the contents of the special-purpose registers (such as the Link Register and the Condition Register)

- the contents of the 32 floating-point registers

Your exception handler can handle the exception in various ways. For example, it might modify the machine state and then resume execution. Similarly, your exception handler might simply transfer control to some other code. In rare instances, however, your exception handler might not be able to handle the exception; when this happens, the exception is usually fatal to your application.

Exception Contexts

In the first version of the system software for PowerPC processor-based Macintosh computers, each application can install its own exception handler, which remains the active handler as long as that application is the current application. In other words, the exception handler of the current application is called for all exceptions not intercepted by the Operating System. In general, this mechanism results in the execution of the appropriate exception handler. It's possible, however, for code you install to cause exceptions that are handled by some other application's exception handler. For instance, exceptions that arise during the asynchronous execution of code (such as VBL tasks, Time Manager tasks, and I/O completion routines) are handled by the exception handler of whatever application happens to be the current application at the time the exception occurs. If that application has not installed an exception handler, the exception might not be handled.

All asynchronous code executed in the first version of the system software for PowerPC processor-based Macintosh computers is executed under the 68LC040 Emulator, in which case the exceptions are handled using the existing 680x0 mechanisms. If, however, a routine executed asynchronously calls some code that is native PowerPC code, and if that native code causes an exception to occur, then the current application's exception handler (if any) is called to handle the exception.

Types of Exceptions

In the first version of the system software for PowerPC processor-based Macintosh computers, the following conditions can cause exceptions while your application or other software is executing in native mode:

■ an attempt to write to write-protected memory

■ an attempt to access (that is, read, write, or fetch) data at a logical address that is not assigned

■ an attempt to execute trap instructions or other instructions that are not part of the supported application programming interface

■ an attempt to execute invalid instructions or an invalid form of a valid instruction

■ an attempt to execute privileged instructions when the system is not in privileged mode

■ in appropriate circumstances, reaching a breakpoint

■ in appropriate circumstances, reaching a trace point

The Exception Manager defines a number of **exception codes** that indicate these and other conditions. An exception code is a constant that indicates which kind of exception has occurred.

```
typedef unsigned long         ExceptionKind;    /*kind of exception*/

enum {
    /*exception codes*/
    unknownException                  = 0,    /*unknown exception type*/
    illegalInstructionException       = 1,    /*illegal instruction*/
    trapException                     = 2,    /*unknown trap type*/
    accessException                   = 3,    /*failed memory access*/
    unmappedMemoryException           = 4,    /*memory is unmapped*/
    excludedMemoryException           = 5,    /*memory is excluded*/
    readOnlyMemoryException           = 6,    /*memory is read-only*/
    unresolvablePageFaultException    = 7,    /*unresolvable page fault*/
    privilegeViolationException       = 8,    /*privilege violation*/
    traceException                    = 9,    /*trace*/
    instructionBreakpointException    = 10,   /*instruction breakpoint*/
    dataBreakpointException           = 11,   /*data breakpoint*/
    integerException                  = 12,   /*unused*/
    floatingPointException            = 13,   /*floating point*/
    stackOverflowException            = 14,   /*stack overflow*/
    terminationException              = 15    /*task is being terminated*/
};
```

Not all of these exception codes are used in the first version of the system software for PowerPC processor-based Macintosh computers; see "Exception Kinds" on page 4-9 for a complete explanation of these constants.

Using the Exception Manager

The Exception Manager provides a routine that you can use to install an exception handler and remove an exception handler. This section describes how to use this routine and how to write an exception handler.

Installing an Exception Handler

You can install an exception handler for your application's context by calling the `InstallExceptionHandler` routine. You pass `InstallExceptionHandler` the address of your exception handler:

```
prevHandler = InstallExceptionHandler((ExceptionHandler)myHandler);
```

The `InstallExceptionHandler` function replaces any existing exception handler already installed for the current execution context (that is, for the current application) and returns the address of that previously installed handler. Listing 4-1 shows a routine that installs an exception handler as part of a wrapper around the `NewEmptyHandle` function.

Listing 4-1   Installing an exception handler

```
static jump_buf *curJmpBuf;

Handle __NewEmptyHandle (ushort trapWord)
{
    Handle              returnVal;
    OSErr               myErr;
    jmp_buf             localJump, *oldJump;
    ExceptionHandler    prevHandler;

    oldJump = curJmpBuf;                        /*save current jump address*/
    curJmpBuf = &localJump;                     /*install new jump address*/

    prevHandler = InstallExceptionHandler((ExceptionHandler)MyHandler);
    if (myErr = setjmp(localJump)) {
        LMSetMemErr(theErr);                    /*set memory error*/
        returnVal = 0;                          /*no bytes allocated*/
    }
```

```
else
    myErr = c_NewEmptyHandle(&returnVal, trapWord);

InstallExceptionHandler(prevHandler);  /*restore previous handler*/
curJmpBuf = oldJump;                    /*restore original jump address*/
return (returnVal);
}
```

You can remove the current exception handler from your application's context by passing the value `nil` as the parameter to `InstallExceptionHandler`, as follows:

```
prevHandler = InstallExceptionHandler(nil);
```

Writing an Exception Handler

An exception handler has the following prototype:

```
typedef OSStatus (*ExceptionHandler) (ExceptionInformation *theException);
```

When your handler is called, the Exception Manager passes it the address of an **exception information record,** which contains information about the exception, such as its type and the state of the machine at the time the exception occurred. The exception information record is defined by the `ExceptionInformation` data type.

```
struct ExceptionInformation {
    ExceptionKind                    theKind;
    MachineInformation               *machineState;
    RegisterInformation              *registerImage;
    FPUInformation                   *FPUImage;
    union {
        MemoryExceptionInformation   *memoryInfo;
    } info;
};
typedef struct ExceptionInformation ExceptionInformation;
```

The `theKind` field contains an exception code. The fields `machineState` and `registerImage` contain information about the special-purpose and general-purpose registers, respectively. The values in the special-purpose registers are contained in a **machine information record,** defined by the `MachineInformation` data type.

```
struct MachineInformation {
    UnsignedWide      CTR;    /*Count Register*/
    UnsignedWide      LR;     /*Link Register*/
    UnsignedWide      PC;     /*Program Counter Register*/
    unsigned long     CR;     /*Condition Register*/
    unsigned long     XER;    /*Fixed-Point Exception Register*/
```

```
    unsigned long        MSR;  /*Machine State Register*/
};
typedef struct MachineInformation MachineInformation;
```

As you can see, this record contains primarily the values in the special-purpose registers. The values in the general-purpose registers are encoded using a structure of type `RegisterInformation`, which is effectively an array of 32 register values.

Note

For a more detailed description of the exception information record and its associated data types, see "Data Structures" beginning on page 4-12. ◆

Your exception handler can perform any actions necessary or useful for handling the exception. You might attempt to recover from the error or simply terminate your application gracefully. The specific actions you perform depend, of course, on the type of exception that has occurred. In general, however, you will probably want to use one or the other of two basic techniques for recovering from the exception.

■ Your exception handler might simply transfer control away from the point of execution. For example, you might jump back into your main event loop or into some error recovery code.

■ Alternatively, your exception handler might attempt to repair the cause of the exception by suitably modifying the state of the machine (as reported to your exception handler in an exception information record). You can alter any piece of that machine state, including the PC register. After you have suitably modified the relevant data, your handler should return, passing back a result code. The Exception Manager inspects the result code you return and determines what further actions to take. If you pass back `noErr`, then the Exception Manager restores the machine state to the state contained in the exception information record and resumes execution. If you pass back any other result code, the Operating System proceeds as if the exception had occurred but no exception handler was present.

Listing 4-2 shows a simple exception handler `MyHandler`.

Listing 4-2   A native exception handler

```
OSStatus MyHandler (ExceptionInformation *theException)
{
    if ((theException->theKind >= accessException)
            && (theException ->theKind <= unresolvablePageFaultException))
        longjmp(*curJmpBuf, memWZErr);
    else
        return (-1);
}
```

As you can see, the `MyHandler` exception handler looks for memory-related exceptions and, if it finds any, transfers control by calling the `longjmp` function.

▲ **WARNING**
Returning a value other than `noErr` from your exception handler is
likely to cause the current application to be terminated. ▲

▲ **WARNING**
Your exception handler must be reentrant if it might itself cause any
exceptions to be generated. For example, if your exception handler
calls the `Debugger` or `DebugStr` routine, the trap exception (of type
`trapException`) is generated. Normally, a debugger intercepts and
handles those kinds of exceptions. If, however, no debugger is installed
in the system, your exception handler might be called repeatedly.
Eventually, the stack will grow to the lowest memory address,
overwriting essential data and causing a system crash. ▲

Exception Manager Reference

This section describes the constants, data structures, and routine provided by the
Exception Manager. See "Using the Exception Manager" beginning on page 4-6
for detailed instructions on using that routine.

Constants

This section describes the constants provided by the Exception Manager.

Exception Kinds

The Exception Manager indicates to your exception handler the kind of exception
that has occurred by passing it an exception code. The exception kind is indicated by
a constant.

Note
Some kinds of exceptions occur only on specific types of
processors or only in specific system software versions. ◆

```
enum {
   /*exception codes*/
   unknownException                  = 0,      /*unknown exception type*/
   illegalInstructionException       = 1,      /*illegal instruction*/
   trapException                     = 2,      /*unknown trap type*/
   accessException                   = 3,      /*failed memory access*/
   unmappedMemoryException           = 4,      /*memory is unmapped*/
   excludedMemoryException           = 5,      /*memory is excluded*/
   readOnlyMemoryException           = 6,      /*memory is read-only*/
   unresolvablePageFaultException    = 7,      /*unresolvable page fault*/
```

4

Exception Manager

```
privilegeViolationException          = 8,     /*privilege violation*/
traceException                       = 9,     /*trace*/
instructionBreakpointException       = 10,    /*instruction breakpoint*/
dataBreakpointException              = 11,    /*data breakpoint*/
integerException                     = 12,    /*unused*/
floatingPointException               = 13,    /*floating point*/
stackOverflowException               = 14,    /*stack overflow*/
terminationException                 = 15     /*task is being terminated*/
};
```

Constant descriptions

unknownException

> Unknown kind of exception. This exception code is defined for completeness only; it is never actually passed to an exception handler.

illegalInstructionException

> Illegal instruction exception. The processor attempted to decode an instruction that is either illegal or unimplemented.

trapException Unknown trap type exception. The processor decoded a trap type instruction that is not used by the system software.

accessException

> Memory access exception. A memory reference resulted in a page fault because the physical address is not accessible.

unmappedMemoryException

> Unmapped memory exception. A memory reference was made to an address that is unmapped.

excludedMemoryException

> Excluded memory exception. A memory reference was made to an excluded address.

readOnlyMemoryException

> Read-only memory exception. A memory reference was made to an address that cannot be written to.

unresolvablePageFaultException

> Unresolvable page fault exception. A memory reference resulted in a page fault that could not be resolved. The theError field of the memory exception record contains a status value indicating the reason for this unresolved page fault.

privilegeViolationException

> Privilege violation exception. The processor decoded a privileged instruction but was not executing in the privileged mode.

traceException

> Trace exception. This exception is used by debuggers to support single-step operations.

instructionBreakpointException

> Instruction breakpoint exception. This exception is used by debuggers to support breakpoint operations.

dataBreakpointException

Data breakpoint exception. This exception is used by debuggers to support breakpoint operations.

integerException

Integer exception. This exception is not used by PowerPC processors.

floatingPointException

Floating-point arithmetic exception. The floating-point processor has exceptions enabled and an exception has occurred. (This exception is not used in the first version of the system software for PowerPC processor-based Macintosh computers.)

stackOverflowException

Stack overflow exception. The stack limits have been exceeded and the stack cannot be expanded. (This exception is not used in the first version of the system software for PowerPC processor-based Macintosh computers.)

terminationException

Termination exception. The task is being terminated. (This exception is not used in the first version of the system software for PowerPC processor-based Macintosh computers.)

Memory Reference Kinds

For each memory-related exception, the Exception Manager returns a memory exception record. The theReference field of that record contains a memory reference code that indicates the kind of memory operation that caused the exception.

```
enum {
   /*memory reference codes*/
   writeReference              = 0,      /*write operation*/
   readReference               = 1,      /*read operation*/
   fetchReference              = 2       /*fetch operation*/
};
```

Constant descriptions

writeReference

The operation was an attempt to write data to memory.

readReference   The operation was an attempt to read data from memory.

fetchReference   The operation was an attempt to fetch a processor instruction. (Not all processors are able to distinguish read operations from fetch operations. As a result, fetch operation failures might instead be reported as failed read operations.)

Data Structures

This section describes the data structures provided by the Exception Manager.

Machine Information Records

The Exception Manager uses a machine information record to encode the state of the special-purpose registers at the time an exception occurs. A machine information record is defined by the `MachineInformation` data type.

```
struct MachineInformation {
    UnsignedWide        CTR;  /*Count Register*/
    UnsignedWide        LR;   /*Link Register*/
    UnsignedWide        PC;   /*Program Counter Register*/
    unsigned long       CR;   /*Condition Register*/
    unsigned long       XER;  /*Fixed-Point Exception Register*/
    unsigned long       MSR;  /*Machine State Register*/
};
typedef struct MachineInformation MachineInformation;
```

Note
The fields `CTR`, `LR`, and `PC` are declared as the 64-bit type `UnsignedWide` to allow compatibility with 64-bit processors. On 32-bit processors, the register values are returned in the low-order 32 bits. The high-order 32 bits are undefined. ◆

Field descriptions

CTR   The contents of the Count Register (CTR).

LR   The contents of the Link Register (LR).

PC   The contents of the Program Counter Register (PC).

CR   The contents of the Condition Register (CR).

XER   The contents of the Fixed-Point Exception Register (XER).

MSR   The contents of the Machine State Register (MSR).

IMPORTANT
The fields of a machine information record are aligned in memory in accordance with 680x0 alignment conventions. ▲

Register Information Records

The Exception Manager uses a register information record to encode the state of the general-purpose registers at the time an exception occurs. A register information record is defined by the `RegisterInformation` data type.

```
struct RegisterInformation {
    UnsignedWide        R0;
    UnsignedWide        R1;
    UnsignedWide        R2;
    UnsignedWide        R3;
    UnsignedWide        R4;
    UnsignedWide        R5;
    UnsignedWide        R6;
    UnsignedWide        R7;
    UnsignedWide        R8;
    UnsignedWide        R9;
    UnsignedWide        R10;
    UnsignedWide        R11;
    UnsignedWide        R12;
    UnsignedWide        R13;
    UnsignedWide        R14;
    UnsignedWide        R15;
    UnsignedWide        R16;
    UnsignedWide        R17;
    UnsignedWide        R18;
    UnsignedWide        R19;
    UnsignedWide        R20;
    UnsignedWide        R21;
    UnsignedWide        R22;
    UnsignedWide        R23;
    UnsignedWide        R24;
    UnsignedWide        R25;
    UnsignedWide        R26;
    UnsignedWide        R27;
    UnsignedWide        R28;
    UnsignedWide        R29;
    UnsignedWide        R30;
    UnsignedWide        R31;
};
typedef struct RegisterInformation RegisterInformation;
```

Field descriptions

R0   The contents of general-purpose register GPR0.

R1   The contents of general-purpose register GPR1.

R2   The contents of general-purpose register GPR2.

R3   The contents of general-purpose register GPR3.

R4   The contents of general-purpose register GPR4.

R5   The contents of general-purpose register GPR5.

R6	The contents of general-purpose register GPR6.
R7	The contents of general-purpose register GPR7.
R8	The contents of general-purpose register GPR8.
R9	The contents of general-purpose register GPR9.
R10	The contents of general-purpose register GPR10.
R11	The contents of general-purpose register GPR11.
R12	The contents of general-purpose register GPR12.
R13	The contents of general-purpose register GPR13.
R14	The contents of general-purpose register GPR14.
R15	The contents of general-purpose register GPR15.
R16	The contents of general-purpose register GPR16.
R17	The contents of general-purpose register GPR17.
R18	The contents of general-purpose register GPR18.
R19	The contents of general-purpose register GPR19.
R20	The contents of general-purpose register GPR20.
R21	The contents of general-purpose register GPR21.
R22	The contents of general-purpose register GPR22.
R23	The contents of general-purpose register GPR23.
R24	The contents of general-purpose register GPR24.
R25	The contents of general-purpose register GPR25.
R26	The contents of general-purpose register GPR26.
R27	The contents of general-purpose register GPR27.
R28	The contents of general-purpose register GPR28.
R29	The contents of general-purpose register GPR29.
R30	The contents of general-purpose register GPR30.
R31	The contents of general-purpose register GPR31.

IMPORTANT
The fields of a register information record are aligned in memory
in accordance with 680x0 alignment conventions. ▲

Floating-Point Information Records

The Exception Manager uses a floating-point information record to encode the state of
the floating-point unit at the time an exception occurs. A floating-point information
record is defined by the FPUInformation data type.

```
struct FPUInformation {
   UnsignedWide        Registers[32]; /*FPU registers*/
   unsigned long       FPSCR;         /*status/control reg*/
};
typedef struct FPUInformation FPUInformation;
```

Field descriptions

Registers   The contents of the 32 floating-point registers. This array is zero-based; for example, the contents of FPR0 are accessed as `Registers[0]`.

FPSCR   The contents of the Floating-Point Status and Control Register (FPSCR).

IMPORTANT

The fields of a floating-point information record are aligned in memory in accordance with 680x0 alignment conventions. ▲

Memory Exception Records

The Exception Manager uses a memory exception record to present additional information about an exception that occurs as the result of a failed memory reference. A memory exception record is defined by the `MemoryExceptionInformation` data type.

```
struct MemoryExceptionInformation {
    AreaID                      theArea;
    LogicalAddress              theAddress;
    OSStatus                    theError;
    MemoryReferenceKind         theReference;
};
typedef struct MemoryExceptionInformation MemoryExceptionInformation;
```

Field descriptions

theArea   The area containing the logical address of the exception. When the memory reference that caused the exception is to an unmapped range of the logical address space, this field contains the value `kNoAreaID`.

theAddress   The logical address of the exception.

theError   A status value. When the exception kind is `unresolvablePageFaultException`, this field contains a value that indicates the reason the page fault could not be resolved.

theReference   The type of memory reference that caused the exception. This field contains one of these constants:

```
enum {
    writeReference = 0,  /*write operation*/
    readReference  = 1,  /*read operation*/
    fetchReference = 2   /*fetch operation*/
};
```

See "Memory Reference Kinds" on page 4-11 for a description of these constants.

IMPORTANT

The fields of a memory exception record are aligned in memory in accordance with 680x0 alignment conventions. ▲

Exception Information Records

The Exception Manager passes an exception information record to your exception handler whenever your handler is called as the result of some exception. The exception information record indicates the nature of the exception and provides other information that might be useful to your handler. An exception information record is defined by the `ExceptionInformation` data type.

```
struct ExceptionInformation {
    ExceptionKind                    theKind;
    MachineInformation               *machineState;
    RegisterInformation              *registerImage;
    FPUInformation                   *FPUImage;
    union {
        MemoryExceptionInformation   *memoryInfo;
    } info;
};
typedef struct ExceptionInformation ExceptionInformation;
```

Field descriptions

theKind
: An exception code indicating the kind of exception that occurred. See "Exception Kinds" on page 4-9 for a list of the available exception codes.

machineState
: The state of the machine at the time the exception occurred. See "Machine Information Records" on page 4-12 for details on the `MachineInformation` data type.

registerImage
: The contents of the general-purpose registers at the time the exception occurred. See "Register Information Records" on page 4-12 for details on the `RegisterInformation` data type.

FPUImage
: The state of the floating-point processor at the time the exception occurred. See "Floating-Point Information Records" on page 4-14 for details on the `FPUInformation` data type.

memoryInfo
: The logical address of the location in memory that triggered the exception.

IMPORTANT

The fields of an exception information record are aligned in memory in accordance with 680x0 alignment conventions. ▲

Exception Manager Routines

You can use the Exception Manager's `InstallExceptionHandler` routine to install an exception handler or to remove an existing exception handler.

InstallExceptionHandler

You can use the `InstallExceptionHandler` function to install an exception handler.

```
extern ExceptionHandler InstallExceptionHandler
                                (ExceptionHandler theHandler);
```

theHandler
> The address of the exception handler to be installed.

DESCRIPTION

The `InstallExceptionHandler` function installs the exception handler specified by the `theHandler` parameter. That handler replaces any existing exception handler associated with the current execution context. The newly installed handler remains active until you install some other handler or until you remove the current handler by calling `InstallExceptionHandler` with `theHandler` set to `nil`.

IMPORTANT

The `theHandler` parameter must be the address of a transition vector for the exception handler, not a universal procedure pointer. ▲

The `InstallExceptionHandler` function returns the address of any existing exception handler as its function result. If there is no exception handler in place for the current execution context, `InstallExceptionHandler` returns `nil`.

SPECIAL CONSIDERATIONS

The `InstallExceptionHandler` function is available to any code executing in the PowerPC native environment. You do not need to call it if your application or other software exists as 680x0 code and hence executes under the 68LC040 Emulator on PowerPC processor-based Macintosh computers.

Application-Defined Routines

This section describes exception handlers, routines that you install using the `InstallExceptionHandler` routine to handle specific types of exceptions.

MyExceptionHandler

An exception handler should have this prototype:

```
OSStatus MyExceptionHandler (ExceptionInformation *theException);
```

theException
> The address of an exception information block describing the exception that triggered the exception handler.

DESCRIPTION

You pass the address of your `MyExceptionHandler` routine to the Exception Manager's `InstallExceptionHandler` function. The Exception Manager subsequently calls your exception handler for all exceptions that arise in your application's context that are not intercepted by the Operating System.

Your exception handler can take whatever steps are necessary to handle the exception or to correct the error or special condition that caused the exception. If your handler is successful, it should return the `noErr` result code. If you pass back `noErr`, the Exception Manager restores the machine state to the state contained in the exception information record pointed to by the `theException` parameter and resumes execution.

If your handler is not able to handle the exception, it should return some other result code. However, if your handler returns a nonzero result code, the current application is likely to be terminated by the Process Manager.

An exception handler uses the same stack that is active at the time an exception occurs. To ensure that no stack data is destroyed, the Exception Manager advances the stack pointer prior to calling the exception handler.

SPECIAL CONSIDERATIONS

An exception handler must follow the same general guidelines as other kinds of asynchronous software. For instance, it cannot cause memory to be purged or compacted, and it should not use any handles that are not locked. See *Inside Macintosh: Processes* for a description of the restrictions applying to interrupt tasks and other asynchronous software.

An exception handler must be reentrant if it can itself generate exceptions.

SEE ALSO

See "Writing an Exception Handler" on page 4-7 for more information about writing an exception handler.

Summary of the Exception Manager

C Summary

Constants

```
enum {
    /*exception codes*/
    unknownException                    = 0,      /*unknown exception type*/
    illegalInstructionException         = 1,      /*illegal instruction*/
    trapException                       = 2,      /*unknown trap type*/
    accessException                     = 3,      /*failed memory access*/
    unmappedMemoryException             = 4,      /*memory is unmapped*/
    excludedMemoryException             = 5,      /*memory is excluded*/
    readOnlyMemoryException             = 6,      /*memory is read-only*/
    unresolvablePageFaultException      = 7,      /*unresolvable page fault*/
    privilegeViolationException         = 8,      /*privilege violation*/
    traceException                      = 9,      /*trace*/
    instructionBreakpointException      = 10,     /*instruction breakpoint*/
    dataBreakpointException             = 11,     /*data breakpoint*/
    integerException                    = 12,     /*unused*/
    floatingPointException              = 13,     /*floating point*/
    stackOverflowException              = 14,     /*stack overflow*/
    terminationException                = 15      /*task is being terminated*/
};

enum {
    /*memory reference codes*/
    writeReference                      = 0,      /*write operation*/
    readReference                       = 1,      /*read operation*/
    fetchReference                      = 2       /*fetch operation*/
};
```

Data Types

```
typedef unsigned long        ExceptionKind;      /*kind of exception*/

typedef unsigned long        MemoryReferenceKind;
```

```
typedef void                   *Ref;

typedef Ref                    AreaID;

typedef Ref                    LogicalAddress;

struct UnsignedWide {
    unsigned long              hi;
    unsigned long              lo;
};
typedef struct UnsignedWide UnsignedWide;

struct RegisterInformation {
    UnsignedWide       R0;
    UnsignedWide       R1;
    UnsignedWide       R2;
    UnsignedWide       R3;
    UnsignedWide       R4;
    UnsignedWide       R5;
    UnsignedWide       R6;
    UnsignedWide       R7;
    UnsignedWide       R8;
    UnsignedWide       R9;
    UnsignedWide       R10;
    UnsignedWide       R11;
    UnsignedWide       R12;
    UnsignedWide       R13;
    UnsignedWide       R14;
    UnsignedWide       R15;
    UnsignedWide       R16;
    UnsignedWide       R17;
    UnsignedWide       R18;
    UnsignedWide       R19;
    UnsignedWide       R20;
    UnsignedWide       R21;
    UnsignedWide       R22;
    UnsignedWide       R23;
    UnsignedWide       R24;
    UnsignedWide       R25;
    UnsignedWide       R26;
    UnsignedWide       R27;
    UnsignedWide       R28;
    UnsignedWide       R29;
    UnsignedWide       R30;
```

```
   UnsignedWide              R31;
};
typedef struct RegisterInformation RegisterInformation;

typedef long                   OSStatus;

typedef OSStatus (*ExceptionHandler) (ExceptionInformation *theException);

struct MachineInformation {
   UnsignedWide                    CTR;   /*Count Register*/
   UnsignedWide                    LR;    /*Link Register*/
   UnsignedWide                    PC;    /*Program Counter Register*/
   unsigned long                   CR;    /*Condition Register*/
   unsigned long                   XER;   /*Fixed-Point Exception Register*/
   unsigned long                   MSR;   /*Machine State Register*/
};
typedef struct MachineInformation MachineInformation;

struct FPUInformation {
   UnsignedWide                    Registers[32]; /*FPU registers*/
   unsigned long                   FPSCR;        /*status/control reg*/
};
typedef struct FPUInformation FPUInformation;

struct MemoryExceptionInformation {
   AreaID                          theArea;
   LogicalAddress                  theAddress;
   OSStatus                        theError;
   MemoryReferenceKind             theReference;
};
typedef struct MemoryExceptionInformation MemoryExceptionInformation;

struct ExceptionInformation {
   ExceptionKind                   theKind;
   MachineInformation              *machineState;
   RegisterInformation             *registerImage;
   FPUInformation                  *FPUImage;
   union {
      MemoryExceptionInformation   *memoryInfo;
   } info;
};
typedef struct ExceptionInformation ExceptionInformation;
```

Exception Manager Routines

Installing Exception Handlers

```
extern ExceptionHandler InstallExceptionHandler
                        (ExceptionHandler theHandler);
```

Application-Defined Routines

Exception Handlers

```
OSStatus MyExceptionHandler
                        (ExceptionInformation *theException);
```

Glossary

32-bit clean   Said of an application (or other software) that is able to run in an environment where all 32 bits of a memory address are used for addressing.

680x0   See **680x0 microprocessor.**

680x0 application   An application that contains code only for a 680x0 microprocessor. See also **fat application** and **PowerPC application.**

680x0-based Macintosh computer   Any computer containing a 680x0 central processing unit that runs Macintosh system software. See also **PowerPC processor-based Macintosh computer.**

680x0 compiler   Any compiler that produces code that can execute on a 680x0. See also **PowerPC compiler.**

680x0 context block   A block of data used by the 68LC040 Emulator to maintain information across mode switches. The structure of this block of data is private.

680x0 microprocessor   Any member of the Motorola 68000 family of microprocessors.

680x0 software   Any software (that is, application, extension, driver, or other executable code) that consists of code only for a 680x0 microprocessor. See also **680x0 application.**

68LC040 Emulator   The part of the system software that allows 680x0 applications and other 680x0 software to execute on PowerPC processor-based Macintosh computers. See also **Mixed Mode Manager.**

A5 world   An area of memory in a 680x0 application's partition that contains the QuickDraw global variables, the application global variables, the application parameters, and the jump table—all of which are accessed through the A5 register. See also **mini-A5 world.**

accelerated resource   An executable resource consisting of a routine descriptor and PowerPC code that specifically models the behavior of a 680x0 stand-alone code resource. Compare **private resource.**

accelerated system software routine   Any Toolbox or Operating System routine that has been rewritten as PowerPC code.

A-line instruction   An instruction that is not recognized by a 680x0 microprocessor and that the Trap Manager uses to execute Toolbox and Operating System routines. The first word of an A-line instruction is binary 1010 (hexadecimal A).

ANSI C language dialect   The C programming language dialect that adheres to the language defined by the document *American National Standard for Information Systems—Programming Language—C*, ANSI X3.159-1989.

application   A file of type 'APPL' that can be launched by the Process Manager. See also **680x0 application** and **PowerPC application.**

application extension   A fragment containing code and data (such as a data-conversion filter, tool, and so forth) that extends the capabilities of an application.

application global variables   A set of variables stored in the application partition that are global to the application.

application heap   An area of memory in the application heap zone in which memory is dynamically allocated and released on demand.

application parameters   Thirty-two bytes of memory in the A5 world of a 680x0 application that are reserved for system use. The first long word is the address of the first QuickDraw global variable.

application partition A partition of memory reserved for use by an application. The application partition consists of free space, along with the application's heap and stack. The application partition for a 680x0 application also contains an A5 world.

A-trap See **A-line instruction.**

backing-store file The file in which the Virtual Memory Manager stores the contents of unneeded pages of memory. See also **file mapping** and **paging file.**

backing volume See **paging device.**

bind To find the referent of an import and place its address in a fragment's table of contents.

bus sizing See **dynamic bus sizing.**

byte smearing The ability of certain members of the 680x0 family of microprocessors to duplicate byte- and word-sized data across all 32 bits of the data bus.

cache See **data cache** or **instruction cache.**

callback routine A routine that is executed as part of the operation of some other routine.

callee A routine that is called by some routine.

caller A routine that calls some routine.

calling conventions A set of conventions that describe the manner in which a particular routine is executed. A routine's calling conventions specify where parameters and function results are passed. For a stack-based routine, the calling conventions determine the structure of the routine's stack frame.

code fragment See **fragment.**

code fragment information record A part of a code fragment resource that provides information about a specific code fragment. There can be more than one code fragment information record in a code fragment resource.

Code Fragment Loader The part of the Macintosh system software that reads containers and loads the fragments they contain into memory. Currently, the application programming interface to the Code Fragment Loader is private. See also **Code Fragment Manager.**

Code Fragment Manager The part of the Macintosh system software that loads fragments into memory and prepares them for execution. See also **Code Fragment Loader** and **fragment.**

code fragment resource A resource of type `'cfrg'` that identifies the instruction set architecture, location, size, and name of an application or import library, as well as version information for import libraries. See also **code fragment information record.**

code patch See **patch.**

code resource See **executable resource.**

code section A section of a fragment that contains executable code. See also **data section.**

code type See **instruction set architecture.**

compile-time library See **definition version.**

Condition Register (CR) A register in the PowerPC processor that holds the result of certain integer and floating-point operations.

connection A link between two fragments.

connection ID A reference number that uniquely identifies a connection. Defined by the `ConnectionID` data type.

container The storage for a fragment. A container is a contiguous chunk of storage that holds a fragment and information describing the location of the parts of the fragment and the format of the container.

context The block of static data (global variables, static variables, and function pointers) associated with one loading of an import library. Each application is loaded into its own context.

context block See **680x0 context block.**

CR See **Condition Register.**

cross-mode call A call to code that is in a different instruction set architecture from the caller's. See also **explicit cross-mode call** and **implicit cross-mode call.**

cross-TOC call A call to code that is in a different fragment from the caller's. A cross-TOC call requires that the Table of Contents Register be changed to the callee's TOC value.

dangling pointer   A pointer that no longer points to the correct memory address.

data cache   An area of memory internal to some microprocessors (for example, the MC68030 and MC68040 microprocessors) that holds recently accessed data. See also **instruction cache.**

data section   A section of a fragment that contains its static data, including the fragment's table of contents. See also **code section.**

de facto C++ standard   The current C++ language definition described in the working paper *American National Standard for Information Systems—Programming Language—C++*, ANSI X3J16.

definition function   A function that defines the appearance and behavior of some user interface element (for example, a control, list, or window). See also **stub definition function.**

definition resource   A resource that contains a definition function. See also **stub definition resource.**

definition version   The version of an import library used by the linker to resolve imports in the application (or other fragment) being linked. The definition version defines the external programming interface and data format of the library. Compare **implementation version.**

disk location record   A data structure that provides information about the location of a fragment in the data fork of a file on disk. Defined by the `DiskFragment` data type.

drop-in   See **application extension.**

dynamically linked library   See **import library.**

dynamic bus sizing   The ability of certain members of the 680x0 family of microprocessors to allow I/O devices with 8-bit and 16-bit data paths to work with the processor's 32-bit data bus.

emulated application   An application whose executable code is not in the instruction set architecture of the CPU. An emulated application relies on an emulator to translate its code into that instruction set. See also **680x0 application.**

emulation   The process by which a microprocessor is able to execute code in an instruction set different from its native instruction set. See also **68LC040 Emulator.**

emulation environment   The 680x0-compatible environment on PowerPC processor-based Macintosh computers provided by the 68LC040 Emulator and the Mixed Mode Manager.

emulator   See **68LC040 Emulator.**

epilog   A standard piece of code at the end of a routine that restores any nonvolatile registers saved by the routine's prolog, tears down the routine's stack frame, and returns to the caller. See also **prolog.**

exception   An error or other special condition detected by the microprocessor in the course of program execution.

exception code   A constant that indicates which kind of exception has occurred.

exception handler   Any routine that handles exceptions.

exception information record   A data structure that contains information about an exception, such as the exception kind, the machine state at the time of the exception, and so forth. Defined by the `ExceptionInformation` data type.

Exception Manager   The part of the Macintosh system software that handles exceptions that occur during the execution of PowerPC applications or other software.

exception stack frame   A block of data placed on the stack automatically by the processor when an exception occurs.

executable resource   Any resource that contains executable code. See also **accelerated resource** and **private resource.**

explicit cross-mode call   A call to code that is in a different instruction set architecture from the caller's, caused by the caller explicitly calling the `CallUniversalProc` function.

export   To make a symbol externally visible. Also, a synonym for **exported symbol.**

exported symbol   A symbol in a fragment that is visible to some other fragments. See also **import library** and **imported symbol.**

Extended Common Object File Format (XCOFF)   A format of executable file generated by some PowerPC compilers. See also **Preferred Executable Format.**

extension   See **application extension** and **system extension.**

external code   Any block of executable code that is not directly contained in an application or other software.

fake definition resource   See **stub definition resource.**

fake handle   A handle that was not created by the Memory Manager but is passed to some Memory Manager routine.

fake pointer   A pointer that was not created by the Memory Manager but is passed to some Memory Manager routine.

fat   Containing or describing code of multiple instruction sets.

fat application   An application that contains code of two or more instruction sets. See also **680x0 application** and **PowerPC application.**

fat binary   Any piece of executable code (application, code resource, trap, or trap patch) that contains code of multiple instruction sets. See also **fat application, fat patch, fat resource,** and **fat trap.**

fat patch   A trap patch that contains executable code in two or more instruction sets.

fat resource   A code-bearing resource that contains executable code in two or more instruction sets. A fat resource begins with a fat routine descriptor.

fat routine descriptor   A routine descriptor that contains routine records for a routine's code in two or more instruction sets.

fat trap   A system software routine that is implemented in two or more instruction sets. In general, the Operating System selects the trap implementation that avoids mode switches. See also **split trap.**

file and directory registry   A list of files and directories that the Code Fragment Manager should search when looking for import libraries. See also **ROM registry.**

file mapping   The process of using a file's data fork as the virtual memory paging file.

Floating-Point Status and Control Register (FPSCR)   A 32-bit PowerPC register used to store the floating-point environment.

FP   See **frame pointer.**

FPSCR   See **Floating-Point Status and Control Register.**

fragment   Any block of executable PowerPC code and its associated data.

fragment initialization block   A parameter block passed to a fragment's initialization routine that contains information about the fragment. Defined by the `InitBlock` data type.

fragment location record   A data structure that provides information about the location of a fragment. Defined by the `FragmentLocator` data type.

frame   See **stack frame** or **switch frame.**

frame pointer (FP)   A pointer to the beginning of a stack frame. See also **stack pointer.**

function prototype   A declaration of the types of parameters expected by a function and of the type of the result it returns. ANSI C requires function prototypes for all functions you define.

global instantiation   The method of allocating an import library's static data in which only one copy of that data is created regardless of how many connections to the library are made. See also **per-context instantiation** and **per-load instantiation.**

global variables   See **application global variables, QuickDraw global variables,** and **system global variables.**

glue routine   A run-time library routine, usually provided by the development environment, that provides the subroutine linkage between high-level language code and a system routine with an interface protocol different from that of the high-level language.

hard import   An imported symbol that must be defined at run time and whose corresponding code or data must therefore be available in an import library on the host machine. Compare **import** and **soft import**.

head patch   A patch that, upon completion, jumps to the next patch in the patch daisy chain. Compare **tail patch**.

heap   An area of memory in which space is dynamically allocated and released on demand, using the Memory Manager. See also **application heap**.

hybrid environment   See **mixed environment**.

implementation version   The version of an import library that is connected at load time to the application (or other fragment) being loaded. The implementation version provides the actual executable code and data exported by the library. Compare **definition version**.

implicit cross-mode call   A call to code that is in a different instruction set architecture from the caller's, caused by the caller executing a routine descriptor.

import   To refer to a symbol located in some other fragment. Also, a synonym for **imported symbol**.

imported symbol   A symbol in a fragment that references code or data exported by some other fragment. See also **exported symbol** and **import library**.

import library   A shared library that is automatically loaded at run time by the Code Fragment Manager.

initialization block   See **fragment initialization block**.

initialization routine   A function contained in a fragment that is executed immediately after the fragment has been loaded and prepared. See also **termination routine**.

input/output (I/O)   The parts of a computer system that transfer data to or from peripheral devices.

instantiation   See **global instantiation**, **per-context instantiation**, and **per-load instantiation**.

instruction cache   An area of memory internal to some microprocessors (for example, the MC68020, MC68030, and MC68040 microprocessors) that holds recently used instructions. See also **data cache**.

instruction set architecture   The set of instructions meaningful to a particular microprocessor or to a family of microprocessors.

interface files   See **universal interface files**.

interrupt   See **exception**.

I/O   See **input/output**.

jump table   An area of memory in a 680x0 application's A5 world that contains one entry for every externally referenced routine in every code segment of the application. The jump table is the means by which the loading and unloading of segments are implemented.

KB   Abbreviation for kilobyte. A kilobyte is 1024 bytes.

leaf procedure   A routine that calls no other routines.

library   See **import library**.

library directory   A directory used by an application or other fragment to store import libraries used by that application or fragment. An application's library directory is specified in the application's code fragment resource.

linkage area   The area in a PowerPC stack frame that holds the caller's RTOC value and saved values of the Count Register and Link Register. See also **parameter area**.

Link Register (LR)   A register in the PowerPC processor that holds the return address of the currently executing routine.

load directory   The directory that contains a fragment being loaded into memory and prepared for execution.

local variable   A variable allocated and used only within the current procedure.

location record   See **fragment location record**.

lock (1) To prevent a relocatable block from being moved during heap compaction. (2) To temporarily prevent a range of physical memory from being paged out or moved by the Virtual Memory Manager.

low-memory global variables See **system global variables.**

LR See **Link Register.**

machine information record A data structure that contains information about the state of the machine at the time an exception occurs. Defined by the `MachineInformation` data type.

Macintosh Operating System The part of Macintosh system software that manages basic low-level operations such as file reading and writing, memory allocation and deallocation, process execution, and interrupt handling.

Macintosh Programmer's Workshop (MPW) A software development system for the Macintosh family of computers provided by Apple Computer.

Macintosh system software A collection of routines that you can use to simplify your development of Macintosh applications. See also **Macintosh Toolbox** and **Macintosh Operating System.**

Macintosh Toolbox The part of the Macintosh system software that allows you to implement the standard Macintosh user interface in your application or other software.

Macintosh User Interface Toolbox See **Macintosh Toolbox.**

main routine A function contained in a fragment whose use depends on the kind of fragment it is in. For applications, the main routine is the usual entry point. See also **main symbol.**

main symbol A symbol whose use depends on the kind of fragment it is in. For applications, the main symbol refers to the fragment's main routine. See also **main routine.**

MB Abbreviation for megabyte. A megabyte is 1024 kilobytes, or 1,048,576 bytes.

memory location record A data structure that provides information about the location of a fragment in memory. Defined by the `MemFragment` data type.

memory management unit (MMU) Any component that performs address mapping in a Macintosh computer. In Macintosh II computers, it is either the Address Management Unit (AMU) or the Paged Memory Management Unit (PMMU). The MMU function is built into the MC68030 and MC68040 microprocessors.

Memory Manager The part of the Operating System that dynamically allocates and releases memory space in the heap.

mini-A5 world An area of memory created and maintained by the Process Manager for a native PowerPC application. A native application's mini-A5 world contains a pointer to the application's QuickDraw global variables. See also **A5 world.**

mixed environment A process execution environment that supports applications and other software written in more than one instruction set.

Mixed Mode Manager The part of the Macintosh system software that manages the mixed-mode architecture of PowerPC processor-based computers running 680x0-based code (including system software, applications, and stand-alone code modules).

MMU See **memory management unit.**

mode switch The process of switching the execution context between the CPU's native context and an emulator (for example, the 68LC040 Emulator). See also **switch frame.**

MPW See **Macintosh Programmer's Workshop.**

nanokernel The lowest-level part of the system software for PowerPC processor-based Macintosh computers.

native application An application whose executable code is in the instruction set architecture of the CPU. See also **PowerPC application.**

nonvolatile register   A register whose contents must be preserved across subroutine calls. If a routine changes the value of a nonvolatile register, it must save the old value on the stack before changing the register and restore that value before returning. See also **saved registers area** and **volatile register.**

opcode   See **operation code.**

Operating System   See **Macintosh Operating System.**

operation code   The part of a machine instruction that encodes the operation to be performed. Often shortened to **opcode.**

page   The basic unit of memory used in virtual memory.

paged memory management unit (PMMU)   The Motorola MC68851 chip, used in the Macintosh II computer to perform logical-to-physical address translation and paged memory management.

page fault   A special kind of bus error caused by an attempt to access data in a page of memory that is not currently resident in RAM.

paging   The process of moving data between physical memory and a paging file.

paging device   A volume that contains the backing-store file or a paging file.

paging file   A file used to store unneeded pages of memory. See also **backing-store file.**

parameter area   The area in a PowerPC stack frame that holds the parameters for any routines called by a given routine. See also **linkage area.**

partition   A contiguous block of memory reserved for use by the Operating System or by an application. See also **application partition** and **system partition.**

patch   Any code used to repair or augment an existing piece of code. In the context of Macintosh system software, a patch repairs or augments a trap. See also **head patch** and **tail patch.**

PC   See **program counter.**

PC-relative   A form of instruction addressing in which the destination instruction is some number of instructions before or after the current instruction.

PEF   See **Preferred Executable Format.**

per-context instantiation   The method of allocating an import library's static data in which one copy of that data is created for each separate application using the library. Using this method, a single application may have only one copy of the static data. See also **global instantiation** and **per-load instantiation.**

per-load instantiation   The method of allocating an extension's static data in which one copy of that data is created for each separate connection to the extension. Using this method, a single client may have multiple copies of the static data. See also **global instantiation** and **per-context instantiation.**

PMMU   See **paged memory management unit.**

PowerPC   See **PowerPC microprocessor.**

PowerPC application   An application that contains code only for a PowerPC microprocessor. See also **680x0 application** and **fat application.**

PowerPC compiler   Any compiler that produces code that can execute on a PowerPC. See also **680x0 compiler.**

PowerPC microprocessor   Any member of the family of PowerPC microprocessors. The MPC601 processor is the first PowerPC CPU.

PowerPC Numerics   The floating-point environment on PowerPC processor-based Macintosh computers. This environment provides floating-point data types and arithmetic operations, plus some advanced numerical functions (such as logarithmic and trigonometric functions). See also **Standard Apple Numerics Environment.**

PowerPC processor-based Macintosh computer   Any computer containing a PowerPC central processing unit that runs Macintosh system software. See also **680x0-based Macintosh computer.**

PowerPC software Any software (that is, application, extension, driver, or other executable code) that consists of code only for a PowerPC microprocessor. See also **PowerPC application.**

Preferred Executable Format (PEF) The format of executable files used for PowerPC applications and other software running on Macintosh computers. See also **Extended Common Object File Format.**

prepare To resolve imports in a fragment to exports in some import library.

private resource Any executable resource whose behavior is defined by your application (or other kind of software) alone. Compare **accelerated resource.**

procedure information A long word that encodes information about a routine's calling conventions, the sizes and locations of the routine's parameters, and the size and location of the routine's result. Defined by the `ProcInfoType` data type.

procedure pointer A reference generated by a compiler when taking the address of a routine. On 680x0-based Macintosh computers, a procedure pointer is the address of the routine's executable code (and is defined by the `ProcPtr` data type). On PowerPC processor-based Macintosh computers, a procedure pointer is the address of the routine's transition vector.

Process Manager The part of the Macintosh Operating System that provides a cooperative multitasking environment by controlling access to shared resources and managing the scheduling, execution, and termination of applications.

processor cache See **data cache** or **instruction cache.**

ProcInfoType See **procedure information.**

ProcPtr See **procedure pointer.**

program counter (PC) A register in the CPU that contains a pointer to the memory location of the next instruction to be executed.

prolog A standard piece of code at the beginning of a routine that sets up the routine's stack frame and saves any nonvolatile registers used by the routine. See also **epilog.**

prototype See **function prototype.**

QuickDraw global variables A set of variables stored in a 680x0 application's A5 world that contain information used by QuickDraw.

reduced instruction set computer (RISC) A microprocessor in which all machine instructions are uniformly formatted and are processed through the same steps. See also **PowerPC microprocessor.**

Red Zone The area of memory immediately above the address pointed to by the stack pointer. The Red Zone is reserved for temporary use by a function's prolog and as an area to store a leaf routine's nonvolatile registers.

reentrant exception handler An exception handler that can be interrupted while servicing an exception, then service a new exception, and then complete servicing the original exception.

register-based routine A routine that receives its parameters and returns its results, if any, in registers. See also **stack-based routine.**

RISC See **reduced instruction set computer.**

ROM registry A list of the import libraries that are stored in the ROM of a Macintosh computer. See also **file and directory registry.**

routine descriptor A data structure used by the Mixed Mode Manager to execute a routine. A routine descriptor contains one or more routine records. Defined by the `RoutineDescriptor` data type.

routine record A data structure that contains information about a particular routine. A routine record specifies, among other things, a routine's instruction set architecture, the number and size of its parameters, its calling conventions, and its location in memory. Defined by the `RoutineRecord` data type.

RTOC See **Table of Contents Register.**

run-time environment The execution environment provided by the Process Manager and other system software services. The run-time environment dictates how executable code is loaded into memory, where data is stored, and how functions call other functions and system software routines.

run-time library See **implementation version.**

SANE   See **Standard Apple Numerics Environment.**

saved registers area   The area in a PowerPC stack frame that holds the saved values of the nonvolatile general-purpose and floating-point registers.

section   A region of memory occupied by part of a loaded fragment. When a fragment is loaded, it is divided into a code section and one or more copies of the data section. See also **code section** and **data section.**

segment   One of several logical divisions of the code of a 680x0 application. Not all segments need to be in memory at the same time.

segment location record   A data structure that provides information about the location of a fragment in the resource fork of a file on disk. Defined by the SegmentedFragment data type.

Segment Manager   The part of the Macintosh Operating System that loads and unloads the code segments of a 680x0 application into and out of memory.

selector-based trap   A system software routine that is called by passing a selector code to a single trap macro.

shared library   A fragment that exports functions and global variables to other fragments. A shared library is used to resolve imports during linking and also during the loading and preparation of some other fragment. A shared library can be stored in a file of type 'shlb'. See also **import library.**

smearing   See **byte smearing.**

soft import   An imported symbol whose corresponding code or data might not be available in any import library on the host machine and which is therefore undefined at run time. Compare **hard import** and **import.**

SP   See **stack pointer.**

split trap   A system software routine that is implemented as 680x0 code in ROM and as PowerPC code in an import library. Because the PowerPC code is contained directly in the import library, you cannot patch the PowerPC portion of a split trap. Compare **fat trap.**

stack   An area of memory in the application partition that is used for temporary storage of data during the operation of an application or other software.

stack-based routine   A routine that receives its parameters and returns its results, if any, on the stack. See also **register-based routine.**

stack frame   The area of the stack used by a routine for its parameters, return address, local variables, and temporary storage.

stack pointer (SP)   A pointer to the top of the stack. See also **frame pointer.**

stale instruction   An instruction in the microprocessor's instruction cache whose corresponding values in RAM have changed. You might need to flush the instruction cache to avoid using stale instructions.

Standard Apple Numerics Environment (SANE) The floating-point environment on 680x0-based Macintosh computers and on Apple II computers. This environment provides floating-point data types and arithmetic operations, plus some advanced numerical functions (such as logarithmic and trigonometric functions). See also **PowerPC Numerics.**

static data   The variables and other data that persist between calls to a particular function or fragment.

stub definition function   Code that dispatches to a definition function contained elsewhere. See also **definition function.**

stub definition resource   An executable resource that contains a stub definition function. See also **definition resource.**

subroutine linkage   The mechanism by which one routine calls another, possibly passing arguments and receiving a function result.

switch   See **mode switch.**

switch frame   A stack frame, created by the Mixed Mode Manager during a mode switch, that contains information about the routine to be executed, the state of various registers, and the address of the previous frame.

symbol   A name for a discrete element of code or data in a fragment.

system extension   A file of type 'INIT' that contains executable code. System extensions are loaded into memory at system startup time.

system global variables   A collection of global variables stored in the system partition.

system heap   An area of memory in the system partition reserved for use by the Operating System.

system partition   A partition of memory reserved for use by the Operating System.

table of contents (TOC)   An area of static data in a fragment that contains a pointer to each routine or data item that is imported from some other fragment, as well as pointers to the fragment's own static data.

Table of Contents Register (RTOC)   A processor register that points to the table of contents of the fragment containing the code currently being executed. On the PowerPC processor, the general-purpose register 2 is dedicated to serve as the RTOC.

tail patch   A patch that invokes the next patch in the patch daisy chain as a subroutine, guaranteeing that the tail patch regains control after the execution of all subsequent patches. Compare **head patch.**

temporary memory   Memory allocated outside an application partition that may be available for occasional short-term use.

termination routine   A function contained in a fragment that is executed just before the fragment is unloaded. See also **initialization routine.**

TOC   See **table of contents.**

tool   See **application extension.**

transition vector   An area of static data in a fragment that describes the entry point and TOC address of a routine. See also **procedure pointer.**

trap   Any of a large set of Macintosh system software routines accessed via A-line instructions. See also **split trap.**

trap dispatcher   The exception handler that deals with the occurrence of A-line instructions, providing the subroutine linkage between the A-line instruction and Macintosh system code.

trap dispatch table   A table of entry points to Macintosh system routines that are invoked with A-line instructions.

Trap Manager   The part of the Macintosh Operating System that provides the subroutine linkage to most Macintosh system software routines.

trap patch   See **patch.**

universal interface files   A set of interface files that you can use with both 680x0 compilers and PowerPC compilers.

universal procedure pointer   A 680x0 procedure pointer or the address of a routine descriptor.

VBL   See **vertical retrace interrupt.**

VBL task   A task executed during a vertical retrace interrupt.

vector   See **transition vector.**

vertical blanking interrupt (VBL)   See **vertical retrace interrupt.**

vertical retrace interrupt   An interrupt generated by the video circuitry each time the electron beam of a monitor's display tube returns from the lower-right corner of the screen to the upper-left corner.

virtual memory   Addressable memory beyond the limits of the available physical RAM. The Operating System extends the logical address space by allowing unused code and data to be stored on a secondary storage device instead of in physical RAM.

Virtual Memory Manager   The part of the Operating System that provides virtual memory.

volatile register   A register whose contents need not be preserved across subroutine calls. See also **nonvolatile register.**

weak import   See **soft import.**

XCOFF   See **Extended Common Object File Format.**

Index

Numerals

32-bit clean 1-4
680x0 applications 1-6 to 1-12
    porting to PowerPC 1-15 to 1-19, 1-31 to 1-34, 1-57 to
        1-65, 1-68 to 1-72, 2-21 to 2-26, 3-12 to 3-13, 4-6 to
        4-9
    structure of 1-32
680x0 compatibility issues. *See* 68LC040 Emulator
680x0 context blocks 1-8, 1-59
680x0 registers. *See also* A0 register; A5 register;
    A6 register; A7 register
    unsupported results 1-10
680x0 run-time environment 1-57 to 1-59
    data alignment 1-63 to 1-65
68851 Paged Memory Management Unit 1-9
68881 floating-point unit 1-9
68882 floating-point unit 1-9
68LC040 Emulator 1-3, 1-6 to 1-12. *See also* Mixed
    Mode Manager
    address error exceptions 1-10
    bus error exceptions 1-11
    byte smearing 1-12
    dynamic bus sizing 1-12
    floating-point instructions 1-9
    instruction cache 1-10
    instruction timings 1-9
    NOP instruction 1-12
    PMMU 1-9
    reserved fields 1-10
    unavailable instructions 1-9
    undefined results 1-10
    virtual memory 1-9

A

A0 register, and the Vertical Retrace Manager 1-62
A5 register, setting and restoring 1-60 to 1-63
A5 world 1-57 to 1-63
    and table of contents 1-28
A6 register 1-42
A7 register 1-42
accelerated resources 1-23, 1-34 to 1-40
    calling at interrupt time 2-26
    data section in 1-38
    limitations on 1-38 to 1-40

    and main symbols 1-38
    and termination routines 1-38
    using global data in 1-39 to 1-40
action procedures. *See* control action procedures
address error exceptions, emulator compatibility
    issues 1-10
alert boxes, displayed by PowerPC applications 1-34
alias resources 3-31
alignment. *See* data alignment
A-line instructions 1-8
'alis' resource type 3-31
ANSI-compliant source code ix, 1-65
APDA xv
AppleShare servers 1-55
'APPL' file type 1-21
application extensions. *See also* fragments
    defined 1-21
application global variables 1-58
application parameters 1-58
application partitions, automatic resizing of 1-55
applications 1-21. *See also* fragments
    file type 1-21
    length of fragment 3-31
    location of fragment 3-31
    specifying instruction set architecture 3-30
    specifying library directory 3-31
    specifying stack size 1-60, 3-31
ApplLimit global variable 1-60
A-traps. *See* A-line instructions

B

backing-store file 1-53
backing volume. *See* paging devices
BCLR instruction 1-12
binding 1-25, 1-28
bit numbering conventions xiii
block headers 1-69
BlockMove procedure 1-70
BSET instruction 1-12
BuildFatRoutineDescriptor macro 2-24
BuildRoutineDescriptor macro 2-23 to 2-24
bus error exceptions, emulator compatibility
    issues 1-11
bus sizing. *See* dynamic bus sizing
byte smearing, emulator compatibility issues 1-12

C

CAAR. *See* Cache Address Register
cache, emulator compatibility issues 1-10
Cache Address Register (CAAR), emulator
    compatibility issues 1-10
Cache Control Register (CACR), emulator
    compatibility issues 1-10
CACR. *See* Cache Control Register
calling conventions 1-41 to 1-47. *See also* procedure
    information
    C routines 1-43, 2-30
    Operating System routines 1-43
    Pascal routines 1-43, 2-30
    PowerPC 1-43 to 1-47
    register-based routines 2-30
    selector-based C routines 2-30
    selector-based Pascal routines 2-30
    680x0 1-42 to 1-43
    special cases. *See* special case routines
    specifying 2-30 to 2-32
    THINK C routines 2-30
CALLM instruction 1-9
`CallOSTrapUniversalProc` function 1-67, 2-42 to
    2-43
`CallUniversalProc` function 1-37, 1-67, 2-42
CCR. *See* Condition Code Register
`'CDEF'` resources 1-36
`'cfrg'` resource type 1-31 to 1-34, 3-12 to 3-13, 3-28 to
    3-31
`CloseConnection` function 1-41, 3-23 to 3-24
closing resource forks 1-70
code, self-modifying 1-53
code fragment information records 3-29 to 3-31
Code Fragment Loader 1-22
Code Fragment Manager 1-22, 3-3 to 3-35
    data structures 3-15 to 3-18
    reading code fragment resources 3-13
    resources 3-28 to 3-31
    routines 3-18 to 3-26
code fragment resources 1-31 to 1-34, 3-12 to 3-13, 3-28
    to 3-31
code fragments. *See* fragments
code patches. *See* patches
code resources. *See* executable resources
code sections 1-23
code types. *See* instruction set architectures
compact discs 1-55
compatibility issues. *See* 68LC040 Emulator
compile-time libraries. *See* definition versions
completion routines 1-18
Condition Code Register (CCR)
    during mode switches 2-14
    specifying in procedure information 2-20
Condition Register (CR) 1-45, 1-46

connection IDs 3-5
connections 3-5
containers
    defined 1-21, 3-4
    specifying location of 3-31
context blocks. *See* 680x0 context blocks
contexts 1-51
control action procedures 1-16 to 1-18
control definition functions 1-16, 1-36
control panel, Memory 1-68
cooperative multitasking environment 1-4
coprocessors 1-9
counting symbols 3-14, 3-25 to 3-26
`CountSymbols` function 3-14, 3-25 to 3-26
CR. *See* Condition Register
cross-mode call. *See* explicit cross-mode calls; implicit
    cross-mode calls

D

data, exchanging between PowerPC and 680x0
    environments 1-64 to 1-65
data, global. *See* global data
data alignment 1-63 to 1-65
data forks 1-21, 1-30, 1-31 to 1-34
data instantiation
    global 1-51
    per-context 1-51
    per-load 1-52
data sections
    and accelerated resources 1-38
    defined 1-23
`Debugger` routine, calling within an exception
    handler 4-9
`DebugStr` routine, calling within an exception
    handler 4-9
default stack size 1-60, 3-31
definition procedures. *See* control definition functions;
    list definition procedures; menu definition
    procedures; window definition functions
definition versions 3-8, 3-30
detaching resources 1-70
`DetachResource` procedure 1-70
device drivers, and the 68LC040 Emulator 1-11 to 1-12
`DiskFragment` data type 3-17
disk location records 3-17 to 3-18
`DISPATCHED_STACK_ROUTINE_PARAMETER`
    macro 2-50
`DISPATCHED_STACK_ROUTINE_SELECTOR_SIZE`
    macro 2-50
`DisposeHandle` procedure 1-69
`DisposePtr` procedure 1-70

`DisposeRoutineDescriptor` function 1-19, 2-21, 2-41
disposing of memory blocks 1-69
disposing of pictures 1-69
draw hook routines, specifying calling conventions of 2-32
drop-ins. *See* application extensions
dynamically linked libraries. *See* import libraries
dynamic bus sizing, emulator compatibility issues 1-12

E

emulator. *See* 68LC040 Emulator
epilog code 1-46
event filter functions 1-18
exception codes. *See* exceptions, types of
exception contexts 4-4
exception frames, created by 68LC040 Emulator 1-11
exception handlers
   defined 4-3
   installing 1-57, 4-6 to 4-7
   limitations on 4-9
   and the Red Zone 1-47
   removing 4-7
   writing 4-7 to 4-9
`ExceptionInformation` data type 4-7, 4-16
exception information records 4-7, 4-16
Exception Manager 1-47, 4-3 to 4-22
   application-defined routines in 4-17 to 4-18
   constants in 4-9 to 4-11
   data structures in 4-12 to 4-16
   routines in 4-17
exceptions
   defined 4-3
   680x0 bus error 1-11
   types of 4-5 to 4-6, 4-9 to 4-11
exchanging data between PowerPC and 680x0 environments 1-64 to 1-65
executable resources 1-34 to 1-41. *See also* accelerated resources; private resources
`ExitToShell` procedure 2-41
explicit cross-mode calls 2-8
exported symbols. *See* exports
exports 1-23, 3-4
   getting information about 3-14
Extended Common Object File Format (XCOFF) 1-22, 1-30
Extensions folder 3-6, 3-7
extensions. *See* application extensions; system extensions
external code 2-4 to 2-5

F

fake definition resources. *See* stub definition resources
fake handles 1-70
fake pointers 1-70
fat applications 1-33 to 1-34
fat patches 1-66 to 1-68, 1-71
fat resources 1-38, 1-71, 2-25
fat routine descriptors 2-24, 2-25
file and directory registry 3-6 to 3-7
file forks. *See* data forks; resource forks
file mapping 1-53 to 1-55
file types
   `'APPL'` 1-21
   `'shlb'` 1-21, 3-6, 3-10
finding symbols 1-38, 3-14, 3-24 to 3-26
`FindSymbol` function 1-38, 1-41, 3-24 to 3-25
F-line instructions 1-8
floating-point data types 1-65
floating-point exceptions, handling 4-3
floating-point information records 4-14
floating-point instructions, emulator compatibility issues 1-9
floating-point parameters 1-72
floating-point registers 1-43, 1-47 to 1-50, 1-72, 4-4, 4-15
Floating-Point Status and Control Register (FPSCR) 4-14 to 4-15
floppy disks 1-55
flushing caches 1-10, 1-70
forks. *See* data forks; resource forks
FP. *See* frame pointer
FPSCR. *See* Floating-Point Status and Control Register
`FPUInformation` data type 4-14
fragment initialization blocks 3-15 to 3-16
fragment location records 3-16 to 3-17
`FragmentLocator` data type 3-16
fragments 1-20 to 1-41, 3-4 to 3-5
   defined 1-5, 1-21, 3-4
   finding symbols in 3-24 to 3-26
   kinds of 1-21
   loading 3-10 to 3-12, 3-19 to 3-22
   special routines in 1-29 to 1-30, 3-26 to 3-28
   specifying names of 3-31
   specifying size of 3-31
   storing 1-30 to 1-34
   structure of 1-22 to 1-23
   unloading 3-23 to 3-24
frame pointer 1-42
frames. *See* stack frames; switch frames
free blocks 1-70
function prototypes 1-72, 2-30

G

general-purpose registers 1-8, 1-26, 1-41, 1-43, 1-45, 1-47 to 1-50, 1-72, 4-4, 4-8, 4-12 to 4-14
Gestalt function 1-25, 1-57
Get1Resource function 3-21
GetApplLimit function 1-60, 1-70, 3-31
GetCurrentISA function 2-44
GetDiskFragment function 3-11, 3-19 to 3-21
GetIndSymbol function 3-14, 3-26
GetMemFragment function 3-11, 3-21 to 3-22
GetNextEvent filter procedures, specifying calling conventions of 2-32
GetPicture function 1-69
GetSharedLibrary function 3-10, 3-22 to 3-23
global data, in accelerated resources 1-39 to 1-40
global instantiation 1-51
global variables. See application global variables; QuickDraw global variables; system global variables
grow-zone functions 1-18
    specifying procedure information for 2-17 to 2-18

H

handles, fake 1-70
header files. See universal interface files
head patches 1-68
hit test hook routines, specifying calling conventions of 2-32
hybrid environment. See mixed environment
HyperCard extensions 1-36

I

implementation versions 3-8, 3-30
implicit cross-mode calls 2-8
imported symbols. See imports
import libraries 1-50 to 1-52. See also fragments
    advantages of 1-51
    checking versions 3-7 to 3-10
    data instantiation 1-51 to 1-52
    defined 1-21
    definition version 3-8
    file and directory registry 3-6 to 3-7
    file type 1-21, 3-6, 3-10
    implementation version 3-8
    length of fragment 3-31
    load directories 3-7

location of fragment 3-31
    ROM registry 3-6
    search order 3-5 to 3-7
    specifying definition version 3-30
    specifying implementation version 3-30
    specifying instruction set architecture 3-30
    specifying update levels 3-30
imports 1-21, 3-4. See also soft imports
InitBlock data type 3-15
InitGraf procedure 1-59
initialization blocks. See fragment initialization blocks
initialization routines 3-15 to 3-18, 3-27
    defined 1-30
in-place data instantiation 1-38
input/output, accessing memory-mapped locations 1-11 to 1-12
Inside Macintosh
    bit numbering conventions xii to xiii
    chapter format xi
    format conventions xii
    format of parameter blocks xiv
InstallExceptionHandler function 4-17
instantiation. See global instantiation; per-context instantiation; per-load instantiation
instruction cache 1-10, 1-70
instruction set architectures
    constants for 2-35 to 2-36
    defined 1-13
    determining 2-44
    specifying for an application 3-30
    specifying for an import library 3-30
instruction timings 1-9
interface files. See universal interface files
interrupts. See exceptions
interrupt time
    calling accelerated resources 2-26
    calling Memory Manager 1-70
I/O. See input/output

J

jump tables 1-58

K

KillPicture procedure 1-69

L

`'LDEF'` resources 1-36
leaf procedures 1-46
libraries. *See* import libraries
library directories 3-6, 3-31
line-start recalculation routines, specifying calling
    conventions of 2-32
linkage area 1-44
Link Register 2-11
list definition procedures 1-35 to 1-36
`LMGetCurDirStore` function 1-57
load directories 3-7
loading code fragments 3-10 to 3-12, 3-19 to 3-23
location records. *See* fragment location records
low-memory global variables. *See* system global
    variables
LR. *See* Link Register

M

`MachineInformation` data type 4-7, 4-12
machine information records 4-7, 4-12
Macintosh Programmer's Workshop xiv, 1-32, 1-38,
    1-57, 1-65, 2-26, 2-30
main routines 3-27
   and accelerated resources 1-38
   defined 1-30
main symbols 3-19, 3-21, 3-22
   and accelerated resources 1-38
   defined 1-30
MakePEF tool 1-26, 1-38
`'MDEF'` resources 1-36
`MemFragment` data type 3-17
memory, organization of 1-52 to 1-65
memory blocks, disposing of 1-69
Memory control panel 1-68
`MemoryExceptionInformation` data type 4-15
memory exception records 4-15
memory location records 3-17
Memory Manager 1-5, 1-68 to 1-70
   disposing of blocks 1-69
   at interrupt time 1-70
   private data structures 1-69
memory operations, types of 4-11
memory reference codes 4-11
menu bar hook routines, specifying calling conventions
    of 2-32
menu definition procedures 1-36
mini-A5 world 1-60
mixed environment 1-3, 1-4

Mixed Mode Manager 1-4, 1-13 to 1-19, 2-3 to 2-50. *See
    also* mixed environment; mode switches; routine
    descriptors; 68LC040 Emulator
   constants in 2-27 to 2-36
   data structures in 2-36 to 2-38
   defined 1-13, 2-3
   introduced 2-4
   limitations of 2-21
   routines in 2-38 to 2-44
mode switches 2-7 to 2-14
   defined 1-13
   overhead 1-66
   in patches 1-66
`MOVE` instruction 1-12
MPW. *See* Macintosh Programmer's Workshop

N

nanokernel 1-4
`NewControlActionProc` function 1-18
`NewFatRoutineDescriptor` function 2-21, 2-40 to
    2-41
`NewPtr` function 1-67
`NewRoutineDescriptor` function 2-15, 2-21, 2-39 to
    2-40
NOP instruction, emulator compatibility issues 1-12
`NSetTrapAddress` procedure 1-67
null events 1-71 to 1-72

O

opcodes. *See* operation codes
operation codes 1-8

P

Paged Memory Management Unit, emulator
    compatibility issues 1-9
paging devices 1-55
parameter area 1-44
parameter blocks, format of xiv
parameter lists, variable 1-72
parameter passing 1-47 to 1-50
patches 1-18, 1-66 to 1-68
   fat 1-66 to 1-68
   head 1-68
   tail 1-68
patching, selector-based traps 1-68
PC. *See* program counter

PEF. *See* Preferred Executable Format
per-context instantiation 1-51
performance 1-70 to 1-73
    avoiding mode switches 1-71 to 1-72
    passing parameters 1-72 to 1-73
    using fat resources 1-71
per-load instantiation 1-52
pictures, disposing of 1-69
PMMU. *See* Paged Memory Management Unit
pointer-based function calls 1-29
pointers, fake 1-70
porting 680x0 applications to PowerPC. *See* 680x0
        applications, porting to PowerPC
PowerPC. *See* PowerPC microprocessor
PowerPC applications, structure of 1-31 to 1-32
PowerPC microprocessor ix, 1-4
    floating-point registers 1-43, 1-47 to 1-50, 1-72, 4-4,
        4-15
    general-purpose registers 1-8, 1-26, 1-41, 1-43, 1-45,
        1-47 to 1-50, 1-72, 4-4, 4-8, 4-12 to 4-14
    special-purpose registers 1-41, 1-44 to 1-46, 4-4, 4-8,
        4-12
PowerPC run-time environment 1-19 to 1-65
    application partitions 1-57 to 1-63
    data alignment 1-63 to 1-65
    organization of memory in 1-52 to 1-65
    system partition 1-56 to 1-57
pragma statements 1-64
Preferred Executable Format (PEF) 1-22, 1-30
prepare 1-22
private resources 1-36, 1-40 to 1-41
procedure information
    constants for 2-27 to 2-33
    defined 1-16, 2-15
    number of specifiable parameters 2-17, 2-20
    specifying 2-14 to 2-21
procedure pointers 2-5 to 2-7
Process Manager, reading code fragment resources 3-12
ProcInfoType. *See* procedure information
ProcPtr. *See* procedure pointers
program counter 1-8, 1-11, 4-8, 4-12
prolog code 1-45
protocol handlers, specifying calling conventions
        of 2-32
prototypes. *See* function prototypes

Q

QDGlobals data type 1-59
QuickDraw global variables 1-58 to 1-60

R

Red Zone 1-46 to 1-47
reentrancy, in exception handlers 4-9
REGISTER_RESULT_LOCATION macro 2-18, 2-50
REGISTER_ROUTINE_PARAMETER macro 2-18, 2-50
RegisterInformation data type 4-8, 4-12 to 4-14
register information records 4-12 to 4-14
registers. *See* PowerPC microprocessor; 680x0 registers
ReleaseResource procedure 1-69
resource-based code. *See also* fat resources
    executing 2-24 to 2-26
resource forks 1-31 to 1-34
    closing 1-70
resources
    accelerated. *See* accelerated resources
    detaching 1-70
    fat 1-71
    private. *See* private resources
    stub. *See* stub definition resources
resource types
    'alis' 3-31
    'CDEF' 1-36
    'cfrg' 1-31 to 1-34, 3-12 to 3-13, 3-28 to 3-31
    'LDEF' 1-36
    'MDEF' 1-36
    'WDEF' 1-36
    'XCMD' 1-36
RESULT_SIZE macro 1-16, 2-16, 2-50
Rez 1-32, 1-38, 2-26, 3-12, 3-13, 3-28, 3-30, 3-31
ROM registry 3-6
RoutineDescriptor data type 2-37 to 2-38
routine descriptor flags 2-27
routine descriptors 1-15 to 1-19, 2-6 to 2-7, 2-37 to 2-38.
        See also universal procedure pointers
    creating 2-39 to 2-41
    defined 1-15, 2-6
    disposing of 1-19, 2-41
    executing code with 2-42 to 2-43
    fat 2-24, 2-25
    global 2-21
    local 2-21 to 2-22
    static 2-22 to 2-24
RoutineRecord data type 2-36
routine records 1-15 to 1-16, 2-36 to 2-37
RTE instruction 1-11
RTM instruction 1-9
RTOC. *See* Table of Contents Register
run-time environment, defined 1-20. *See also* PowerPC
        run-time environment; 680x0 run-time
        environment
run-time libraries. *See* implementation versions

S

SANE. *See* Standard Apple Numerics Environment
saved registers area 1-45
sections 1-22. *See also* code sections; data sections
`SegmentedFragment` data type 3-18
segment location records 3-18
Segment Manager 1-32
selector-based traps 1-68
self-modifying code 1-53
`SetA5` function 1-62 to 1-63
`SetApplLimit` procedure 1-60, 1-69, 1-70, 3-31
`SetCurrentA5` function 1-63
`SetGrowZone` procedure 1-69
`SetOSTrapAddress` procedure 1-67
`SetToolTrapAddress` procedure 1-67
`SetTrapAddress` procedure 1-67
shared libraries. *See* import libraries
`'shlb'` file type 1-21, 3-6, 3-10
68881 floating-point unit 1-9
68882 floating-point unit 1-9
68851 Paged Memory Management Unit 1-9
680x0 registers. *See also* A0 register; A5 register;
    A6 register; A7 register
  unsupported results 1-10
`SIZE_CODE` macro 1-16, 2-50
smearing. *See* byte smearing
socket listeners, specifying calling conventions of 2-32
soft imports 1-25 to 1-26
SP. *See* stack pointer
`SPECIAL_CASE_PROCINFO` macro 2-50
special case routines 2-30 to 2-32
special-purpose registers 1-41, 1-44 to 1-46, 4-4, 4-8,
    4-12
Special Status Word (SSW) 1-11
split traps 1-68
SSW. *See* Special Status Word
stack, specifying minimum size of 1-60, 3-31
stack frames 1-41, 1-42 to 1-47. *See also* switch frames
    parameter area 1-44
stack pointer 1-8, 1-42, 2-10
`STACK_ROUTINE_PARAMETER` macro 1-16, 2-50
stale instructions 1-10
Standard Apple Numerics Environment (SANE) 1-9
stub definition resources 1-35
switches. *See* mode switches
switch frames
    PowerPC-to-680x0 2-13 to 2-14
    680x0-to-PowerPC 2-10 to 2-12
symbols 3-4
    counting 3-14, 3-25 to 3-26
    finding 1-38, 3-14, 3-24 to 3-26
System 7.1 1-4
system extensions, defined 1-21

system global variables 1-56 to 1-57, 1-69
system partition 1-56 to 1-57
system software
    patching 1-66 to 1-68
    for PowerPC processor-based Macintosh
        computers 1-4 to 1-6

T

table of contents 1-26 to 1-29
    defined 1-26
    maximum size of 1-29
Table of Contents Register (RTOC) 1-26, 1-27, 1-29,
    1-45, 1-46, 2-11
tail patches 1-68
temporary memory 1-55
termination routines 3-28
    and accelerated resources 1-38
    defined 1-30
text display routines, specifying calling conventions
    of 2-32
text width hook routines, specifying calling
    conventions of 2-31
THINK C calling conventions 2-30
32-bit clean 1-4
Time Manager tasks 1-18, 1-60
TOC. *See* table of contents
tools. *See* application extensions
`TrackControl` procedure 1-17, 2-21
transition vectors 1-26 to 1-27
    defined 1-26, 2-5
    and exception handlers 4-17
trap patches. *See* patches
traps
    selector-based 1-68
    split 1-68

U

universal interface files 1-18 to 1-19, 1-57, 1-65, 2-6 to
    2-7, 2-15, 2-17
universal procedure pointers 1-17 to 1-19, 2-6 to 2-7,
    2-37. *See also* routine descriptors
    and accelerated resources 1-37, 2-24 to 2-26
    defined 2-6
    executing code with 2-42 to 2-43
    and fat patches 1-66
    and universal interface files 2-15
    used in stub definition functions 1-36
    using 2-21 to 2-22
unloading code fragments 3-23 to 3-24

`UnloadSeg` procedure 1-6
update levels, specifying for an import library 3-30
`USESROUTINEDESCRIPTORS` compiler variable 2-14,
    2-39

V

variable parameter lists 1-72
VBL tasks 1-18, 1-60 to 1-63
vectors. *See* transition vectors
versions
    of import libraries 3-7 to 3-10
    of routine descriptor 2-38
Vertical Retrace Manager 1-61 to 1-63
virtual memory 1-53 to 1-55
    emulator support for 1-9
Virtual Memory Manager 1-4, 1-53

W

`WaitNextEvent` function 1-71
`'WDEF'` resources 1-36
weak imports. *See* soft imports
width hook routines, specifying calling conventions
    of 2-31
window definition functions 1-36
word sizes xiii, 1-63

X

`'XCMD'` resources 1-36
XCOFF. *See* Extended Common Object File Format

Z

zone headers 1-69

THE APPLE PUBLISHING SYSTEM

This Apple manual was written, edited, and composed on a desktop publishing system using Apple Macintosh computers and FrameMaker software. Proof pages were created on an Apple LaserWriter IINTX printer. Final page negatives were output directly from text files on an Optrotech SPrint 220 imagesetter. Line art was created using Adobe™ Illustrator. PostScript™, the page-description language for the LaserWriter, was developed by Adobe Systems Incorporated.

Text type is Palatino® and display type is Helvetica®. Bullets are ITC Zapf Dingbats®. Some elements, such as program listings, are set in Apple Courier.

WRITER
Tim Monroe

DEVELOPMENTAL EDITOR
Jeanne Woodward

ILLUSTRATOR
Shawn Morningstar

ART DIRECTOR
Betty Gee

PROJECT LEADER
Patricia Eastman

COVER DESIGNER
Barbara Smyth

Special thanks to Richard Clark, Erik Eidt, Dave Falkenburg, Bruce Jones, Alan Lillich, Mikey McDougall, Dave Radcliffe, Brian Topping, and Eric Traut.

Acknowledgments to Eric Anderson, Scott Boyd, Joanna Bujes, Jeff Crawford, Gary Davidian, Peri Frantz, Miki Lee, Wayne Meretsky, Brian Strull, Beverly Zegarski, and the entire *Inside Macintosh* team.

About Inside Macintosh

Inside Macintosh is a collection of books, organized by topic, that describe the system software of Macintosh computers. Together, these books provide the essential reference for programmers, designers, and engineers creating applications for the Macintosh family of computers.

Inside Macintosh: Overview

This book provides a general introduction to the Macintosh Operating System, the Macintosh Toolbox, and other system software services. It illustrates how to write a Macintosh application by gradually dissecting the source code of a sample application. The book also provides guidelines for writing software that is compatible with all supported Macintosh computers.

272 pages, ISBN 0-201-63247-0

Inside Macintosh: Macintosh Toolbox Essentials

This book describes how to implement essential user interface components in a Macintosh application. The Macintosh Toolbox is at the heart of the Macintosh, and every programmer creating a Macintosh application needs to be familiar with the material in this book. This book explains how to create menus; create windows, dialog boxes, and alerts boxes; create controls such as buttons and scroll bars; and create icons for an application and its documents. This book provides a complete technical reference for the Event Manager, Menu Manager, Window Manager, Control Manager, and Dialog Manager.

928 pages, ISBN 0-201-63243-8

Inside Macintosh: More Macintosh Toolbox

A companion to *Inside Macintosh: Macintosh Toolbox Essentials*, this book describes important features such as how to support copy and paste, provide Balloon Help, and create control panels. This book provides a complete technical reference to the Resource Manager, Scrap Manager, Help Manager, List Manager, Component Manager, Translation Manager, and Desktop Manager.

928 pages, ISBN 0-201-63299-3

Inside Macintosh: Imaging With QuickDraw

This book describes QuickDraw, the part of the Macintosh Toolbox that performs graphics operations, and the Printing Manager, which allows applications to print the images created with QuickDraw. This book explains how to create images, display them in black and white or color, and print them.

832 pages (tentative), ISBN 0-201-63242-X

Inside Macintosh: Text

This book describes how to create applications that can perform all kinds of text handling—from simple character display to complex, multi-language text processing. It provides a brief introduction to the unique Macintosh approach to text handling and shows how to draw characters, strings, and lines of text; how to work with fonts in any size, style, and language; how to use utility routines to format numbers, dates, and times; and how to use the WorldScript technology to design an application that handles text in any language.

1120 pages, ISBN 0-201-63298-5

Inside Macintosh: Files

This book describes the parts of the Macintosh Operating System that allow you to manage files and other objects in the file system. It describes how to create an application that can handle the commands typically found in the File menu. This books also provides a complete technical reference for the File Manager, the Standard File Package, the Alias Manager, the Disk Initialization Manager, and other file-related services provided by the system software.

544 pages, ISBN 0-201-63244-6

Inside Macintosh: Memory

This book describes the parts of the Macintosh Operating System that allow you to directly allocate, release, or otherwise manipulate memory. It shows how an application can manage the memory partition that it is allocated and perform other memory-related operations. This book also provides a complete technical reference for the Memory Manager, the Virtual Memory Manager, and other memory-related utilities provided by the system software.

312 pages, ISBN 0-201-63240-3

Inside Macintosh: Processes

This book describes the parts of the Macintosh Operating System that allow you to manage processes and tasks. It shows in detail how an application can manage processes and tasks and provides a complete technical reference for the Process Manager, the Notification Manager, the Time Manager, the Deferred Task Manager, and other task-related services provided by the system software.

208 pages, ISBN 0-201-63241-1

Inside Macintosh: Operating System Utilities

This book describes the parts of the Macintosh Operating System that allow you to manage low-level aspects of the Operating System. It describes how you can get information about the available software features, how to manage operating-system queues, get information about parameter RAM settings, and manipulate the trap dispatch tables. It also describes other utilities, such as mathematical and logical utilities; date, time, and measurement utilities; and the System Error Handler. This book provides a complete technical reference to the Gestalt Manager, Trap Manager, Start Manager, and Package Manager.

400 pages (tentative), ISBN 0-201-62270-X

Inside Macintosh: Devices

This book is a companion volume to both *Guide to Macintosh Family Hardware* and *Designing Cards and Drivers for the Macintosh Family*. It is written for anyone writing software that interacts with built-in and peripheral hardware devices and covers critical hardware and device programming topics including the Device Manager, SCSI Manager, Power Manager, ADB Manager, Serial Driver, and Slot Manager.

560 pages (tentative), ISBN 0-201-62271-8

Inside Macintosh: Interapplication Communication

This book explains how to create applications that work with other applications to give users even greater power and flexibility in accomplishing their tasks. It provides an introduction to how applications work together in a cooperative environment and discusses how they can share data with other applications, request information or services from other applications, and respond to scripts written in a scripting language. This book provides a complete technical reference to the Apple Event Manager, the AppleScript component, the Program-to-Program Communications Toolbox, and the Data Access Manager.

1008 pages, ISBN 0-201-62200-9

Inside Macintosh: Networking

This book describes key concepts of networking the Macintosh with other computers. It describes in detail the components and organization of AppleTalk, how to select an AppleTalk protocol, and how to write software that uses AppleTalk networking protocols.

592 pages, ISBN 0-201-62269-6

Inside Macintosh: QuickTime

This book describes how to create applications that can use QuickTime, Apple's system software extension that supports time-based data in the Macintosh desktop environment. Time-based data is any information that changes over time, such as sound, video, or animation. *Inside Macintosh: QuickTime* discusses how to manipulate time-based data in the same way that you work with text and graphic elements, and it describes how to use the Movie Toolbox to load, play, create, edit, and store objects that contain time-based data. It also explains how to use image compression and decompression to enhance the performance of QuickTime movies in an application.

736 pages, ISBN 0-201-62201-7

Inside Macintosh: QuickTime Components

This book is a companion to *Inside Macintosh: QuickTime*. It describes how you can use or develop QuickTime components such as clock components, image compressors, movie controllers, sequence grabbers, and video digitizers.

848 pages, ISBN 0-201-62202-5

Inside Macintosh: Sound

This book describes the parts of the Macintosh Toolbox that allow you to manipulate sound and speech. It shows how to use the Sound Manager, the Sound Input Manager, and the Speech Manager to create and record sounds, and to convert written text to speech.

432 pages (tentative), ISBN 0-201-62272-6

Inside Macintosh: AOCE Application Interfaces

This book describes the application interfaces to the Apple Open Collaboration Environment (AOCE), the technology behind the PowerTalk system software. This book is intended for anyone who wants to add mail services, messaging services, catalog services, digital signatures, or authentication services to their application. It also shows how to write templates that extend the Finder ability of display information in PowerTalk catalogs.

Inside Macintosh: AOCE Service Access Modules

A companion book to *Inside Macintosh: AOCE Application Interfaces*, this book is required reading for anyone developing software modules that give users and PowerTalk-enabled applications access to a new or existing mail and messaging service or catalog service. It also describes how to provide an interface that lets a user install and set up the service.

Inside Macintosh: PowerPC System Software

This book describes the new process execution environment and system software services provided with the first release of PowerPC processor-based Macintosh computers. It describes the 68LC040 Emulator, which allows existing 680x0 applications to execute unchanged on PowerPC processor-based Macintosh computers, as well as the Mixed Mode Manager, which handles switching between the PowerPC and 680x0 environments. It also documents the Code Fragment Manager and the Exception Manager.

224 pages (tentative), ISBN 0-201-40727-2

Inside Macintosh: PowerPC Numerics

This book describes the floating-point numerics provided with the first release of PowerPC processor-based Macintosh computers. It provides a description of the IEEE Standard 754 for floating-point arithmetic and shows how PowerPC Numerics complies with it. This book also shows how to create floating-point values and how to perform operations on floating-point values in high-level languages such as C and in PowerPC assembly language.

336 pages (tentative), ISBN 0-201-40728-0

Inside Macintosh QuickDraw GX Library

QuickDraw GX is the powerful new graphics architecture for the Macintosh that provides a unified approach to graphics and typography, and that gives programmers unprecedented flexibility and power in drawing and printing all kinds of shapes, images, and text. This extension to Macintosh system software is documented in a suite of books that are themselves an extension to the Inside Macintosh series. The Inside Macintosh QuickDraw GX Library contains volumes that are clear, concise, and organized by topic. They contain detailed explanations and abundant programming examples.

Inside Macintosh: Getting Started With QuickDraw GX

This book provides an introduction to the QuickDraw GX development environment. It begins with an overview of QuickDraw GX and the key elements of QuickDraw GX programs and then moves on to illustrate these features using practical programming examples.

Inside Macintosh: QuickDraw GX Objects

This book gets you started in understanding how to work with QuickDraw GX and how to create the objects that underlie all of its capabilities. It focuses on the object architecture as a whole, and how to use the objects that make up a QuickDraw GX shape: the shape object, the style object, the ink object, and the transform object.

640 pages (tentative), ISBN 0-201-40675-6

Inside Macintosh: QuickDraw GX Graphics

This book shows you how to create and manipulate the fundamental geometric shapes of QuickDraw GX to generate a vast range of graphic entities. It also shows you how to work with bitmaps and pictures, specialized QuickDraw GX graphic shapes.

655 pages (tentative), ISBN 0-201-40673-X

Inside Macintosh: QuickDraw GX Typography

This books shows you how to create and manipulate the three different types of text shapes supported by QuickDraw GX, and how to support sophisticated text layout, including text with mixed directions and multiple language text.

672 pages (tentative), ISBN 0-201-40679-9

Inside Macintosh: QuickDraw GX Printing

This book shows you how to support basic printing features including desktop printers, and how to use QuickDraw GX printing objects to customize printing and perform advanced printing-related tasks.

480 pages (tentative), ISBN 0-201-40677-2

Inside Macintosh: QuickDraw GX Printing Extensions and Drivers

This book shows you how to extend the printing capabilities of QuickDraw GX by creating a printing extension that can work with any application and any kind of printer. It also shows how to create a QuickDraw GX printer driver.

512 pages (tentative), ISBN 0-201-40678-0

Inside Macintosh: QuickDraw GX Environment and Utilities

This book shows you how to set up your program to use QuickDraw GX, how QuickDraw GX relates to the rest of the Macintosh environment, and how to handle errors and debug your code. It also describes a public data format for objects, and documents several managers that extend the object architecture and provide utility functions.

640 pages (tentative), ISBN 0-201-40676-4

Inside Macintosh

Book title	Information on
Inside Macintosh: Macintosh Toolbox Essentials	Control Manager; Dialog Manager; Event Manager; Finder Interface; Menu Manager; Window Manager
Inside Macintosh: More Macintosh Toolbox	Component Manager; Control Panels; Desktop Manager; Help Manager; Icon Utilities; List Manager; Resource Manager; Scrap Manager; Translation Manager
Inside Macintosh: Imaging With QuickDraw	Color QuickDraw; Cursor Utilities; Graphics Devices; Offscreen Graphics Worlds; Printing Manager; QuickDraw
Inside Macintosh: Text	Dictionary Manager; Font Manager; International Resources; Keyboard Resources; QuickDraw Text; Script Manager; TextEdit; Text Services Manager; Text Utilities; WorldScript Extensions
Inside Macintosh: Files	Alias Manager; Disk Initialization Manager; File Manager; Standard File Package
Inside Macintosh: Memory	Memory Management Utilities; Memory Manager; Virtual Memory Manager
Inside Macintosh: Processes	Deferred Task Manager; Notification Manager; Process Manager; Segment Manager; Shutdown Manager; Time Manager; Vertical Retrace Manager
Inside Macintosh: Operating System Utilities	Control Panel Extensions; Date, Time, and Measurement Utilities; Gestalt Manager; Mathematical and Logical Utilities; Package Manager; PRAM Utilities; Queue Utilities; Start Manager; System Error Handler; Trap Manager
Inside Macintosh: Devices	Apple Desktop Bus Manager; Device Manager; Disk Driver; Power Manager; SCSI Manager; Serial Driver; Slot Manager
Inside Macintosh: Interapplication Communication	Apple Event Manager; AppleScript Component; Data Access Manager; Edition Manager; Program-to-Program Communications Toolbox
Inside Macintosh: Networking	AppleTalk Data Stream Protocol (ADSP); AppleTalk Filing Protocol (AFP); AppleTalk Session Protocol (ASP); AppleTalk Transaction Protocol (ATP); AppleTalk Utilities; Datagram Delivery Protocol (DDP); Ethernet, Token Ring, and FDDI Drivers; Link-Access Protocol (LAP) Manager; Name-Binding Protocol (NBP); Zone Information Protocol (ZIP)

Inside Macintosh (continued)

Book title	Information on
Inside Macintosh: QuickTime	Image Compression Manager; Movie Toolbox
Inside Macintosh: QuickTime Components	Clock Components; Derived Media Handler Components; Image Compressor Components; Movie Controller Components; Movie Data Exchange Components; Preview Components; Sequence Grabber Components; Standard Image-Compressor Dialog Components; Video Digitizer Components
Inside Macintosh: Sound	Sound Input Manager; Sound Manager; Speech Manager
Inside Macintosh: AOCE Application Interfaces	AOCE Utilities; Authentication Manager; Catalog Manager; Digital Signature Manager; Interprogram Messaging Manager; Standard Catalog Package; Standard Mail Package
Inside Macintosh: AOCE Serrvice Access Modules	Catalog Service Access Modules; Messaging Service Access Modules
Inside Macintosh: QuickDraw GX Objects	Color Objects; Ink Objects; Shape Objects; Style Objects; Tag Objects; Transform Objects; View Objects
Inside Macintosh: QuickDraw GX Graphics	Bitmap Shapes; Geometric Operations; Geometric Shapes; Geometric Styles; Picture Shapes
Inside Macintosh: QuickDraw GX Typography	Fonts; Glyph Shapes; Layout Shapes; Text Shapes; Typographic Shapes; Typographic Styles
Inside Macintosh: QuickDraw GX Printing	Dialog Box Customization; Page Formatting; Printing
Inside Macintosh: QuickDraw GX Printing Extensions and Drivers	Printer Drivers; Printing Extensions; Printing Functions; Printing Messages; Printing Resources
Inside Macintosh: QuickDraw GX Environment and Utilities	Collection Manager; Debugging; Mathematical Functions; Memory Management; Message Manager; Stream Format
Inside Macintosh: PowerPC System Software	Code Fragment Manager; Exception Manager; Mixed Mode Manager
Inside Macintosh: PowerPC Numerics	Conversions; Environmental Controls; Numeric Operations and Functions

Please keep me informed about future volumes in
New Inside Macintosh.

Name   _____

Company _____

Address _____

         _____

City   _____

State   _____

Zip   _____

Please tear out card, put in an envelope, and mail to:
Chris Platt
Addison-Wesley Publishing Company
One Jacob Way
Reading, MA 01867

APDA

Your main source for Apple development products

Get easy access to *New Inside Macintosh* and over 300 other programming products through APDA, Apple's worldwide source for Apple and third-party development products. Ordering is easy. APDA offers convenient payment and shipping options.

Call today for your FREE APDA Tools Catalog

1-800-282-2732	U.S.
1-800-637-0029	Canada
(716) 871-6555	International

Site licensing is available for many of the development tools. For information, contact Apple Software Licensing at (408) 974-4667.

© 1992 Apple Computer, Inc. Apple, the Apple logo, APDA, and Macintosh are registered trademarks of Apple Computer, Inc.